Fire on the Mountain

Fire on the Mountain

*Past Renewals, Present Revivals, and the
Coming Return of Israel*

Louis Goldberg, M.A., Th.D.

Messianic Jewish Publishers
a division of
Lederer/Messianic Jewish Communications
Baltimore, Maryland

Unless otherwise noted, all Scripture quotations are taken from the *Complete Jewish Bible*. Copyright by David H. Stern, Jewish New Testament Publications, Inc., 2000.

Also quoted are the NIV and NEB.

Cover design by Now You See it! graphics

05 04 03 02 01 00   6 5 4 3 2 1

ISBN 1-880226-85-5
Library of Congress classification number 00-90046

Messianic Jewish Publishers
a division of
Lederer/Messianic Jewish Communications
6204 Park Heights Avenue
Baltimore, Maryland 21215
(410) 358-6471

Distributed by
Lederer/Messianic Jewish Resources International
Individual order line: (800) 410-7367
Trade order line: (800) 773-MJRI (6574)
E-mail: lederer@MessianicJewish.net
Website: www.MessianicJewish.net

Contents

List of Illustrations vii

Preface ix

Acknowledgements xi

Chapter One
    Introduction.. 1

Chapter Two
    Moses At Sinai 11
        The Man Who Wanted to See the Glory of the Lord

Chapter Three
    Samuel at Mizpah.. 37
        The Man Who Was a Testimony to Ebenezer

Chapter Four
    Asa, the Defender of Judah... 63
        The Man Who Did What Was Right as His Father David

Chapter Five
    Elijah at Carmel 87
        The Man Who Heard God's Gentle Whisper

Chapter Six
    Jonah at Nineveh... 113
        The Man Who Ran Away From the Lord

Chapter Seven
    Hezekiah and the Temple of the Lord 133
        The Man Who Opened the Temple Doors

Chapter Eight

Josiah, Near the End of the First Temple Period 159
The Man Who Tore His Clothes When the Scriptures were Read

Chapter Nine

Nehemiah at the Wall 179
The Man Who Said, "The Joy of the LORD *is your strength"*

Chapter Ten

From the End of the Period of the Tanakh and
During the Intertestamental Period 207

Chapter Eleven

A Brief Overview of Renewal
During the Age of the Body of Messiah 217

Chapter Twelve

The Coming Return of Israel to the Lord God 231

Chapter Thirteen

Conclusion: The Encouragement to Reach Out 243

Endnotes 247

List of Illustrations

Figure 1: Overview of all the revivals in Israel and Judah .... xii–xiii

Figure 2: Israel—People of God 6

Figure 3: The Life of Moses Amidst the Egyptians and Israelites 13

Figure 4: World of Samuel and the Spiritual Renewal Under his Ministry 39

Figure 5: Spiritual Link Between Asa and Samuel and David 71

Figure 6: Elijah's World and Work 89

Figure 7: Jonah, *Shaliach* (sent one) to the Gentiles 115

Figure 8: God's Gracious Renewal Under Hezekiah 135

Figure 9: God's Mercy in a Renewal before the End of the First Commonwealth 161

Figure 10: Renewal in the Post-Exilic Period 181

Preface

Some time ago it was my privilege to preach a series of messages in a Lynchburg, Virginia, church. One afternoon the pastor and I went up on a ridge overlooking the city. It was autumn, and the sight from the sides and top of the mountain was dazzling. Trees stood straight, with their trunks pointing to heaven, their fingers of leaves decorated with brilliant colors of yellow, gold, and various hues of red. I remember one tree in particular whose leaves were a bright, fiery crimson. The pastor and I stood in awe, voicing our deep thankfulness to God for such breathtaking beauty he alone can create.

Late in the afternoon, as we drove away from the mountain ridge, the setting rays of the sun touched the mountain with a reddish hue, and I exclaimed, "It looks like a fire on the mountain!"

That statement, "Fire on the mountain," remained in my thoughts across the years and, instinctively, I felt that it could aptly describe a major address or series of messages at an appropriate time.

Several years later, I gave a series of messages on the spiritual renewals of Old Testament believers in Israel. Many friends then urged me to put these messages into a book. As I put together the manuscript on these messages, God reminded me again of that experience on the mountains around Lynchburg. "Fire on the Mountain" seemed an apt description of the great spiritual renewals of the Old Testament.

Many times, the great revivals in Israel took place on prominent heights or mountains. Or, in many cases, the men whom God called came from settlements or cities on high hills. God's fire came on Mount Sinai as he spoke to the sons of Israel. Often, God's fire in spiritual renewal came upon the hill on which Jerusalem is situated, symbolically called Mount

Zion. When Elijah was on Mount Carmel challenging the people of Israel to choose between the *ba'alim* or the Lord, the fire of God fell on the sacrifice, consuming it, and Israel's leaders were startled at the Lord's awesome presence. God has not changed. In the past, he had worked in the hearts of his believers in Israel to renew them; he gave them a keen sense of the presence of his Spirit in their hearts, and then led them out to reach multitudes, even thousands, for his sake. There is reason to believe that he will work in the same way today.

Do we believe that God wants to revive our faith and have us reach our neighbors for him? Do we believe that God wants to heal us, as well as our neighbors, of maladies such as alcoholism, materialism, and the humanistic philosophies that lead us into such vices?

Perhaps ours can be the generation that experiences what the Lord promised to King Solomon so long ago at the dedication of the first Temple:

> [I]f my people, who bear my name, will humble themselves, pray, seek my face and turn from their evil ways, I will hear from heaven, forgive their sin and heal their land. (2 Chron. 7:14)

This possibility was held out to Israel as God's people; and there is every reason to believe that our unchanging God offers to apply the same principles in the lives of his people today.

Acknowledgements

Heartfelt thanks must be expressed by every sensitive believer for the way God works among his people. Often, when a group of believers, a congregation, or several congregations come to a very low spiritual level, God's Spirit, in response to the prayers of the handful of concerned believers, comes on the believers. He warms their hearts, and then an outreach begins so that unbelievers accept Yeshua the Messiah and begin to live for him. Concerned believers are truly grateful for the way God works, and even if he does not move in congregations, individual believers can be involved in the work of God with a continuous touch of his presence.

Grateful acknowledgment also is given to the congregations in Israel who have been inspired with the series of lessons in this book and have asked that they be placed in printed form. I am thankful also to Mildred Cooper, Donna Sundblad, and Dawn Kolodin, who typed the first draft of the manuscript; to Ed Pollock, who provided the graphics; and to Pam Rather, Mitchell and Dawn Kolodin, who provided the final form of the manuscript.

I pay special tribute to my wife, Claire, gone to be with her Messiah and now enjoying her reward, who encouraged me in the ministry of writing so that the hearts of many people can be touched, particularly with the spiritual emphasis portrayed in this book.

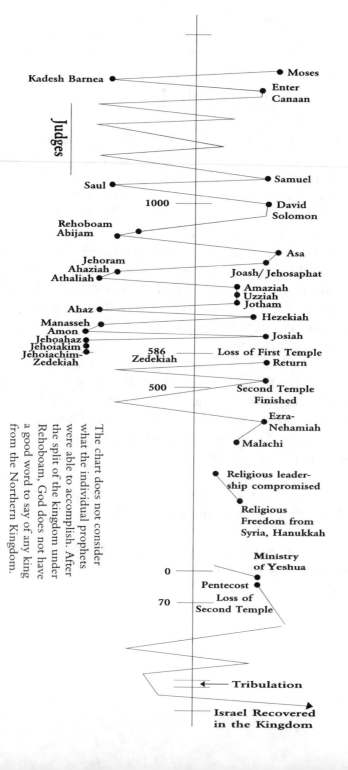

Kadesh Barnea ●　　　　　　　　　● Moses

　　　　　　　　　　　　　　　　● Enter
　　　　　　　　　　　　　　　　Canaan

Judges

Saul ●　　　　　　　　　　　● Samuel

　　1000 —　　　　　　　● David
　　　　　　　　　　　　Solomon

Rehoboam
Abijam ●　●

　　　　　　　　　　　　　● Asa

Jehoram
Ahaziah ●
Athaliah ●　　　　　Joash/Jehosaphat

　　　　　　　　● Amaziah
　　　　　　　　● Uzziah
　　　　　　　　● Jotham

Ahaz ●　　　　　　　　● Hezekiah

Manasseh ●
Amon ●　　　　　　　　● Josiah
Jehoahaz ●
Jehoiakim ●
Jehoiachim- ●
Zedekiah　　586
　　　　　Zedekiah — Loss of First Temple
　　　　　　　　　　　　● Return

　　　　500 —　　　Second Temple
　　　　　　　　　　Finished

　　　　　　　　　　● Ezra-
　　　　　　　　　　Nehamiah

　　　　　　　● Malachi

　　　　　● Religious leader-
　　　　　ship compromised

　　　　　　　● Religious
　　　　　　　Freedom from
　　　　　　　Syria, Hanukkah

　　　　　　　　Ministry
　　　　　　　　of Yeshua
　　　0 —　　　　　●
　　　　　　Pentecost ●
　　　70 —　　Loss of
　　　　　Second Temple

　　　　　　　←— Tribulation

　　　　　　　Israel Recovered
　　　　　　　in the Kingdom

The chart does not consider
what the individual prophets
were able to accomplish. After
the split of the kingdom under
Rehoboam, God does not have
a good word to say of any king
from the Northern Kingdom.

Leaders and kings marked with an * below are those who managed to keep the nation on a high spiritual level.

*Moses	(1527-1407 B.C)	Now show me your glory (Exodus 33:18)
*Samuel	(1100?-? B.C.)	All Israel from Dan to Beersheba recognized that Samuel was attested as a prophet (1 Samuel 3:2)
Saul	(1051-1011 B.C.)	I am grieved that I have made Saul king because he has turned away from me (1 Samuel 15:11)
*David	(1100-971 B.C.)	From that day on, the Spirit of the Lord came upon David in power (1 Samuel 16:13)
Soloman	(971-931 B.C.)	Give your servant a discerning heart ... his wives turned his heart (1 Kings 3:9; 11:4)
Rehoboam	(931-913 B.C.)	Judah did evil in the eyes of the Lord (1 Kings 14:22)
Abijam	(913-911 B.C.)	He committed all the sins his father had done (1 Kings 15:3)
*Asa	(911-870 B.C.)	He did what was right in the eyes of the Lord as his father David had done (1 Kings 15:11)
*Jehoshaphat	(873-848 B.C.)	He did what was right in the eyes of the Lord (1 Kings 22:43)
Jehoram	(853-841 B.C.)	He walked in the ways of the kings of Israel (to the north) (2 Kings 8:18)
Ahaziah	(841 B.C.)	He did evil in the eyes of the Lord (2 Kings 8:27)
Athaliah	(841-835 B.C.)	She destroyed the whole royal family (except for Joash) (2 Kings 11:1-2)
*Joash	(835-796 B.C.)	He did what was right in the eyes of the Lord all the years of Jehoiada (2 Kings 12:2)
*Amaziah	(796-767 B.C.)	He did what was right in the eyes of the Lord but not as his father David had done (2 Kings 14:3)
*Uzziah(Azariah)	790-739 B.C.)	He did what was right in the eyes of the Lord just as his father Amaziah had done (2 Kings 15:3)
*Jotham	(750-731 B.C.)	He did what was right in the eyes of the Lord just as his father Uzziah had done (2 Kings 154)
Ahaz	(743-715 B.C.)	Unlike David his father, he did not do what was right in the eyes of the Lord his God (2 Kings 16:2)
*Hezekiah	(728-686 B.C.)	He did what was right in the eyes of the Lord just as his father David had done (2 Kings 18:3)
Manassah	(687-642 B.C.)	He did evil in the eyes of the Lord (2 Kings 21:2)
Amon	(642-640 B.C.)	He did evil in the eyes of the Lord, as his father Manassah had done (2 Kings 21:20)
*Josiah	(640-608 B.C.)	He did what was right in the eyes of the Lord and walked in all the ways of his father David, not turning aside to the right or to the left (2 Kings 22:2)
Jehoahaz	(608 B.C.)	He did evil in the eyes of the Lord, just as his fathers had done (2 Kings 23:22)
Jehoiakim	(608-597 B.C.)	And he did evil in the eyes of the Lord, just as his fathers had done (2 Kings 23:27)
Jehoiachin	(597 B.C.)	He did evil in the eyes of the Lord, Just as his father had done (2 Kings 24:9)
Zedekiah	(597-586 B.C.)	He did evil in the eyes of the Lord, just as Jehoiakim had done (2 Kings 24:19)
	516 B.C.	Second temple completed at the urgings of the prophets Haggai and Zechariah
*Ezra, Nehemiah	(444 B.C.)	For the joy of the Lord is your strength (Nehemiah 8:10)

For the intertestimonial period, see Fig. 9 p. 161

Peter	(A.D. 30)	The promise is for you and your children and all who are far off (Acts 2:39)

Figure 1 Overview of all the revivals in Israel and Judah

National Spiritual Levels of Israel before the rupture of the Kingdom and of Judah after the rupture. What is interesting to note is that spiritual renewal, or the slide to spiritual ruin was in the hands of the kings or other civil authorities.

CHAPTER ONE

Introduction

"ADONAI, I have heard the report about you.
ADONAI, I am awed by your deeds.
Bring your work to life in our own age,
make it known in our own time."
(Hab. 3:2)

Some Observations Concerning Renewal

Sometimes, God's people have peculiar notions about the word "revival." Some may feel this is the time when, in special meetings, believers become "high," jump up on the pews, shout at the top of their voices, and roll down the aisles in some sort of a worked-up ecstasy. While these phenomena occasionally occur, and though no fair-minded person wants to prejudge, this description is hardly the experience of a genuine, God-wrought and Spirit-led renewal that changes the core of a believer's being.

Moishe Rosen, leader-emeritus of Jews for Jesus, declared that "revival" is the "ronngh word," purposely misspelling the word to emphasize his point:

> We should never use the term revival to describe successful evangelism. What was never *alive* cannot be revived! . . . I reiterate: We should not use the term "revival" to describe evangelism because true evangelism informs, inspires, and invites those who do not have a saving knowledge of God. . . . Revival *could* come to the church, which consists of those who already believe, but are not enjoying the benefit of their faith.[1]

What shall we say, however, concerning the multitude of churches that, year after year, conduct "revival meetings"? Is this revival in its truest sense? Philip Newell observed, "This word 'revival' has acquired an erroneous, unhappy connotation in recent years. Certainly it does not mean a pre-scheduled, well-publicized, and highly organized series of religious meetings . . ."[2] When a congregation schedules such "revival meetings," and when no genuine noticeable result takes place, the end experience of seeing a church sink into the same old apathy after their "revival" is over is distressing. For the people of a congregation to go through such an exercise falls far short of the authentic experience of a spiritual renewal.

The Genuine Event of Renewal

The Psalmist spelled out the true meaning of revival: "Won't you revive us again, so your people can rejoice in you?" (Ps. 85:6) The Hebrew word used in this passage for "revive" is from the verb *shuv*, or, "turn back, turn."[3] One must, therefore, turn back to God, agree with what he says about our sins, and call on him for a change in our hearts in order to have the Spirit's fullness. One observation becomes quite clear: David was praying for himself and other *believers* within Israel who already had entered into the experience of atonement. This plea was echoed by many of the men whom God used in the renewals in Israel and Judah, as we shall see in succeeding chapters. But the truth is ever the same for the body of the Messiah. Newell said, "'Reviving' to the church must mean the recovery of spiritual blessing already possessed but not held fast—or never fully appreciated."[4]

And yet, suppose a believer earnestly seeks to live every day in accordance with the light God provides in his Word. He humbles himself, has a Spirit-filled prayer life, and earnestly seeks the lost and even leads many to the Lord. Will renewal come to the congregation to which this believer belongs? Will his community experience an awakening? As we read many of the books on revival, some suggest that if believers are faithful to follow the directions for revival, a congregation-wide or community-wide awakening will occur as a result. Charles Finney thought as much:

> In truth a revival should be expected whenever it is needed. If we need to be revived it is our duty to be revived. If it is our duty and it is possible, we should set about being revived ourselves, and, relying on the promise of Christ to be with us in making disciples always and everywhere, we ought to revive Christians and convert sinners, with confident expectation of success. Therefore, whenever the church needs reviving they ought and expect to be revived, and to see sinners converted to Messiah. When those things are seen . . . let Christians and ministers be encouraged and know that a good work is already begun.[5]

While no one can detract from the way God used Finney, and an awakening did follow in the train of his ministry, his suggestion that if we meet all the conditions a revival will come may be too optimistic.

From what we will see in the renewals of the people of Israel, a sense of God's providence prevails when awakenings occurred. Likewise, renewals within Messiah's body came at specific times in the past as God directed. Lewis A. Drummond has well observed the following:

> It is important to understand that we must permit God to promote the awakening in any way and by whatever instruments *He chooses*. At times we are very willing to have a revival provided we run it as we see it. But God . . . has His ways. They may be quite different from ours. He will often take the most unlikely people and thereby glorify Himself.[6]

It would appear that believers cannot pray down a Holy Spirit revival any time they choose, even though we desperately crave one. A delicate balance exists between human responsibility to meet God's requirements and the mysterious providence of God to send one.

Principles for Renewal

Most scholars who write about revival indicate many of the same principles necessary for an awakening of God's people. Throughout his book, Newell builds on the formula for renewal found in Solomon's prayer recorded in 2 Chronicles 7:14 at the dedication of the Temple. The conditions are as follows: God's people will (1) humble themselves, (2) pray, (3) seek God's face, and (4) turn from their evil ways.[7] Finney states the principles in much the same way: (1) Believers confess their sins. (2) A spirit of prayer prevails. (3) Ministers are burdened for revival (but lay people also need to be involved in prayer for their pastors). (4) Believers disciple new believers after an awakening comes.

Individual Responsibility

What if believers meet the conditions for revival but the awakening does not come? Does it mean failure? Not at all. Remember the mysterious element of God's timing. To insist that a revival must come while ignoring God's part can lead only to extremism. In the long run, a person who does so will become obsessed with a one-sided issue and will not be able to function adequately in the full range of the Lord's work.

George Verwer, leader of Operation Mobilization, touched on this very issue in a chapel message at the Moody Bible Institute's Founder's Week. His challenge on that occasion was that believers avoid extremism, seek to be personally filled with God's Spirit, and be involved in the work of evangelism. "It just might be," said Verwer, "God will be gracious and honor a believer's plea for revival in his church and community if he meets all the principles. And yet, if the revival does not come, at least the believer can be filled with the Spirit of God in his own soul and have power in his service for the Lord."

His advice is sound, and certainly is what undergirds him and his associates in his organization as they seek to reach the world for Messiah. We will see exactly this pattern as we consider the awakenings in Israel. In some instances believers, lay people, and prophets who met all the conditions for renewal as individuals were present and were used of God in many ways, and yet no national renewal took place. On other occasions, however, God brought about his movement for revival in his timing through specially selected men.

The Renewals of Israel and Judah

Although many books have been written on the spiritual renewals of the past several hundred years, and many surveys have been made of its principles, the *Tanakh* (Old Testament) is the best textbook on how God works in awakening his people spiritually. The people of Israel have been the ones among whom God intervened in the past in such a telling way. As we examine most of the movements that took place—the circumstances under which they occurred, the men involved in the awakenings, and the factors that are connected with any movement of God—we have the best laboratory in which to consider how God might work today.

But some people might ask, "Are not the people of Israel a chosen people, so that in a special sense all of them knew the Lord?" Or, on the other hand, some people interpret the Old Testament in such a way that one wonders if, apart from the prophets called to preach to their generations, any believers existed in Israel.

Perhaps the best way to understand Israel as a specially selected people is through the following diagram:

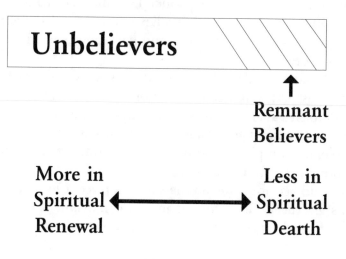

Figure 2

Israel was called to be a people of God, selected from the nations to receive God's revelation, and from whose ranks the Messiah was to come. But by no means can we infer that every individual in Israel knew the Lord. Nor was it a nation in which no one except the prophets knew the Lord.

The Message of Salvation According to Moses

Did the Spirit regenerate people in Old Testament times so that their hearts were changed, and they repented as they turned to the Lord? Certainly a work of the Holy Spirit existed; we know because no one could be born again without the Spirit's involvement in changing his heart, and no believer could do God's work without his empowerment.

The Principles of Atonement

We do know that the lessons concerning atonement for sin were present already in the Mosaic Covenant through the sin offering. There, as each one brought his particular animal, four major principles were attached.[8]

1. *Substitution*: As each worshipper brought his animal, he had to regard it as his particular *substitute*.
2. *Identification*, where the offerer put his hand on the animal's head and confessed his sins. The sins of the offerer were symbolically transferred to the animal-substitute, thereby making it sin. It had become identified with his sins.
3. *The death of the substitute*, which called for the offerer himself to actually kill the animal. No doubt, the officiating priest helped the offerer to do so, but it was the latter's res-ponsibility to learn that his own particular sin caused the substitute to die in his place.
4. The principle of *the exchange of life*: While this is not spelled out clearly in the book of Leviticus, later prophets described that as the animal died, it gave *its* life, free of sin, to the offerer.

Four Possible Responses by the People of Israel

Four noted responses occurred in those who made these sin offerings:

1. Some *did not care* at all for what Moses had prescribed for the forgiveness of sin, and instead, in an act of rebellion, went off to worship at the pagan shrines.
2. Others brought the called-for animal because they knew that was what Moses had prescribed, but they went through the worship as *a ritual*. The prophets condemned this kind of worship because no change was forthcoming with such a heart attitude (see Isa. 1:10–15).
3. Still others brought their animals, realizing that they had to be obedient to what Moses prescribed, but they took a *legalistic* stance toward offering the animal. For them, wor-

ship had descended to a tit-for-tat relationship with the Almighty. No doubt these people thought they had done what God asked him to do and, therefore, God owed them something.

4. *The Response by the Remnant*: God worked in every generation to reach individuals so that a remnant who trusted and served him wholly was always present. Sometimes the remnant was numerous, particularly in times of spiritual renewal. At other times, the number of believers was small, as in Elijah's day, when God declared that only 7,000 were present (see 1 Kings 19:18). The message here is that God never abandoned his people. At certain points in Israel's history, God's Spirit worked in spiritual renewal to encourage, strengthen, and empower his believers to have an outreach so that a remnant again could grow significantly.

With the first three responses, nothing occurred in the people's hearts; they remained unregenerate, even though the Spirit could have been at work, convicting them of sin and judgment. However, as seen in the fourth response, God wanted the people to *respond in faith*, to personalize these four principles attached to these offerings. Then, *because of their faith*, the Spirit would work in their hearts to change them.

Needs Can Vary in Different Generations

Some generations, such as that of Moses and those who experienced the Exodus, were faced with great decisions that provided opportunities to learn about God. In order to save a remnant of believers in a later generation that had turned away from him, God uprooted them from their homeland and exiled them to slavery in Babylon. In the days following Messiah's death and resurrection, God's Spirit inspired the disciples as they waited and prayed during the days before

Pentecost. In this unique revelation by God during the formation of Messiah's body, such an outpouring of the Spirit occurred that thousands came to know the Lord.

Considering the Renewals of Israel and Judah

My approach will be to look at the spiritual renewals in the history of Israel and Judah under Moses, Asa, Elijah, Jonah, Hezekiah, Josiah, and Nehemiah. Each of these renewals requires an understanding of its historical background. Examining the background of each of these eras might seem tedious, but it is important to note to what depths a nation can go before God's Spirit reaches his people.

A thumbnail sketch of the men God used will also be provided to help understand how God prepared and used specially selected men. Some, such as Moses, were uniquely trained. Others were lay people—even ordinary people—chosen by God to be the channels through whom he worked. We often tend to view these men as "spiritual giants," and lament that no such giants exist anymore. But the men God used were very human indeed, subject to the same passions we have. So human were they that at times they could say to God, "choose someone else," as Moses and Jonah did, or even deny him as Peter did. What set them apart was the providential way in which the Lord intervened in their lives, preparing them to be the channel for the work of his Spirit in the great spiritual renewals.

I hope this book will help us to appreciate how fire from God came on Israel's mountains to transform many generations. May we also see the Holy Spirit work in convicting power in our hearts to bring about spiritual renewal in our congregations, our communities, our nation, and even soon, *Eretz Yisra'el* (the Land of Israel).

CHAPTER TWO

Moses at Sinai

The Man Who Wanted to See the Glory of the Lord

(Exod. 32:1–33:23)

"But Moshe [Moses] said, 'I beg you to show me your glory.'"

(Exod. 33:18)

One of the first times God brought spiritual renewal to his people occurred at Sinai, and it provides lessons that will assure today's believers of a closer walk with the Lord. At the same time, the experiences of what happened to Israel at Sinai also teach us that we too, like Moses, can be God's witnesses to our society. We too may intercede in prayer so that many can be reached with the Good News of Messiah and change can take place on every level within our nation.

Historical Background

For this occasion, we go back some 3,400 years. Solomon ascended the throne in 971 B.C.E.,[9] and in the fourth year of his reign, 967 B.C.E., he began to build the Temple (see 1 Kings 6:1). But the biblical text demonstrates the connection between the beginning of its construction and the Exodus, which occurred in "the 480th year after the people of Israel left the land of Egypt" (1 Kings 6:1). The Exodus occurred, therefore, during 1447 B.C.E., after the slaying of the firstborn of the Egyptians. That experience of being delivered from Egypt became an occasion that always was to be remembered during the Passover festival, when the lambs were slaughtered, while the Temples stood, and even after the loss of the Second Temple in 70 C.E.

God's Power

The Israelites traveled for about two months before they reached the traditional site of Mt. Moses (Sinai) in the southern third of the Sinai (see Exod. 19:1). During that time they saw some of the greatest evidences ever of the mighty display of God's power—his omnipotence as well as his love and mercy.

The generation that came out of Egypt, with the relentless Egyptian army behind them and the Red Sea (Sea of Reeds) before them, was between the proverbial rock and a hard place (see Exod. 14:5–9). God showed his power in two ways: First, he divided the waters of the sea, making a pathway for the people of Israel to cross as on dry ground. Then, he also placed his pillar of cloud in front of the armies of Egypt, accentuating the darkness of night in their midst. Once the Israelites were across, the pillar of cloud was withdrawn, and the Egyptian army pursued them in earnest through the divided waters of the sea. As the Israelites stood on the east bank of the sea, they saw the divided waters return, drowning the Egyptian officers and soldiers. Egypt lost the flower of its army, but Israel was safe. In an exultation of commemoration, Moses led Israel in a grand victory celebration because the majestic right hand of God had wrought deliverance on behalf of his people (see Exod. 15). Miriam, sister of Moses and Aaron, also led the women in song and dance, praising God for the great victory he gave to his people.

Man's Failure—God's Provision

The events that subsequently took place on the way to Sinai reflect two direct opposites: *man's failure and God's gracious provision*. These contrasts are just as evident today, even among God's people in the body of the Messiah.

When the Israelites tried to slake their thirst at the waters of Marah, they found the water bitter and began to grumble (see Exod. 15:22–24). God then told Moses to throw a certain piece of wood into the water. When Moses did so, the water became sweet.

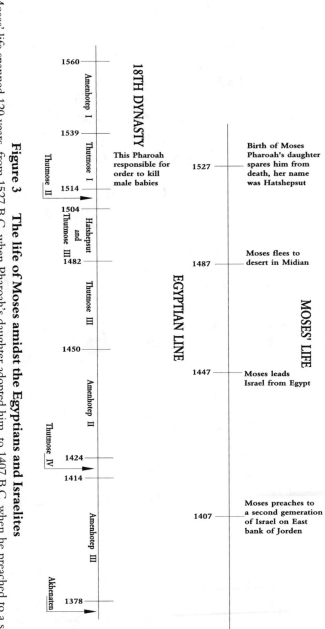

Figure 3   The life of Moses amidst the Egyptians and Israelites

18TH DYNASTY

EGYPTIAN LINE

Amenhotep I

1560

Thutmose I

1539

Thutmose II

1514

This Pharoah responsible for order to kill male babies

Hatshepsut and Thutmose III

1504

1482

Thutmose III

1450

Amenhotep II

Thutmose IV

1424

1414

Amenhotep III

Akhenaten

1378

MOSES' LIFE

1527 — Birth of Moses Pharoah's daughter spares him from death, her name was Hatshepsut

1487 — Moses flees to desert in Midian

1447 — Moses leads Israel from Egypt

1407 — Moses preaches to a second generation of Israel on East bank of Jorden

Moses' life spanned 120 years, from 1527 B.C. when Pharoah's daughter adopted him, to 1407 B.C. when he preached to a second generation of Israelites, poised and ready to enter Canaan.

Spiritual renewal came soon after the Israelites arrived at Sinai, on the heels of a moral and spiritual breakdown. They remained at Sinai for eleven months and five days (Numbers 10:11).

Tragically, the renewal did not last long, reminding us that such experiences are never self-sustaining. Within only one month after leaving Sinai and arriving at Kadesh Barnea, many in the nation made their tragic and sinful error which kept Israel in the desert for 37½ years. One wonders how wide-spread the renewal was in such a situation.

In the Desert of Sin, the entire community constantly complained to Moses and Aaron because they had nothing to eat in the desert. Looking back, by comparison, they described the abundance of food they had in Egypt when they were slaves (see Exod. 16:1–3). And yet, God's gracious response to such lack of faith was to miraculously provide manna, not only once, but for almost forty years while Israel was in the desert and until the day they crossed the Jordan into Canaan. God also gave his people quail meat for their evening meals (see Exod. 16:13).

As they marched along the dry and hot paths in the desert, the Israelites grumbled again because there was no water. They even pressured Moses to the point that he had to chide them because they were always testing the Lord. But God patiently did a miracle for Israel when Moses struck the rock in Rephidim and waters gushed forth, sufficient for all the people as well as for the Egyptians who elected to come along with the Israelites (see Exod. 17:1–7).

The only record of military victory during this period occurred in the battle against the Amalekites. As long as Moses' hands were held high before God, Israel was victorious in the conflict. Joshua, the army commander, as well as the troops who fought with him, and those of Israel who took God seriously, learned the great lesson of the name of God that was revealed in the battle: *ADONAI nissi* (The Lord is my Banner). With the sign of the uplifted hand, God's graciousness was revealed so that he himself became the mantle of victory on behalf of his people.

Israel at Mt. Sinai

The culmination of all the physical deprivation and spiritual experiences for Israel—and the reason for which they had been called out of Egypt—was to meet God at Mount Sinai (see Exod. 19). At the mountain, the Israelites consecrated themselves according to God's instructions communicated to Moses, and there they were confronted by God's holiness as he descended on Sinai in the fire. The people heard the loud claps of thunder and saw the threatening lightning flashes as the entire mountain range trembled violently (see Exod. 19:16–19). God revealed himself to his people to impress them with his holiness, power, and authority. In turn, the people were warned not to cross the boundary line between the sacred and profane and touch the mountain; in so doing they would risk their very lives.

After God communicated the Ten Commandments and the Book of the Covenant, and with the ratification of the latter (see Exod. 20:22–24:8), God called Moses up to the mountain for forty days. Moses set out with Joshua, his aide, leaving the elders of Israel and particularly Aaron and Hur in charge of the camp (see Exod. 24:12–15). Joshua probably went only part of the way, while Moses proceeded on to the top of the mountain. Joshua must have waited at an agreed-upon location, because he seems to have had no knowledge of what happened subsequently in the camp (see Exod. 32:17). During the forty days, God instructed Moses concerning what was necessary for Israel's lifestyle and worship.

What occurred in the camp while Moses was on top of the mountain, particularly after the great display of God's holiness in the thunder, lightning, fire, and smoke, seems incredible and difficult to comprehend. On the verge of entering into its greatest opportunities to serve the living God, Israel suffered one of her greatest failures. The problem with that generation—those twenty years and older—was not in taking them out of Egypt, with all of the miracles that occurred in making the Exodus possible. No, the real difficulty was to take Egypt out of their hearts!

Rebellion against God

Idolatry—While for forty days Moses was being instructed concerning the various facets of the covenant on the mountain, God abruptly announced that the Israelites remaining in the camp had committed a great sin: They actually were worshipping a golden calf! (See Exod. 32:1–6.) This worship of the bull idol—which many of the people were involved in making—appeared to be a representation of the cult associated with the Egyptian worship of Horus, where the bull was the sign of strength and fertility.[10]

What appears most astounding is that upon Aaron's seeming faint-hearted approval, he had announced, "Tomorrow there will be a festival to the Lord." How does one fashion a bull, erect an altar in front of it, and call this a preparation for the *Lord's* worship? The people had reduced the true God to the same level as the Egyptian bull object of worship. And when the unbelievers in Israel's ranks—as well as the Egyptians with them—saw the bull, it reminded them of what was involved in the Egyptian religion. Was Aaron trying to soften the impact by creating a synthesis between the two worship systems and calling it the worship of the Lord? His decisions led to sacrilege—taking Israel's God, the sovereign Lord of the entire earth, and bringing him down to the level of the gods of the nations. No wonder God interrupted his instructions to Moses for proper worship. No divine revelation could continue at the top of the mountain while at the same time every activity in the camp contradicted what God was teaching Moses.

Immorality—The twin in the religions of the ancient Middle East was also a gross offense: sexual immorality! After presenting the fellowship offering at this idol, the people sat down to eat the fellowship meal and then they rose up to indulge in revelry, which also included acts of sexual immorality. Once the people lost sight of God's holiness symbolized by his fire that touched the mountain, the door was then open to commit gross sins.

Moses' actions reflected his horror with all the wrongdoing, because, as he approached the camp and saw the calf and the lewd dancing, his immediate response was to throw the tablets to the ground, breaking them in pieces at the foot of the mountain (see Exod. 32:19). How could Moses bring these holy commandments from the Lord into the camp while his people were breaking every one of them? God's holiness cannot be brought into sin's presence! Even Moses' brother, Aaron, though he would not approve of such behavior, was charged with allowing the people to run wild (see Exod. 32:25).

Death in the Camp—The climax of Moses' horror came when he stood at the entrance to the camp and cried, "Whoever is for *ADONAI*, come to me" (Exod. 32:26). The gravity of the situation required drastic action, before God's judgment would fall. To their credit, Moses' brethren, the Levites, stood with Israel's leader, slaying 3,000 of their rebellious relatives, fellow Israelites. It appears incredible, Israelis killing Israelis. But God is holy, and he requires holiness among his people. One New Testament counterpart is the affair of Ananias and Sapphira, whose trivializing of God's commandments cost them their lives. We cannot tamper with God's holiness and his purposes without suffering the consequences.

For this and other circumstances, God called Moses to minister to his people. Moses did not have an easy task in leading Israel from Egypt, but he knew that he was not alone in his ministry. God enabled him also to be victorious. Consequently, the first generation out of slavery had an opportunity to experience spiritual renewal after passing through the depths of degradation.

The Man God Used

Preparing the Man of God; 40 years[11]

God prepared his man for the great task of leading Israel through the wilderness to the borders of the Promised Land. He also taught Moses how his people are to worship the one true and holy God. Mention Moses to Jewish people or Messianic believers and get a quick response: "He is our teacher!" Non-Jewish believers view him as the lawgiver, as do Muslims.

But Moses was a many-dimensioned man. God chose Moses and worked with him, bringing him to the point where he could be Israel's divinely appointed leader. The same lessons apply today in preparing leaders.

His Childhood—Moses was born soon after the beginning of Egypt's 18th dynasty.[12] Being 80 years old when he led Israel from Egypt in 1447 B.C.E., he was, therefore, born in 1527 B.C.E., soon after the time when this dynasty placed Israel under ruthless slavery (see Exod. 1:13). In addition, the Egyptians issued decrees to control the Israeli population by killing the infant boys (see Exod. 1:15, 16). It was not the first time that men under Satan's control had tried to destroy Israel, but through the circumstances, God always works via those he raises up to deliver his people.

Moses' parents saw that he was a "fine child," someone special, and so his mother hid him for three months after his birth (see Exod. 2:2). When it was no longer possible to conceal him, she made a papyrus basket and placed her son in it, setting it along one of the many banks of irrigation canals fed by the Nile. In a sense, Israel's future hung on the fate of a little boy floating in his basket on the canal, crying in the midst of his circumstances. God has often worked through small and insignificant ways that seem incredible afterward.

As a Young Man—Pharaoh's daughter, who found the baby, was the woman in God's design; and after the weaning period by Moses' mother (see Exod. 1:7–10), this woman of royalty reared him as her own son. In God's plan, his man was to be trained in all the wisdom of Egypt, which included the academic disciplines of the Middle East—the languages, laws, diplomatic relationships with other nations, military tactics, economics, and many other areas of learning (see Acts 7:22).

When Moses reached his fortieth birthday, he went out to see the Hebrew slaves. Why? Had his parents instilled in him, even before he was weaned, that he belonged to Israel?

Or, did he simply become dissatisfied with worldly pleasures and Egyptian wisdom and, consequently, turn again to the very people from whom he came? For whatever reason, Moses made a turn at a very crucial point in his life, and we cannot overlook God's omniscient hand in it all.

Moses killed an Egyptian overseer who had mistreated a Hebrew slave. The next day, when he thought he could be an arbitrator between two fighting Israelites, he found that his interest in the slaves would get him into trouble. What was he, an Egyptian of royalty, doing among the Hebrew slaves? The exposure of Moses' true identity as an Israelite—who had killed an Egyptian—ended his phase of education in Egypt's royal courts.

So when Pharaoh tried to kill Moses upon learning of the affair (see Exod. 2:15), Moses ran away into the Sinai desert, where he spent the next forty years as a lonely shepherd. There he married and had two sons (see Exod. 18:2–5).

Grinding the Man of God

We may wonder at Moses' fate. After his education and easy life in Egypt, why did God cause such an abrupt turn, where for forty years Moses seemingly became a nobody? Or did he? Alexander Whyte described what was also essential in Moses' training: reducing and subduing the "too-high-temper" and weaning him "from the sham and sweetness of this world" where eyes and hearts "suffer the loss of all things for the recompense of the reward in heaven."[13] This seemingly difficult experience was essential for Moses' own good before God could entrust to his servant the leadership of a nation. Only through the "valley trials" could this servant of the Lord learn to be quiet before him and develop hidden qualities—qualities that never would surface while reveling in the wisdom and pleasures of Egyptian society.

But the time in the Sinai also was for more mundane reasons. Across the forty years, Moses learned where every water hole and every oasis existed in the dreary desert—and where every valley and pathway led so as to get through this barren land. All this information was necessary if he was going to lead some two to three million people to Mt. Sinai as well as go from there to the Promised Land.

One day, as God led him through his "desert lessons," Moses was attracted to a burning bush, which, strangely, was never consumed. When he went to observe this odd sight, he was suddenly confronted by God's presence calling to him from the midst of the bush. Forty years had gone by as Moses became the contemplative shepherd while Israelites were suffering in their misery as slaves.

Now, however, the time had come for action. Once before, Moses tried to be a leader in his own way. But this time, remembering what had already happened, he recoiled and tried every possible excuse to turn away from the responsibility God wanted to place on his shoulders. After all the arguments Moses could muster (see Exod. 4), he finally yielded to God's will and went in God's power and strength, ready to deliver Israel and lead them from their slavery to become a free people. The confirmation of the divine promise came when, as God had declared, Moses' brother Aaron just "happened to be in the desert" when Moses returned to Egypt. Moses now knew that he was to begin a new phase, a new task, for God.

Moses' Ministry: 40 Years

Moses the Intercessor—We also have insight into Moses' character as he pleaded with God for Israel. On the mountain, for the first forty-day period, God announced to Moses that the people had gone astray with the bull worship in the camp. Then the Lord declared that because of this horrendous sin he was going to destroy Israel and make of Moses a great nation (see Exod. 32:10). The choice was quite plain: Either Moses intercedes on behalf of Israel, guilty of a heinous crime against God's holiness, or he is given the prominence of being the father of a new nation. But was this choice real? How could

God go back on his promises made to the Patriarchs? Would this not demean his very nature? Moses understood God's challenge, but in a way it was a test of how Moses would respond. It was used to see how sensitive Moses was to God's Word, and to test his resolve to do God's will.

This man of God interceded on behalf of his people, calling God's attention to the promises made to the forefathers: to Abraham (see Gen. 17:7), to Isaac (see Gen. 26:3, 4), and to Jacob (see Gen. 35:10–12). He knew quite well that the Lord could never entertain a proposal of cutting off Israel and giving Moses the dubious honor of fathering a new nation. God's promises must never be mocked, but Israel's leader spoke out in defense of his people. He submerged his own personal desires to that of the nation's interests and God's glory (see Exod. 32:11–13). No wonder God greatly respected Moses and listened to his plea of intercession on behalf of Israel.

God's Great Answer—After Moses had led the people of Israel in purging their sin—which included exterminating 3,000 people (see Exod. 32:28)—he returned to the Lord, saying, "These people have committed a terrible sin: they have made themselves a god out of gold. Now, if you will just forgive their sin! But if you won't, then, I beg you, blot me out of your book which you have written!" (Exod. 32:31, 32) This testimony was the sign of Moses' greatness: He would rather be banished to an eternity of separation from God than to permit Israel to be judged further. Only one other human being had the courage to pray such a prayer. Rav Sha'ul (Paul the *shaliach*, or messenger) also declared, "I could wish myself actually under God's curse and separated from the Messiah, if it would help my brothers, my own flesh and blood, the people of Isra'el" (Rom. 9:3, 4).

How could Moses pray such a prayer? When Moses was a baby, hidden in a basket on the banks of the irrigation canal, who but God could know what eventually would be in the heart of Israel's leader to pray so selflessly and with such complete trust in God's promises, righteousness, and glory? But God knows what he is doing when he selects people for his tasks, and even though the human vessel must be prepared to do his will, yet in the end the divine and human interests combine to serve his purposes. The Lord can then have complete confidence in his servants as they lead a community or nation in spiritual renewal.

Moses the Preacher—Moses made his share of mistakes, even to the point that he was not permitted to enter the Promised Land (see Num. 20:12). Yet he was a man of great faith, with a deep trust in God. He asserted himself as a great preacher of the messages of Deuteronomy (after his brother Aaron had passed off the scene). He prepared the people of the second generation for their future commitment, teaching them again the great lessons of the *Torah* (the Word of God) as they were poised on the East bank of the Jordan River ready to cross into Canaan. When he was 120 years old and at the point of death, his physical stamina and spiritual strength were epitomized by these words: "With eyes undimmed and vigor undiminished" (Deut. 34:7). No wonder, then, one of the finest blessings anyone can offer in Hebrew is the benediction that reflects on the greatness of Moses the man, *ad me'ah ve'esrim*, may you live "until one hundred and twenty!"

The focal point of that generation of Israel came at Sinai when it had sinned so greatly; but out of that experience came the possibility for one of the greatest renewals of a people. We marvel at God's lovingkindness and his patience when he took the pains to restore his people, and Moses his servant became the instrument through whom he worked.

The Challenges of Spiritual Renewal

God issued several challenges to the nation in one of its most trying experiences, so that the people could experience renewal in their personal lives; but these truths also are applicable personally for each of us today for a vital, healthy, spiritual experience with the Lord.

A Sense of Need

The first challenge is to sense our spiritual needs. No spiritual renewal will take place unless we *know* we have fallen short of God's standards of holiness. The cumulative effect of the small acts of disobedience makes us less and less perceptive to our fellowship with the Lord, and once a believer pursues this course, the ultimate result will be the gross sin that will then be common knowledge for an entire community. To pretend we are all right spiritually when actually we have become detestable in God's sight is really to play blind man's bluff with him! We have to realize our need.

The Shock Treatment—God had to speak dramatically to Moses' generation to make them realize their need. "You will go to a land flowing with milk and honey; but I myself will not go with you, because you are such a stiffnecked people that I might destroy you on the way" (Exod. 33:3). The warning of the removal of God's presence was calculated to be a shock to wayward people. They could make their plans to go to the land of Canaan, but God's presence would not be in their midst. Many times in our experiences with the Lord we too need to say, "Lord, ever keep us sensitive to your presence. We want to face you as a friend, rather than have you confront us in controversy."

What was God trying to do with that generation and perhaps even with some of us? The need for conviction of sin and wrongdoing is evident. He cannot work with unclean vessels and, therefore, he had to shock that generation of Israel. The same drastic reaction occurred when Yeshua had to speak to a spiritually bereft and materialistic farmer, "You fool! This very night you will die" (Luke 12:20). The farmer, too, was insensitive to his eternal welfare and felt instead that all his riches were of his own doing and that he was going to live forever.

The Drastic Problem—But why this drastic approach with Israel? We do not have to look very far for the answer; God put his finger on the problem: "You are a stiffnecked people" (Exod. 33:5). This generation was stubborn in its sins and blind to God's desires. They already had seen God's mighty works: He had parted the Sea of Reeds; he gave them water in the desert; he gave them manna bread to eat; he gave them quail, meat that they needed; he fought for and gave Israel victory against the Amalekites. He even revealed himself in his holiness on the mountain, causing it to shake because of his presence. In view of all of these mighty acts of God's power, why did many in that generation turn away and compromise their worship by creating a synthesis between God as their Lord and one of the gods of Egypt? God detested their stubbornness and pride and warned the people that he was going to remove his presence from them.

God is not different today; he still has a way of putting his finger on the reprehensible deeds in our lives. In a congregation where I served as a spiritual leader many years ago, one couple many times sought to thwart God's will in the life of that congregation. On every occasion and at every turn, they stood against the wishes of the leader and blocked the spiritual progress of the fellowship of God's people. The wife was pregnant at the time, and when the child was born, I well remember going to visit her in the hospital. The baby was born dead, with the cord wrapped around his neck, and upon learning what had happened, I could only go out into the hospital hall and cry, saying to myself, "Does it have to take such circumstances for God to speak to some hearts?"

God wants to work in our lives, but we have to be open to his probe of our shortcomings. If we resist him, he cannot work in power in our midst. The challenge, therefore, is to sense the deep needs in our hearts and then be completely transparent to him so that he can bring renewal in our hearts.

The Word of God

The second challenge to that generation of Israel occurred when Moses shared God's Word. No spiritual renewal occurs without God's Word being proclaimed. The Torah must always be central so that he can speak to us.

Teaching and preaching the Word—The Lord said to Moses, "Tell the people of Isra'el" (see Exod. 33:5). Many times we have to be reminded of what God desires of us, and how he feels about our decisions and deeds. So he raises up men to speak his word and help us to know his will. The Word of God is "like fire . . . like a hammer shattering rocks" (Jer. 23:29). The man of God has no desire to hurt the people he serves, but the Spirit of God takes the Word and applies it to peoples' hearts. The Lord spoke to that generation in Israel, shocking them by saying, "You are stiffnecked," that is, "Your pride is showing." So God had to declare, "I will not go with you."

The Word speaks today with no less power. Too often we are caught up serving ourselves, much too interested in materialism, willing to criticize the brethren, and hardly involved with the outreach among the people in our communities. Then when leaders, elders, men called of God to speak his Word, speak to our shortcomings, we are swift to react and reject their admonitions. Sometimes, rebellious believers find it easier to put out the leader or elder than to change their ways. But we must realize that the men of God today who selflessly preach his Word have been sent by him to awaken his people.

What are the characteristics of the Word of God?—While the Torah has its effect at many levels within the human psyche, Hebrews 4:12, in the New Covenant, specifies some of the ways in which the Word operates:

A. **THE WORD OF GOD IS LIVING.**

Because the Word is God-breathed, it comes from a living person—in this case, God. Yes, the words are on paper, but aside from inerrancy, which guarantees the truth of what is being written, these words are from God, and so the words are more than mere written symbols on a sheet of paper. As we read the Torah, as we hear it, and as we use it, we will find that the Spirit of God takes this Word and applies it so that lives are changed as a result.

B. **THE WORD OF GOD IS ACTIVE**

This Word is energized and is calculated to stir us. Just as the trumpet blast of reveille shook me awake each morning at 4:30 when I was in the army, so the Word is calculated to shake people out of their lethargy and get us going. The Word deeply stirred King Josiah; he cried and tore his clothes, and as we shall yet see from that encounter, renewal came to Judah.

C. **THE WORD OF GOD IS SHARP AND PIERCING**

The Word is sharper, by comparison, than the double-edged sword used by the Roman soldier. And it is sharper than the knife used by the Jewish priests when they dissected the sacrifices; it's even sharper than the laser beam used by a surgeon in an operation. This Word can penetrate to divide soul and spirit and the joints and marrow, and it penetrates into a person's deepest core. This Word is so effective when it is used, because it can convict and touch people where we with our words of wisdom cannot.

D. **THE WORD OF GOD IS A JUDGE**

We find it easy to be critical of people—our families, friends, unbelievers, and even believers. But the one place in Scripture where the Word is regarded as a judge or critic is in the very definition of the Word. So, as we read the Torah every morning, and as it judges and criticizes us, we will be less apt to criticize others!

The Call for Repentance

"Turn around"—The next challenge for spiritual renewal is the call for us to repent of our sins. As already noted, the basic meaning of repentance is "turn around," and it is a picture of how a right heart attitude can prompt a person to turn from his sin and also turn toward God. But no element of works by unbelievers can be attached to genuine repentance; one does not claim atonement from sin merely because he or she no longer *practices* the old ways of sin. In the experience of the new birth, God regenerates a person's heart and implants in him or her a new life; at the very same moment, however, the person is also repentant, turning from ways that are merely self-serving. God's Spirit will then have greater freedom to work out his will in the repentant person's heart.

But *shuv*, "turn back," is also the same word David had used for "revive." As already noted, when believers are renewed, they actually "turn back" to the Lord, and no element of mere self-effort will avail. The believer needs to change his attitude toward wrongdoing, and also to agree with God's assessment of his or her lifestyle before God's Spirit can work in fullness to effect a revival in the heart.

Internal Changes—The repentance of this particular generation of Israel can be seen in two dimensions. An internal change occurred: "When the people heard this bad news, they went into mourning" (Exod. 33:4). The word for "bad" in this passage is the Hebrew *ra*, normally translated "evil" or "wrong," but it also can be translated as "sorrowful." The NIV translates it "distressing," which captures the meaning of the word in the context. True repentance somehow is always related to a sorrow for sin: "Godly sorrow brings repentance" (2 Cor. 7:10, NIV). While tears can be associated with sorrow, it is not the measure of tears that will make the difference, but rather one's basic heart attitude. People can shed copious tears when they hear pastors and evangelists preach powerful messages, but what matters is the salvation of the individual and the internal change weeks and months after the Word has spoken to him or her.

Three thousand of that generation of Israel had died, and one can imagine how scores and even hundreds of families were affected in that judgment of God. They paid a disastrous price because of the terrible sin that had been committed in the Lord's very presence, bringing with it the prospect of the removal of his presence. God's Spirit was faithful, however, and began to work in believers' hearts, producing an internal change, a sorrow for sin. What's more, many unbelievers turned toward God for the salvation of their souls.

External Consequences—But repentance also has consequence for external change. "So from Mount Horev onward, the people of Isra'el stripped themselves of their ornaments" (Exod. 33:6). These were the garments of sin, the very same clothes in which many of the people had worshiped the Egyptian deity, made their sport in drunken revelries, and, possibly, even had committed adultery. These very clothes and jewels had become the sign of desecration, an offense to God, and shedding these garments was the direct effect of the internal change that worked itself out to an external change in appearance.

In later centuries, crowds of Israelis came to hear the preaching of John the Baptizer. They were curious about a man who had a ministry in the Desert of Judea instead of the Temple in the capital city. And yet, as the Spirit of God spoke in power, the multitudes repented, confessed their sins and were baptized in the Jordan River. But when the Baptizer saw some of the religious leaders, Pharisees and Sadducees, as well as other people, just standing there and listening to his proclamation of the Word, he cut through their curiosity, proclaiming, "If you have really turned from sins to God, produce fruit that will prove it!" (Matt. 3:7, 8) Even the religious leaders of Israel and curious bystanders had to demonstrate some external change resulting from the struggle for inward change after listening to what John was saying. The preaching of genuine repentance and atonement from sin called for a radical change: Move away from a religion of man-made rules, or some kind of a ritual lifestyle. Live a moral lifestyle that reflects Scriptural standards and an energized spiritual experience that will lead to worship of the Holy One.

As that generation in Moses' day heard their leader call for internal and external changes—and because of the shock that God could remove his presence from them—people's hearts were touched and they turned from themselves to face God. They tore from themselves the very garments in which they had been involved in sin.

A Call for change—We believers know all the statistics of the football games, but we hardly spend five minutes a day in prayer. We can spend hundreds of dollars on our wardrobes or insist on the latest electronic gadgets, but give only a pittance to the poor. We take pride in and comfort ourselves that the United States is the richest country on earth, but if this country goes down the economic drain, many nations will go likewise.

We also fail to have the greater vision of a world in spiritual need. Most of the centers for spiritual outreach are located in this country. However, when we focus on our own lives, these centers will be removed from the West to the third world, where people from those areas will carry on the work of outreach, even if the believers in the United States fail. God is not duty-bound to always favor this country. If we learn anything from Moses, we must learn that our wrongdoing is incompatible with God's holiness, justice, and righteousness. And he can judge us today even as he did with that generation of Israel so long ago.

However, Moses also proclaimed that God is faithful, he is the God of mercy and love, and he is ready and willing to do more for his people than they are even able to ask for. God's call for repentance is for a greater dependence on him, whereby he has the opportunity to work through us in power. Many of our younger generation see a desperate need for standards; they observe that our permissive excesses are harmful. Perhaps God is calling today to our younger generation for total dependence on him and complete involvement in his work. We may see God bring about a gracious renewal in our congregations through them.

A Revitalized Worship Experience

The fourth challenge for spiritual renewal is a revitalized worship experience. "Moshe would take the tent and pitch it outside the camp. He called it the tent of meeting. Everyone who wanted to consult ADONAI would go out to the tent of meeting, outside the camp" (Exod. 33:7). The focus of God's power was at the tent of meeting, where God was pleased to speak.

Scripture indicates that the tabernacle had not yet been erected, but this tent, with the peculiar designation as "tent of meeting," was a simple one. It was pitched outside the camp, further indicating that the worship center could not in any way be placed within the camp of Israel, where sin was present. The way back to God meant separation from sin; but it also revitalized worship and called for a new approach to God.

A sincere desire to meet with God—The Word strongly urged that "anyone inquiring of the Lord" must go outside the camp to the tent of meeting. The challenge to do so was personal; and while, unfortunately, not all went out, many—probably the believers—did go because they really wanted to worship the Lord and be separate from sin.

As the people viewed this tent, they also were forced to ask themselves what they wanted from God. Many among that generation of Israel had never made a decision to live for the Lord, and the presence of the tent meant they had to draw near to him and find atonement for their sins. Even for the believer an earnest question was posed: "How serious is my commitment to the Lord, and how can my worship of him be revitalized?"

The record of the failures of the first generation at Sinai and a people's need to repent is not a dry history-book lesson. The challenge of confrontation by a holy God means that we too have to tear ourselves away from our apathy, our luxuries and gadgets, and listen with a fresh interest in God's Word. When we sense a deep need for spiritual renewal, we can then be led into a new and revitalized worship experience. Such worship will bring again the joy of the Lord into our hearts with a continual anticipation that God is going to speak and work through us for a greater outreach among unbelievers.

Taking away the barrier—God was yet to reveal to Moses the full impact of worship within the tabernacle when it finally would be erected. But its lessons still serve as a reminder of one's salvation: The ark, and the mercy seat upon it, which are located within the veil or curtain, are always focused on meeting with God. "There above the cover between the two cherubim that are over the ark of the Testimony, *I will meet with you*" (Exod. 25:22, NIV, emphasis added). In any spiritual renewal, believers gain a new and deeper understanding of sin and salvation. We must never take our salvation for granted, nor should we forget that unbelievers in every facet of life also need to meet with God at his mercy seat.

Our lives don't belong to us—God also meets us in a revitalized aspect of worship at the altar of burnt offering, which stands outside of the tabernacle. The burnt and grain offerings, with their call to lay down one's life in sacrifice and to enter into the blessing of doing God's will, now become the focus of what worship entails. Spiritual renewal will never be genuine apart from total and complete consecration. At this altar God declared, "*I will meet with you* to speak with you. There I will

meet with the people of Isra'el; and the place will be consecrated by my glory" (Exod. 29:42, 43, emphasis added).

Daily fellowship—A revitalized worship experience also must
include daily communion with God. The sweetness of the incense was a reminder that in the tabernacle, at the altar of incense, God fellowshiped with his people daily. The sweetness
of his presence encouraged believers to do his will and find
the comfort of his presence, no matter the experience he led
them through. If we only spend a few minutes with God a
day, then we have yet to learn what the sweetness of real communion is all about.

The Place of Prayer

Community prayer—Finally, the fifth challenge for spiritual renewal is the place of prayer. When the people of that generation of Israel, in their restoration, wanted to pray before God,
they had to go to the tent of meeting outside the camp (see
Exod. 33:7). It became, therefore, a focal point for corporate
prayer by the community of renewed believers.

Private prayer—But there was also the necessity of private
prayer: "When all the people saw the column of cloud sta-
tioned at the entrance to the tent, they would get up and prostrate themselves, each man at his tent door" (Exod. 33:10).
The presence of the pillar of cloud at the tent of meeting was
God's visible manifestation, and each Israelite was encouraged
to pray at his own tent entrance. When a purified people stood
to pray, having turned from their evil ways and then seeing
God's visible presence at the tent of meeting, Moses, God's
man, could then face the Lord and seek his presence among
Israel, and his blessing of them as well.

Moses began to intercede for his people, crying before God,
"Now please, if it is really the case that I have found favor in
your sight, show me your ways; so that I will understand you
and continue finding favor in your sight. Moreover, keep on

seeing this nation as your people" (Exod. 33:13). Once again we see Moses' selflessness in his intercession for a renewed Israel. How did God reply to him after great numbers within Israel had repented? The Lord replied, "Set your mind at rest—my presence will go with you, after all" (Exod. 33:14). He had applied the shock treatment to Israel, declaring that he would withdraw his presence from his people, but after the spiritual renewal he graciously announced that his presence would indeed be with Israel to lead them on their way to the Promised Land. We cannot question God's methods of handling rebellious people; rather, we must recognize that there are occasions when the shock treatment has value in accomplishing his purposes.

Praying the seemingly impossible—This shock treatment was not the end of the experience of communion with God. Moses was assured that that generation had been restored; but will he now be content? No! Moses was still hungry and thirsty for more of God, and this intense desire for a greater intimacy with the living God became reflected in his boldness in prayer, "I beg you to show me your glory!" (Exod. 33:18) Had Moses lost his senses? Was he "hitching his wagon to the stars," asking for the impossible? Moses, along with other servants of the Most High God, always have made those seemingly impossible petitions.

Sometimes we make requests that may be too big for us personally; but God delights in the fact we ask, even though he may have to limit the extent. George Washington Carver once asked God to show him the secrets of the universe. God replied, "Scale down your request." This devout scientist then requested, "Show me the secret of the peanut." The lowly peanut. With that, God was pleased to open to his servant the universe of the peanut. A renewed heart bombards the gates of heaven and the throne of God's grace to ask for help and power to do God's work!

What the Lord did for Moses because of his boldness and daring is amazing. God honored his servant Moses because the man had chosen to be faithful in his prayer on behalf of Israel and not grasp for his own personal glory in a new nation that would be established from his line. In loving response, God made it possible for Moses to see his back. (Moses had to be satisfied with an indirect view, for he would not have been able to withstand the intensity of God's direct glory.) Moses' persistence for the restoration of Israel as well as his own intense desire to see God led him to be just one step removed from actually viewing God's face!

Will We Turn?

Do we want to see God's presence so as to do great exploits for him? Do we want to see him work in great power? If we long for such involvement with the Lord, we need to turn from our set ways, mend the broken fellowship with God, face him, and listen to his Word—even if he puts his finger on some questionable areas in our lives. His design is for us to turn to him and expect him to do great and wonderful things for us.

Some time ago, at a Founder's Week conference at Moody Bible Institute, Joni Eareckson was one of the main speakers. Many of us have read her life story: As a teenager, a diving accident left her paralyzed. Although she has some motion in her shoulders, from that point down in her back to her feet, she has absolutely no feeling.

In her book *Joni*, she describes the experiences she passed through while in the hospital and during her therapy. Prior to her accident, she had the usual teenager's ideas about God. She knew the pat phrases on how to approach him, and to behave as a believer and as a good member of a congregation. Left alone, she probably would have gone through the usual apathy of the average believer in an exercise of fruitless service.

But God had other plans. During her long ordeal in physical rehabilitation of her remaining functioning muscles, she rebelled against God; she struggled with how any good could ever come out of the depth of her valley. Ever so slowly, however, he worked in her heart as she gradually opened herself up to him. She began to realize that he has his ways of working with every individual, including Joni, even though she was in such an apparently pitiful condition. When Joni finally made peace with the Lord, she found she could be triumphant over her paralysis. Then God was ready to use her.

As Joni spoke to her audience at the conference, she sat in a wheelchair. She could not use her hands, she could not walk, and she needed two attendants to care for her. But she spoke with God's power as he touched people's hearts. Many pitied her as they saw her, sitting so helpless. But as God began to speak through her as she spoke his Word, it was not long before many people took their eyes off her and allowed God to shock and remind them that they might be the ones to be pitied in their desperate need for spiritual renewal. The wheelchair she sat in became "the prison God used to set her spirit free." And her words sparked a wave of confession of sin by believers and a new appreciation for worship. Through the renewal of many hearts in the atmosphere of that meeting, many unbelievers also found the Lord.

Even as God worked in Moses' generation, God can still work today. While the rebellion at Kadesh Barnea would soon test the effectiveness of the spiritual renewal (see Num. 14), what occurred at Mt. Sinai is, nonetheless, real and vital. We need to be open to what God wants to say to us, because his desire is to bring us to the place where, like Moses, we can ask him for the seemingly impossible. What do you want from God?

CHAPTER THREE

Samuel at Mizpah

The Man Who Was a Testimony to Ebenezer

"*ADONAI* has helped us until now"
(1 Sam. 7:12)

"Sh'mu'el [Samuel] kept growing, *ADONAI* was with him, and he let none of his words fall to the ground. All Isra'el from Dan to Be'er-Sheva became aware that Sh'mu'el had been confirmed as a prophet of *ADONAI*."
(1 Sam. 3:19, 20)

"From the day that the ark arrived in Kiryat-Ye'arim a long time elapsed, twenty years; and all the people of Isra'el yearned for *ADONAI*"
(1 Sam. 7:2)

Moses died at about 1407 B.C.E. and was succeeded by his servant Joshua, the tactical commander of Israel's forces who led in the conquest of the major portions of Canaan. Joshua lived 110 years (see Josh. 24:29), and his death may have been around 1390 B.C.E. (No data exists as to Joshua's birth or his age when he began to lead Israel after Moses' death.) The record further indicates that "Isra'el served *ADONAI* throughout Y'hoshua's [Joshua's] lifetime and throughout the lifetimes of the leaders who outlived Y'hoshua and had known all the deeds that *ADONAI* had done on behalf of Isra'el" (Josh. 24:31). The death of the last of the elders is placed around 1375 B.C.E.

Israel then entered a period known as the time of the Judges when, except for a few isolated instances, any semblance of morality was absent. The last judge was Samuel, whose ministry began in 1075 B.C.E. Samuel was a contemporary of another judge, Samson, as well as King Saul. He also anointed young David as the future king. Israel's period of the judges can be reckoned from 1375 B.C.E., from the time of the death of the last of the elders under Joshua, until the days of Samuel, when Saul began his reign in 1051 B.C.E. (although Samuel lived during a good part of Saul's kingship).[14] This period lasted about 325 years.

Historical Background for Samuel's Ministry of Renewal

As the second generation out of the slavery was poised on the east bank of the Jordan, ready to enter the Promised Land, God told Moses he would not be permitted to cross the Jordan (see Deut. 3:23–28; Num. 20:11, 12). Instead, Joshua was commissioned to assume the responsibility of leading Israel into Canaan and conquering it.

The essence of Moses' message on the east bank forms most of the book of Deuteronomy. In three great messages contained in the first thirty chapters of Deuteronomy, Israel's lawgiver expanded upon the Sinaitic covenant (see Exod. 20 to 23 and Leviticus) and charged those of the second generation to stay faithful to the Lord once they entered the land of Canaan. Deuteronomy chapter 31 contains Moses' account of how Joshua was to succeed him, as well as the reading of the Torah and a prediction that Israel would rebel against the Lord. Chapters 32 and 33 are personal reminiscences of how God had been good to Israel. They also include promises that if the people would remain faithful to him, his goodness would bless that second generation in its conquest of Canaan and the experience of a new life within that land. With the exception of the minor incident at Ai (see Josh. 7), the second generation who left Egypt, as well as their children, remained faithful to the Lord for more than thirty years, until the death of the elders who outlived Joshua.

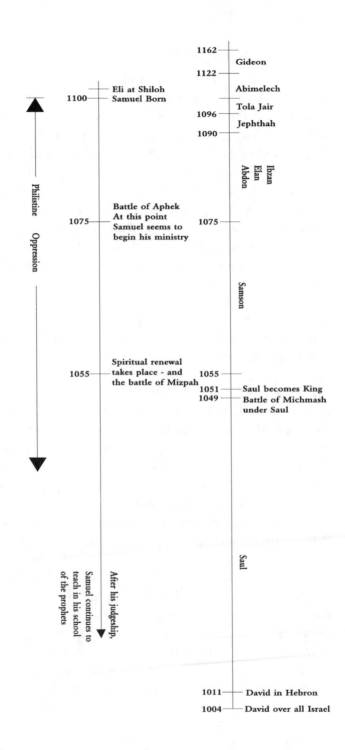

Figure 4   World of Samuel and the Spiritual Renewal Under His Ministry

The Time of the Judges

Sadly, the period of the Judges recounts one failure after
another when people had no firsthand experience with the
wilderness journey and the conquest of the land by their fathers. Tragically, new generations had to learn how to relate
to the God of Israel through their failures and the sorrow of
encountering his judgments; and yet God was merciful. In
one part of the country after another, tribes or groups of tribes
broke faith with God and then suffered defeat at the hands of
their enemies who attacked and conquered them. Only God's
grace and loving guidance brought each of them out of their
spiritual and moral failures. A consideration of apostasy and
renewal can be charted as follows:

When relations with the Lord are productive—One or several tribes
were faithful to the Lord and enjoyed his *blessing*, and the
spiritual level was high.

When people turn away—When a spiritual renewal ran its
course, after three or four generations, with no attempt made
to retain the momentum, increasing numbers of believers
grew cold and worship became a ritual. Believers were always
the key in setting the example, but with a weakened spiritual
testimony, the danger was that pagan worship would then fill
the gap and become the choice for an increasing number of
unbelievers. The choices of worshipping foreign gods meant a
dangerous spiritual low among the clans of Israel.

A judgment by God—Subsequently, God had to bring about a
judgment, usually by allowing neighboring pagan peoples to
conquer the area in which the apostate tribe or tribes were located. The invaders severely pressured the people, taxing
them heavily, usually through food allocations, leaving the Israelites with very little to eat and little else besides. God purposely permitted the pressure to become heavy in order to
provoke his people to realize what was causing their distress.

The need for repentance—With cries of repentance an Israelite tribe (or tribes) then turned to God in the midst of their intense suffering. When a people understood how greatly they had sinned against their God (who wanted to be their benefactor), they were ready to turn back to him.

God calls for his leader—God responded to the cry of repentance from his people by raising up his representative, a judge, who then led the people in spiritual renewal. The testimony of the judge, as a regent of God, was that Israel's God was unique. He is the Lord.

Victory over the enemies—When renewal had taken place, and believers turned wholeheartedly to the Lord, the tribe or tribes were restored to fellowship with God. Unbelievers then could be reached with the biblical message of truth. Finally, the people then could drive out their conquerors, triumphing over their enemies.

A spiritual high and a time of rest—Once the tribe or tribes were restored to a period of blessing again, they enjoyed rest for a number of years, usually for two or three generations. Unfortunately, when a new generation came along who knew only second- or third-hand what it meant to walk with God, and the testimony of the believers was again very weak, this new generation had to learn again the lessons of knowing and walking with God. If God's people do not learn from the mistakes of the past, they will be doomed to repeat them again.

So it went for some 300 years. One might perceive that everyone in the country had gone astray in this period and that Israel lacked faithful believers who sought to live for God on a high spiritual level. But God gives us a small glimpse into the lives of some of his people who really trusted him. The book of Ruth is a pleasant and delightful interlude in the midst of depressing and sad events. In Bethlehem were godly people who remembered God's Word and lived to honor him.

It does not take many to be salt for the earth, and a few, such as Boaz and Ruth, were examples to the believers and a testimony to those who had not yet entered into an atonement experience with the Lord.

The Philistines

The worst of the pagans confronting Israel were the Philistines, whose cities were in the southwest part of the country, mostly along the plain of the seacoast. They had a warlike tradition, and, being newcomers in the Canaanite region, they were ready to challenge and press their conquest vigorously. Evidence exists that they fought against the Canaanites and took land from them as far north as the Esdraelon Valley (running generally east to west across Israel) and even through the valley eastward to the Jordan River. The full oppression began just after 1100 B.C.E., and for some forty years they dominated many parts of Israel (see Judg. 13:1). We also know that Saul began his reign about 1051 B.C.E. and waged many campaigns to drive out the Philistines.

Samson—Just prior to Saul, Samson also served as a judge. He was born in Zorah, near the boundary line between Israel and the Philistines, and from his birth he was called to be a Nazirite and was set aside for the purpose of driving out the Philistines.

Samson's strategy of attack against the Philistine oppressors was not to lead an army against them but rather to work alone in their midst. Because of his tremendous strength, he confounded Israel's enemies through his feats of physical prowess. His tragic downfall was in Delilah's barbershop where he unwittingly told her the source of his strength—his long hair (see Judg. 16:16), which was the sign of his dedication as a Nazirite. When his hair was cut, he no longer had his God-given strength; he was captured, his eyes were gouged out, and he became a pathetic mill grinder.

Only in the end, when his hair had grown back and after his cry of repentance and spiritual restoration, did his strength once more return. On a day when the Philistines offered sacrifice to their god Dagon for Samson's capture, they called for him to entertain them. Little did they realize how God was to answer his repentant servant. As Samson stood, braced between the two central columns of the Temple, he cried to God to help him and the Lord gave him the strength to cause the building to collapse. More Philistines were killed at the time of Samson's death than in all of his previous exploits (see Judg. 16:28–31).

Samson was an enigma. Certainly God had called him to *begin* Israel's delivery (see Judg. 13:5), and he did win some victories over the Philistines. In many ways, Samson served the God of Israel and made the Philistines respect the God who could give him so much power. On the other hand, his life was hardly what one could call disciplined.

He took honey from the carcass of a dead lion, a practice that was forbidden by the kosher laws under ordinary circumstances, but even more so since he was a Nazirite (see Judg. 14:9). He had a lust for women, on one occasion visiting a prostitute (see Judg. 16:1). Then he insisted on marrying a foreign woman—a decision that brought his parents a lot of grief.

Even though he had been dedicated a Nazirite, we can only conclude that there were times when his heart was completely insensitive to God's desires. However, since he judged Israel for some twenty years, there is evidence that for most of this period he did have some kind of testimony. But only by God's mercy was Samson listed in God's honor roll of faith (see Heb. 11:32).

Samuel—Samuel, a contemporary with Samson, was one of Israel's great leaders. Because he had sons old enough to act as judges in Beersheba (see 1 Sam. 8:1, 2)—even before Saul began to reign in 1051 B.C.E.—Samuel's birth date could not be much later than 1100 B.C.E. This was just about the beginning of the Ammonite and Philistine oppressions of portions of Israel.

Samuel was born to Elkanah, a Levite in Ramah, within the territory of Benjamin. While the Scriptures indicate that Elkanah was from the hill country of Ephraim (see 1 Sam. 1:1), the record also states that Elkanah and Samuel were both of Levitical lineage (see 1 Chron. 6:33–35). Samuel's mother was Hannah, one of Elkanah's two wives, but she had no children prior to Samuel's birth. On one yearly occasion, when she and her husband made a pilgrimage to the tabernacle at Shiloh, Hannah prayed in anguish before the Lord, asking for a son, and God heard her desperate cry. He enabled her to conceive and give birth to a son. She named the boy Samuel, which in Hebrew means, "heard of God," a fitting designation for such a direct answer to prayer. When Samuel was weaned at about age three, his mother brought him to the tabernacle and, true to her promise to God, she dedicated him for ministry, placing him under the tutelage of the priest Eli.

A.   REMOVAL OF THE LINE OF ITHAMAR AS PRIESTS

However, the spiritual level of the people in that part of the country was questionable, and what passed for worship, particularly at the tabernacle, was going from bad to worse. Eli, as high priest, was a descendant of Aaron through Ithamar. When Samuel came under Eli's care, the priest was already old, and his sons, Hophni and Phinehas, ministered as priests alongside him. While Eli himself could be considered an earnest follower of the Lord, his testimony as a father was sullied: He had completely failed in his responsibilities in rearing his own children.

When Hophni and Phinehas reached the age for ministry, they became wicked, thereby making despicable the worship at the altar. But instead of severely disciplining his sons, Eli failed to exercise his spiritual discrimination by barring them from their high office. Because of their perversion of the worship services, they discouraged Israelis from seeking the Lord, even driving them away. God not only had to judge these sons, but also to cut off their father's line. A prophet arose to warn Eli, not even offering him the opportunity to repent. Instead, he delivered the message of doom that not only would every one of this family line perish, but the full line of Ithamar eventually would be removed from serving even as priests (see 1 Sam. 2:27–36) and in the end would serve only as Levites.

B. SAMUEL'S TRAINING

Meanwhile, God prepared Samuel to lead Israel. As a mere child, he began his training at the tabernacle, and was told that when he matured he would take the place of Eli and his two sons. The message he shared with the high priest was serious and would take place soon enough. If Samuel was about ten years old when God revealed himself to him, then the date was about 1090 B.C.E. Fifteen years later, the prophecy was fulfilled when a disastrous battle took place between Israel and the Philistines at Aphek, around 1075 B.C.E. (see Sam. 4).

Aphek was located in the plains of Sharon and is associated with the later Roman site of Antipras. The site today is just east of the modern city of Tel Aviv, which meant that the Philistines had control of a good part of the coastal area of the country.

C. ISRAEL DEFEATED, AND ELI'S LINE CUT OFF

In an initial encounter between the armies of Israel and the Philistines, some 4,000 Israelites soldiers were killed. So as to insure victory, a message was sent back to Eli at the tabernacle, requesting permission to bring the sacred Ark of the Covenant into the battle area. Permission was granted, and Eli's sons, Hophni and Phinehas, brought the ark into the military camp, a distance of some twenty-three miles from Shiloh. Treating the ark in such fashion was not only contrary to God's will, it was also another symptom of how low was the spiritual level of the people of Israel in this part of the country.

One wonders why the ark of God was treated in this fashion. Did the people see it as some kind of good luck charm? When Moses came down from Mount Sinai with the tablets in his hands and stood at the edge of the camp, he was appalled at what he saw. He took one look at what was going on in the camp and did not even dare enter with these symbols of God's holiness among a people who were so indifferent to God's will. Instead, he smashed the tablets of commandments at the entrance to the camp. Moses' response shows how such worthless men as Hophni and Phinehas should have been treated. How could these "sons of perdition" even dare bring the sacred ark among the soldiers? The sons of Eli were completely bereft of any kind of spiritual perception.

No wonder the battle went against Israel. Some 30,000 troops fell, including Eli's sons; and the Philistines captured the Ark of the Covenant. The tragic prophecy against the house of Eli began to unfold so devastatingly that when the elderly priest Eli heard the news, he fell backward off his chair, broke his neck and died. His daughter-in-law was pregnant at the time, and when she heard the news, she went into labor and then died in childbirth. The child that was born was named Ichabod, meaning "No glory," suggesting in a sense that the glory had departed from Israel through the capture of the ark of God. In one of the nation's most dire moments in history, Israel was left seemingly helpless and alone. And yet, at such a calamitous time, God intervened to bring about restoration.

The Philistines were unable to keep the ark in their midst. Even the priests of Israel's enemy recognized that their unlawful possession of the Ark of the Covenant posed a grave danger to them and their god, Dagon (see 1 Sam. 5). So they sent the ark back to Israel, where it finally found a resting place among the people of Kiriath-Jearim, remaining there until the day when David brought it to Jerusalem about seventy years later. The fact that Samuel did not return the ark to the tabernacle at Shiloh when he became the ministering judge is very significant. How was it possible to focus on a worship center where the religious leaders were so irresponsible? That irresponsibility in turn led to the disastrous defeat for Israel when so many died on the battlefield.

In the midst of such deplorable spiritual circumstances, God had his man prepared to lead the nation in spiritual renewal. But before we consider the specifics of this particular renewal, we need to take another look at Samuel, a person unique in Israel's history, as well as the home from which he came.

The Man Samuel

A Home Where Parents were Believers

Because Samuel was the answer to his mother's prayer, we already have some idea about the home that played a vital role in the background of Samuel's ministry. His parents, Elkanah and Hannah, were among the handful of people who knew the Lord amid such spiritual poverty; and this aspect of the home life reveals how the parents had a vital *personal relationship* with the Lord. Hannah, Samuel's mother, praised God for his faithfulness in providing her with a son, exclaiming, "My heart exults in ADONAI" (1 Sam. 2:1). For a woman to make such a statement can only mean that she had come to a personal relationship with the living God. How important it was for this mother to know the Lord and thereby have a sensitivity to encourage Samuel and her other children! Of Elkanah, Samuel's father, the record says he went "from his city every year to worship and sacrifice to ADONAI-*Tzva'ot* [the LORD of Hosts] in Shiloh" (1 Sam. 1:3), which was a sign of his obedience to the Word. His faithfulness to God would also have its impact on Samuel's ministry.

Believing parents have a crucial opportunity and responsibility to influence their children for the Lord.

A Meaningful Prayer Life

Samuel's home also reflected his parents' genuine *prayer life*. His father "worshiped ADONAI," a statement that suggests prayer. His mother knew how to cling desperately to God as she prayed for a son—Samuel's name and life are testimony to her prayers.

Parents need to face the challenge of earnestly praying for their children. Even before the children are born, they should be dedicated to the Lord, even as Hannah did. God uniquely entrusts parents with children for the purpose of rearing them to know the Lord and to serve him joyfully. Prayer then becomes important, enabling a father and mother to have wisdom for the multitude of perplexing circumstances of child rearing and training. These days, parents need Solomon's wisdom, Job's patience, Elijah's prayer life, Sha'ul's (Paul's) dedication, and God's grace!

Spending Time with our Children

Parents must take time to *know* their children. Samuel's parents were devoted people, and until Samuel was weaned they no doubt made every effort to be with their son. After Elkanah and Hannah turned over Samuel to Eli, to be trained by him, they still visited him at Shiloh. We can also assume that they spent time with their other children, but the relationship of Hannah and Elkanah with Samuel took on a special heart-touching significance. Every year they visited Samuel at the usual period; and for each occasion Hannah made a little robe, bringing it with her to clothe her son (see 1 Sam. 2:19). We can well imagine how this mother took special care in preparing the cloth, each year making it a little larger to care for the body of a growing boy. While no trace is left of these robes, they became the sign of a mother's deep feelings for her son who had been dedicated to the ministry in such a sacrificial way. Samuel's parents never forgot him. They took the time to visit him, understand his longings, needs, joys, and hope for future service. They genuinely loved Samuel and gave him their wholehearted support.

Do parents today really know their children? Do they know what is on their minds? I have often listened to young people talk among themselves, at the Institute where I taught and in the congregations I had the privilege to serve. And I had cause to wonder if the parents really knew what was on the hearts and minds of their children. For parents to understand their children's interests, their beliefs, and values, it is necessary to spend quality time with sons and daughters, thereby encouraging a two-way conversation. Parents who do so will then be able to mold and guide their children to grow up to be men and women of God.

God's Specially Prepared Man

Samuel knew he had his parents' full support. Because of what he received from his godly home, Samuel had a spiritual perception, knowing how to relate to all kinds of people; and, therefore, he had confidence in his work. He was not afraid to rebuke Israel's leaders and people for their poor choice of Saul as king. He spelled out exactly what would happen if the wrong man should take office (see 1 Sam. 8). His farewell address as a judge, when he charged King Saul and the nation to be faithful to Israel's real King, had the ring of integrity characteristic of a man of God. The high honor of anointing David as God's choice to be the future king of Israel went to Samuel (see 1 Sam. 16). Toward the end of his life he conducted a school of prophets in his old hometown of Ramah, preparing for Israel the men of God who would be their future spiritual leaders (see 1 Sam. 19:18–20).

We can well appreciate the enormous task Samuel faced as God led him to restore a nation. Israel's enemies had humiliated her. Because the Ark of the Covenant had been displaced, the nation's spiritual nerve center was severed. God, however, was more than able and ready to re-establish spiritual fellowship with Israel at just the right moment, when his prophet was ready to face the challenge.

The Imperatives of Spiritual Renewal

God had prepared Samuel to lead Israel in its spiritual renewal, but before the Philistines or any other enemy could be defeated on the battlefield, the nation had to be restored in its relationship to the Lord. Only when we are right with God can we be physically and spiritually victorious over our enemies.

Importance of God's Word

Powerfully proclaiming God's Word is imperative for renewal. God's Word played a key role in the days of Moses at Mt. Sinai. But the personal experience with the power of the Word would prove no less true for Samuel and Israel as God spoke to the desperate need of the nation in one of its darkest hours.

The record states, "Sh'mu'el [Samuel] addressed all the people of Isra'el" (1 Sam. 7:3). The Israelites didn't have television sets that received telecasts from satellite communications so that one message could reach the entire nation. To enable all the people to hear the Torah, Samuel became an itinerant preacher, moving about from Shiloh in the north to the area of his hometown in Ramah, near to what later was to be Jerusalem, and then on to Mizpah, Gilgal, and as far south as Bethlehem. All Israel heard the prophet's message.

The Word creates a hunger in the heart—As Samuel ministered the Torah, he sensed the longing in people's hearts for a national spiritual restoration. The Ark of the Covenant rested at Kiriath-Jearim for some twenty years after the battle of Aphek (1075–1055 B.C.E.). "Twenty years" can represent an entire generation, or at least a good part of it, and the Scripture states that "all the people yearned for ADONAI" (1 Sam. 7:2). No doubt, Samuel's preaching created an even greater thirst and hunger in people's hearts as they realized the ark was not readily accessible and, therefore, there was no central place to go for their worship.

Likewise, preaching, teaching, and hearing God's Word creates a desire for more of the Lord's presence in our lives. Across the centuries, Israel had a central sanctuary where they went to worship God. Today, in the body of the Messiah, each believer is a temple wherein the Holy Spirit lives (see 1 Cor. 6:19). Yet the Holy Spirit's fullness is not automatic; he will never force his way in to fill a person's heart. Only as we study the Word and seek to worship him in the beauty of his holiness will his presence be enjoyed, and then the Holy Spirit will fill the sincere seeker.

The requirements by the Word—What does God's Word need so that it can work in the depths of believers' hearts?

A. THE WORD NEEDS TO BE READ EVERY DAY

Believers need to read God's Word daily. This practice will prove to be one of the greatest joys possible in this life. Many of God's people, in the midst of the daily round of their lives, will say in essence, "We're too busy. We don't have time to read the Scriptures every day." I am reminded of what one well-known preacher said: "Beware of the barrenness of a busy life!" If we are too busy, then it is most important that some of this business be set aside so as to make time to read the Word and allow it to speak to us.

B. THE WORD NEEDS DIRECT USE

Daily, believers need to be immersed in reading the Scripture, devouring entire chunks of it, perhaps two, three, and four chapters a day. It is much like the butcher who carves large chunks of meat before he ever cuts them into the small pieces to be sold to customers. As a believer reads large blocks of the Word, he seeks for God to speak very specifically on a number of areas in his life. This kind of reading leads one to zero in on particular areas for specific study, which is the next usage of the Scriptures.

C. THE WORD NEEDS A DETAILED USE

After the butcher has cut the larger chunks of meat, he then takes a large piece and cuts it into smaller pieces for his customers to purchase. A chef then cooks these and they end up on a dinner plate as food to be cut into even smaller pieces.

This procedure also applies as one carefully investigates smaller portions of the Scriptures. After one handles the larger chunks of the Word, these then need to be cut down into very small pieces so that the believer's heart can absorb them in specific and unique ways. We can claim applicable promises in God's Word (see Ps. 37:4, about ADONAI giving his loving followers the desires of their hearts, for example). When a command (such as Prov. 3:5–6, about trusting ADONAI wholeheartedly) is emphasized, then we need to obey it, sensing that God can bless and make paths straight when believers seek to serve him.

When precepts are laid down in the Word, guidance will be given to follow them (such as in Ps. 119:11, which reveals the purifying influence of God's Word). When God provides warnings, it calls for responsible action to heed them (such as in Yeshua's parable about the nobleman who gave his servants money to invest, see Luke 19:13). God's warning makes it urgent for unbelievers to give heed to the message of salvation through the Messiah (see 1 Cor. 6:2). The Scriptures provide us with many examples of holy living, encouraging us to enter into some of their experiences, as for example, the meaning of intercession as Abraham pleaded for his wayward nephew Lot (see Gen. 18:22f).

Every generation of believers needs to meditate on the Word, but often tension can arise. We can have every intention to act on what God is saying, but at the same time we can struggle with doing it (see Gal. 5:17). We have to get into the Word through the "spiritual knife-and-fork drill"; as we do, we will grow and not backslide.

D. DOING WHAT THE WORD SAYS

The call in Samuel's day was for people to be obedient to what the Torah declares—a message that applies for our day as well. So the prophet set out to preach and teach this Word everywhere. He had *one message*, and it was *to the point*, "If you are returning to ADONAI with all your heart, then be done with the foreign gods and *'ashtarot* that you have with you" (1 Sam. 7:3). While the Holy Spirit worked in the hearts of the believers in their longing for restoration, he also led Samuel to put his finger on some of the more glaring problems among the unbelievers. At the appropriate moment, with believers restored, the unbelievers would be ready to listen and respond to the Word.

Preaching can single out what is wrong. And the man of God, as he preaches the Word, is only trying to correct attitudes and lifestyles among believers that are a definite block to spiritual renewal. Even as God worked in Samuel's day, he is also at work in our day. As believers yearn for fullness of God's Spirit in our lives, we need to put away any practice or relationship that will detract from this spiritual goal. Secular and unconcerned people also need to listen to the Word and turn away from the deities of our age, such as affluence, immorality, drugs, the occult, and a host of others, all of which only leave the human heart empty.

But notice Samuel's *commanding* message in the same verse: "Serve only him" (v. 3). The prophet called people to turn to the true and living God and give him our ultimate attention. He is a jealous God and will not allow for any rival among the lives of his followers or among unbelievers. The nation was on the verge of renewal, and Samuel wanted to ensure this spiritual effort so that his hearers would not "blow it."

Call for a National Convocation

Another imperative for spiritual renewal was the call for a national convocation. Many in Israel had been obedient to Samuel's proclamation and had "banished the ba'alim and the 'ashtarot and served only ADONAI" (1 Sam. 7:4). However, Samuel challenged the believers of his day: "Do you want to really meet God?" So he issued a summons reflecting the sentiments of such a question, "Gather all Isra'el to Mizpah, and I will pray for you" (1 Sam. 7:5). The prophet called all Israel to gather at one of its key locations for a meeting with Israel's King—the Lord.

While the purpose of the convocation was to face God in repentance and then to seek to do his will without reservation, Israel also faced the problem of how such a large convocation would appear to the Philistines. Their Philistine overlords might interpret a large gathering as a revolt. For forty long years Israel had been under the thumb of the Philistines (see Judg. 13:1), going back to 1095 B.C.E. And except for the faithful few who no doubt were praying for renewal, the nation had become a spiritual desert. Now, however, God was going to answer the prayers of believers, and his judge-deliverer had come in answer to their call. Because they had earnestly sought God, the promise by the prophet was for complete deliverance from the Philistine tyrants.

Similarly, as believers face today's problems, each of us needs to ask, "Am I living in victory every day?" "Do I know God's deliverance as I face the extreme tests of an illness that can cripple, of financial reverses, or of difficult experiences with unbelievers in a family who can make life a hell for those who come to the faith?" Sometimes we may not *feel* victorious in the battle, but God gives us the opportunity to be overcomers. We have the promise that we possess all spiritual blessings in heavenly places in the Messiah (see Eph. 1:3). As we lay hold on these blessings, a battle can ensue to attain them because we wrestle with the spiritual forces of darkness who are also in the heavenly places (see Eph. 6:12).[15] Nothing worth achieving in the spiritual realm is without a battle, but the God who gave the promise for victory in Samuel's generation is the same Lord who will work mightily today for every believer who desires the best.

The Elements for Spiritual Renewal in Samuel's Day

Every renewal has certain elements that are common, but at times there are specific ones that command our attention.

The element of total commitment—One of Samuel's first pleas was for believers to make a total commitment to the Lord God of Israel. The record describes a most unusual circumstance: As many in Israel had assembled at Mizpah, "they . . . drew water and poured it out before *Adonai*" (1 Sam. 7:6). This act is seen nowhere else in Scripture, although an occasion in David's life does lend some understanding about what took place (see 2 Sam. 23:14–17).

David was confined in the cave of Adullam while a Philistine military force was in the Valley of Raphaim, as well as in the nearby town of Bethlehem. With David completely surrounded and cut off from any possible human help, he began to reminisce. He recalled nostalgically many of his boyhood experiences, including drinking fresh cold water from the well near the gate of Bethlehem on a warm day. As he thought of the cool, refreshing water that had satisfied him so thoroughly as a lad, he uttered in a wistful tone, "Oh, that someone would get me a drink of water from the well," even though he and his men already had plenty of water.

When three of David's mightiest warriors heard their master's wish, they took their leave and, slipping through the Philistine lines at great risk to their lives, drew water from that well and brought it back to David. When he looked at the water and understood that it had been obtained at the risk of the lives of his closest men, he could not drink it. Rather, he poured it out on the ground before the Lord because he regarded this water as a symbol of the great dedication of his closest warriors, whose only thought was to please their king.

The only other incident of pouring out water was mentioned later, when, on the last day of the Feast of Tabernacles, a group of priests went out of the Temple area to the pool of Siloam. They drew water in a golden pitcher and carried it back to the Temple area; then they poured the water into a basin west of the great altar.[16] Later, the water—along with wine—was poured out at the altar, and everyone present began to sing the passage from Isaiah 12:2, 3.[17] But this symbolic action conveyed the great message of eternal life and where it can be found, especially when Yeshua made such an emphasis of it in John 7:37, 38.[18]

Samuel poured out the water at Mizpah, in the sight of the entire congregation, as the drink offerings were "poured out" at the altar. This action depicted one pouring out his life before the Lord[19] in an act of dedication, especially when fasting and confession also were associated with it. So the prophet declared to the people of his generation that they had to yield to the sovereign God of Israel if he ever was going to drive out their enemies before them and grant them his blessings. One of the elements of any spiritual renewal is the call for God's people to be dedicated to him wholeheartedly, without any reservation.

The element of fasting—In addition, the people also fasted (see 1 Sam. 7:6). As the people prayed and waited upon the Lord, they urgently asked him to work in a mighty way. Going without food did not mean that the people in Samuel's day (or in ours) should strut about and pat themselves on the shoulders and announce to the world at large, "We are fasting!" No merit can be acquired by boasting about a spiritual exercise. But so intense were the congregants in their pursuit of God's blessings that they voluntarily set aside their food.

Some today might suggest that fasting was a spiritual exercise in "Old Testament days," and that it is unnecessary for today because Yeshua never required his disciples to fast. The phrase *and fasting* is not found in the best Greek manuscripts of Mark 9:29 (where the Lord was talking to his disciples about casting out stubborn demons). Nor is it found in similar passages, such as Acts 10:30; 1 Cor. 7:5 or Matt. 17:21, where the phrase is omitted entirely in the best texts.[20]

Some scholars, however, allow for personal fasting if it is done in secret and with a sincere heart. I agree. Congregational or national revival, or a nation's abysmal lack of moral consciousness, can be a legitimate concern by believers as they engage in prayer and, yes, even fasting.

The element of confession of sin—The nation in convocation at Mizpah also confessed its sins (see 1 Sam. 7:6), as believers and others cried out, "We have sinned against ADONAI." Perhaps they remembered the great sin of taking the Ark of the Covenant out to the battle of Aphek, but they also could have been reminded of the presence of false gods in their midst.

Every Israeli had to recognize his or her part in a large household, and that each one was responsible for his fellow citizen. Hophni and Phinehas were personally responsible for their despicable lifestyle and also for taking the Ark of the Covenant onto the battlefield. At the same time, however, each member of the nation was responsible for the entire community's sins. That confession, which began with the word, "we," was the prayer of intercession: Each Israelite felt that he was confessing the nation's sins. This statement was certainly no new phenomenon; actually, this kind of prayer on behalf of the nation reflected a well-known concept. Moses had done so previously (see Exod. 33:13), and Daniel also had to confess the sins of the forefathers, even though he himself was not responsible for the waywardness that led the nation into exile (see Dan. 9). Intercessory prayer and confession of sin represents one of the greatest spiritual exercises believers can be engaged in, and it is always an element in spiritual renewal.

Taking time to wait upon the Lord—Samuel was also the *leader*, as well as *judge* of Israel at Mizpah, acting as God's regent and adjudicating specific cases brought before him. No doubt, there were many in that generation who came before the congregation and Samuel to seek counsel for their personal lives in areas of spiritual lack and need. It was as if they had come before God to ask for help in their personal lives, confess their sins, and seek for a more meaningful personal relationship with the Lord. The congregation took the time to wait upon God.

Engaging the enemy—The convocation must have been at Mizpah for quite some time, although it is difficult to ascertain just how long. The record explains, "When the P'lishtim [Philistines] heard that the people of Isra'el had gathered together at Mizpah, the leaders of the P'lishtim marched up against Isra'el; and when the people of Isra'el heard about this, they were afraid of the P'lishtim" (1 Sam. 7:7). It took time for word to get back to their cities and leaders. Upon hearing of such an assembly, the enemy felt that Israel had gathered together to oppose them, so the Philistines deployed their military units to attack and break up this convocation. Yet, Israel's prayer and confession of sin was just what God had in mind in order to prepare for battle with these invaders. Little did the Philistines realize their danger; with Israel in a new relationship and worship before God, the Lord could then fight and destroy his people's enemies.

Even today, believers who take the time to wait upon God and seek his counsel for the day's activities can have the same experience—even though the enemy of our souls will be mustering all the forces of evil. After all, who can prevail against the Lord God of heaven? Congregations and individual believers often fall down in their witness and ministry because so few of God's people are praying. Only a few have the fullness of the Spirit in their hearts, which is why the Body of Messiah has such a low level of expectation for what God can do.

Victory

When Israel had met the two imperatives of *listening to God's Word* and *gathering together before the Lord to seek his face*, victory then could be the expected outcome.

God worked at just the right time—For forty years Israel had been under Philistine oppression. Until about five years before Saul became king, the Philistines had controlled the seacoast of Israel, north to the Esdraelon Valley, across the center of Israel as far east as the Jordan River. The battle of Mizpah was, therefore, just prior to the anointing of Saul as king over Israel. While Samson began to deliver Israel, Israel's first king led the first victorious battle against the Philistines, after spiritual renewal had come to the people of Israel (see 1 Sam. 11).

An enemy on the run—As the invaders approached, the terrified people had the presence of mind to call on Samuel to pray on behalf of the nation. So, even "[a]s Sh'mu'el was presenting the burnt offering, the P'lishtim advanced to attack Isra'el" (1 Sam. 7:10). As the Israelis worshiped, God took action against the Philistines and "thundered with loud thunder" against these invaders, hurling a great storm of lightning, rain, and possibly hail at them. The Philistine enemies themselves realized that powerful spiritual forces were gathered against them, so they panicked, broke ranks, and ran back to their cities as fast as they could go.

Did the Israelites come to worship at Mizpah fully armed with their weapons? Hardly! The worshipers came to face God, and they realized only too painfully that they were indeed weak before their enemies and needed God's protection. But after the Israelites dedicated themselves to the Lord, the Philistines were put to flight because of the storm, leaving their weapons behind them. The men of Israel were able to use their enemies' own weapons to kill them! The enemy left their dead all along the way to a point below Beth Car, in the foothills, well out of the central mountain range of the country. From there, the stragglers continued to flee to their cities in the plain along the Mediterranean.

The sign of great spiritual renewal was in Israel's celebration of victory over the Philistines, and was memorialized when Samuel set up the stones between Mizpah and Shen. The word "Shen" means "tooth," and probably refers to some rock or peak by that name where Israel's soldiers left off pursuing their enemies. The stones that Samuel erected were called "Ebenezer," meaning "Stone of Help," and the place was designated as a remembrance or testimony to God for the great victory he wrought on Israel's behalf. So, at the right moment, when a large number of believers in Israel greatly yearned for and earnestly turned back to God, the nation's relationship with him was restored. Then the great victory took place. No doubt, many unbelievers also were reached because of the great outpouring of God's Spirit on his people. For that reason, the hand of the Lord was against the Philistines throughout the rest of Samuel's lifetime (see 1 Sam. 7:13).

Samuel's heritage of a godly home and the part his parents played in their son's experience with God, was important in preparing the man God would use. While the elements of renewal and the message by the prophet are brief, they are no less powerful than what God had accomplished through Moses in his day. Finally, the account of the great victory, in renewal as well as the defeat over the Philistines, is a tribute to what God can accomplish through dedicated hearts in renewal. The hearts of believers today can also be turned when there is a hunger for God and for his interests—provided there is the willingness to sincerely do his will in claiming unbelieving family members, communities, and even the nation for the Lord! Who knows? Perhaps we can again see an outpouring of the Spirit upon our nation today as the *Mizpah* conditions are met.

I remember when I was in seminary in the early 1950s, during the renewal that occurred on the campuses of our Christian colleges and seminaries. I would imagine that all who attended chapel one particular day will never forget the seminary president leading in prayer. When he finished, he hesitated, saying nothing. He remained standing quietly for more than a couple of minutes. A hush fell in the chapel, and the more than 300 young men and women felt what we later perceived as the invading presence of the Lord. In the midst of that silence, God's Spirit prompted a young woman to stand, and with tears on her cheeks, she confessed considerable ill will toward one of her professors. No one moved, and the chapel remained silent as the Holy Spirit moved to search our hearts. The president continued to stand quietly. Soon, a young man stood to his feet and also confessed to having much the same attitude as the young woman.

After that, it was as if the dam that had held back unconfessed sin broke loose. For the next several hours, students confessed sins, one after another. Faculty and administration also confessed sinful attitudes and actions. With tears, we sought God's face as we waited on him to cleanse us. Most remained in chapel for the rest of the day. Toward evening the spirit of praise came upon us, and we began to glorify God for what he had accomplished in our hearts when we were clean and pure before him.

I look back on that experience as a movement of the Spirit that changed so many of our lives and gave us great victory in our ministry. Today, many from that seminary class have served and continue to serve in diverse fields in the world, reaching unbelievers. But it all goes back to that day when, after a heart-searching prayer, the fire of God's Spirit fell in our midst, and we were on our faces before him.

CHAPTER FOUR

Asa, The Defender of Judah
The Man Who Did What Was Right as His Father David

(1 Kings 15:9–24; 2 Chron. 14:2–16:14)

"*ADONAI*, there is no one besides yourself, strong or weak, who can help. Help us, *ADONAI* our God, because we are relying on you, and we are coming against this vast throng in your name. You are *ADONAI* our God; don't let human beings stop you."
(2 Chron. 14:11)

"Then he gathered all Y'hudah and Binyamin, along with those from Efrayim, M'nasheh and Shim'on who were staying with him (for they had defected to him in large numbers upon seeing that *ADONAI* his God was with him)."
(2 Chron. 15:9)

"All Y'hudah was full of joy at this oath; for they had sworn with all their heart and had sought him with all their will; and they found him, and *ADONAI* gave them rest all around."
(2 Chron. 15:15)

We now jump across the centuries from the days of Samuel to King Asa, a period of some 400 years (see Figure 5, page 71). This timespan included some of the nation's greatest triumphs as well as some of its worst tragedies. The nation had strength in the days of the united kingdom under David and Solomon. But after Solomon, the kingdom split—with tragic consequences—into Israel of the north and Judah of the south (perhaps better known as the Northern Kingdom and the

Southern Kingdom). God had no good word for any king of the north, but after David and Solomon, Asa was the first of eight Judean kings (out of a total of nineteen) who were declared to be good before the Lord. Not all of these eight kings did only what was pleasing to God, but they nevertheless sought to be faithful to him and his Word.

Historical Background

After Samuel's service as a judge, he continued in his ministry as a spiritual link with Asa. He lived concurrently with Israel's first two kings, through most of Saul's life, and during the early part of David's life. The Lord pronounced judgment against Israel's first king when he removed his presence from him (Saul certainly was not God's choice, see 1 Sam. 15:26–28). The consequent tragedy was concluded when Saul and his son Jonathan died on the battlefield fighting the Philistines (see 1 Sam. 31).

King David

David began his reign in Hebron over Judea and Benjamin (1011–1004 B.C.E.). Then, with a political, military, and economic agreement with the leaders of the northern tribes, David also was accepted as king over all Israel in 1004 B.C.E., reigning until 971 B.C.E. For most of his tenure, the king conducted himself as a godly and spiritual man. The exceptions were his evil deeds of lust with Bathsheba and the subsequent murder of Uriah (see 2 Sam. 11) and the element of pride in his census taking when he desired to know how many fighting men were in his army (see 2 Sam. 24).

As a military tactician, David was able to extend Israel's borders almost to what God had promised to Abraham (see Gen. 15:18). As a songwriter and musician, he had few peers. The lyrics of his Psalms have left a legacy for all mankind to worship the Lord. Because of his interest in a national center where Israel could worship the Lord, he brought the Ark of the Covenant from Kiriath-Jearim—where it had been for seventy years—to the city of Jerusalem, placing it in a tent amid great rejoicing as the sacrifices were offered. He also had an intense desire to build a temple, but God did not permit him to do so because he was a man of war (see 2 Sam. 7:1–17; 1 Chron. 17:1–15; 2 Chron. 22:7–9).

Instead, God made a covenant with David, guaranteeing him a house, a throne, and a kingdom over which one day the Messiah would preside. David could have been disappointed because he was not permitted to build the Temple; nevertheless he humbled himself before the Lord and thanked him for his blessings for singling out his family for such honor (see 2 Sam. 7:18–29; 1 Chron. 17:16–27). He then gathered together great quantities of material (see 1 Chron. 22:1–5, 14–16), and made preparations to enable his son Shlomo (Solomon) to build the Temple that would properly house the ark.

King Solomon

When Solomon ascended the throne in 971 B.C.E., he had the heritage and the potential to be an exemplary leader. God revealed himself to the new king and granted him his prayerful request for wisdom to govern "this great people" (see 1 Kings 3). Solomon also was promised riches and honor so that he was without an equal among the kings of the ancient Middle East in his day. To his credit, he built the Temple named after him, and then dedicated it in his well-reasoned prayer of blessing and hope for all peoples (see 1 Kings 8:23–53). But this was not to be the end of Solomon's building activities: Among his many projects, he also built the royal palace as well as the fortifications of Hazor, Megiddo, and Gezer.

Solomon failed, however, because his many wives turned him away from the Lord. Wanting to please their religious preferences, he had pagan shrines built where his wives could worship their gods (see 1 Kings 11). As a result, "he was not wholehearted with *Adonai* his God, as David his father had been" (see 1 Kings 11:4). God became angry with Solomon for creating a syncretism between true worship of the Lord and the false religious practices in the capital city of Israel. Consequently, God disciplined the king and the nation, bringing many adversaries against them.

Slowly but surely, Israel lost control of more and more of the territory that David had conquered. Despite God's favor, Solomon had not honored Israel's Lord, so the Lord judged him. God also predicted through his prophet Ahijah that the kingdom was going to be split in two. In the south, Judah and Benjamin remained intact, and also included the tribe of Simeon, who lived on Judah's land, as well as the Levites who served in the Temple. Solomon's successor would have only a portion of the land of Israel over which he could rule, but at least the lamp before the Lord in the Temple would be kept intact for a while (see 1 Kings 11:29ff). What a sad price to pay for disobedience!

The Kingdom is split in half

When Solomon died, Rehoboam ascended the throne and, with a new administration, a new day and a new beginning could have taken place, starting with the hope for economic reform. Solomon's building projects and rich lifestyle had required a severe tax load on the people, and now the leaders of the tribes earnestly asked the new king to "lighten the harsh service . . . and ease his heavy yoke" that had been placed on them. With relief granted for a legitimate request, the representatives of the nation gave their promise that all Israelites would gladly yield their allegiance to Rehoboam (see 1 Kings 12:4). Solomon's council of elders urged the new king to listen and provide for a necessary and welcome relief from the people's tax burden. Such a humane gesture would endear the king to his subjects.

But the younger men who had grown up with Rehoboam, sitting in the lap of luxury and enjoying what seemed an unlimited money supply, also gave their vain advice: *Do not lighten the tax load; rather, make it even heavier!* When Rehoboam listened to the words of his young and foolish friends who were nothing more than pleasure seekers and "playboys," he revealed a complete lack of sensitivity for his people who were so sorely oppressed. After all, when a ruler cares for what God desires, he will also be sensitive to the social and economic needs of his disadvantaged subjects. The result was a tragedy when the kingdom split. At least eight of the northern tribes made Jeroboam their king, while Judah, Benjamin, and Simeon in the south along with the priests and Levites from all Israel remained loyal to the house of David.

The spiritual course of the Northern Kingdom from that day on was down, down, and down. God had nothing good to say of any king of any dynasty in the Northern Kingdom. Their first king, Jeroboam, put his policy of separation into effect by sealing off the north from any contact with the Temple at Jerusalem. He built temple-shrines at Dan and Bethel and set up his own priests to officiate there, thereby providing alternative worship centers. Jeroboam's successors were evil, and the Northern Kingdom quickly adopted many of the idol-worship systems of the other nations in the Middle East, offering sacrifices to pagan gods. They ignored the Lord, although, even in the worst of times and occasions, God still had his witness to these wayward people. Chapters 5 and 6 will reveal that the Lord tried not only once, but many times, particularly in the ministries of Elijah, Elisha, Jonah, and other prophets, to reach Israel with the message of redemption.

Rehoboam and Abijam

In the south, Rehoboam's reign began when he was forty-one years old, and it lasted for seventeen years (931–913 B.C.E.). This sham of a king was unworthy to succeed David; he did only evil in the eyes of the Lord (see 1 Kings 14:22), mimicking particularly the spiritual sins his father Solomon had committed during the "spiritually down" years of his life.

God disciplined Rehoboam by permitting Shishak, king

of Egypt, to attack Judah. And while the Egyptian records do not indicate an assault on Jerusalem proper, the Egyptian monarch possibly took many sites in southern Judah. In order to keep the Egyptian monarch from actually penetrating any farther into the country, Rehoboam may have given him many of Jerusalem's treasures, including all of the gold shields that Solomon had made.

Rehoboam's son Abijam (sometimes called Abijah, see 2 Chron. 13:1) ruled for only three years (913–911 B.C.E.). The conflict continued between Israel and Judah, making this rivalry a tragedy, because, after all, these peoples all belonged to the same household and spoke the same language. Perhaps it would appear that Abijam exalted the Lord, in that he declared that the kingship of Judea was really the kingdom of the Lord (see 2 Chron. 13:8). He even appeared to condemn the fact that Jeroboam had driven out the priests of the Lord, the sons of Aaron, and the Levites, and had made priests of his own choosing. But Abijam's words also could reflect that Abijam was speaking as a politician rather than as a man of God. Elsewhere, the Scriptures declare that Abijam had a serious lack of spiritual grasp: "He committed all the sins his father had committed before him; he was not wholehearted with ADONAI his God, as David his forefather had been" (1 Kings 15:3).

God honored his Word, insuring Judah's position as a bona fide kingdom of the Lord; and so he also disciplined Jeroboam, routing his armies through the forces of Abijam, so that Judah captured a number of towns in Israel, including Bethel. At the same time, the record condemns Abijam's failure in that he did not take away the idols in Judah. Instead, his son Asa was the one who took seriously God's Torah, and removed the idols of the land (see 2 Chron. 14:3).

With the spiritual level of Judah already beginning to deteriorate during the latter part of Solomon's reign and into the reigns of Rehoboam and Abijam, the nation was ready for a spiritual renewal. Such a renewal also would impact many in the north, despite Jeroboam's utter disregard for the kingdom of Judah in the south.

The Man Asa

"Asa did what was good and right," reigning for some forty-one years, from 911 until 870 B.C.E. Asa was nothing like Rehoboam and Abijam. His first act as king was to remove all the foreign altars and have the male shrine prostitutes thrown out of the land. This king even zealously deposed his grandmother Maacah from her position as queen mother, because she kept a sacred pole to the goddess Asherah as an object of worship. Asa acted boldly because he felt a burning desire that the Lord's interests must come first. No doubt a spiritual hunger pervaded the king's soul, but he also sensed that Judah's strength must be entirely in the Lord God of Israel if any further blessings were to come upon the nation.

When one person takes a stand for God, generally he will be able to rally other believers around him. Not only did Asa gather believers around him, but he also became a beacon light of encouragement to many in the Northern Kingdom. Jeroboam already had put out the priests and the Levites from the kingdom of Israel (see 2 Chron. 13:9). Yet the record indicates that priests and other folks had come over to Asa from Israel when they saw that the Lord was with him (see 2 Chron. 15:9). The people of the south and the north needed a leader, and Asa was the very man God could use to touch the lives of countless numbers of people in spiritual renewal.

Because of his stand for the Lord and his utter reliance on him when foreign nations attacked Judah, the prophet Azariah encouraged this king who sought to honor Israel's God. Significantly, Asa "did what was right as his father David"!

For most of his forty-one years as king, Asa remained true and faithful and was able to sustain the spiritual renewal that God had graciously brought to Judah. But renewal also carried with it a forewarning—its blessings are never self-sustaining. One must also keep up the personal relationship with the Lord and ever seek his help. Tragically, this king relied more and more on himself, his schemes, and his own strength. Even Asa had to learn that the evil one craftily works to build a sense of self-sufficiency in people.

The Encouragement for Spiritual Renewal

Affirming our Faith

Torah must take precedence—The first element of encouragement for spiritual renewal is to keep on affirming our faith in God's instructions, as already noted in previous renewals. We always seem to have a problem doing what we know to be right. Believers continually need to be on guard, with the task of closing the gap between *knowing* what is needed and actually *doing* it. Ya'akov (James) sets forth the challenge, "Anyone who knows the right thing to do and fails to do it is committing a sin" (James 4:17).

The negative affirmations—Asa affirmed his faith with action when he removed the foreign altars and the high places (see 2 Chron. 14:3). Telling people that they are wrong—and correcting their errors—does not win popularity contests. Nonetheless, the king had to point out what was spiritually wrong with Judah and insist that people turn away from their worship of the detestable fertility cult of immorality (see 2 Kings 15:12). Pagan worship desecrated the moral and spiritual well-being of the nation; and because this king had a burden to honor the Lord, he felt compelled to speak as he did.

The only place where anyone, north or south, had a legitimate place to worship the God of Israel was in Jerusalem, at the Temple, which was dedicated to the Lord by Solomon in a day when he was a tower of spiritual strength (see 1 Kings 8). Only at this altar could the legitimate lessons of atonement be learned. The false altars with shrines to Ba'al, Asherah, and other false gods will fail for anyone seeking to find a spiritual home and rest. For believers to proclaim today that Yeshua is the only way to come to the living God seems so bigoted! But the lessons of atonement did not begin with Yeshua the Messiah; they already were in place in the Torah given by the Lord to Moses, who in turn gave it to the people of Israel as their legacy.

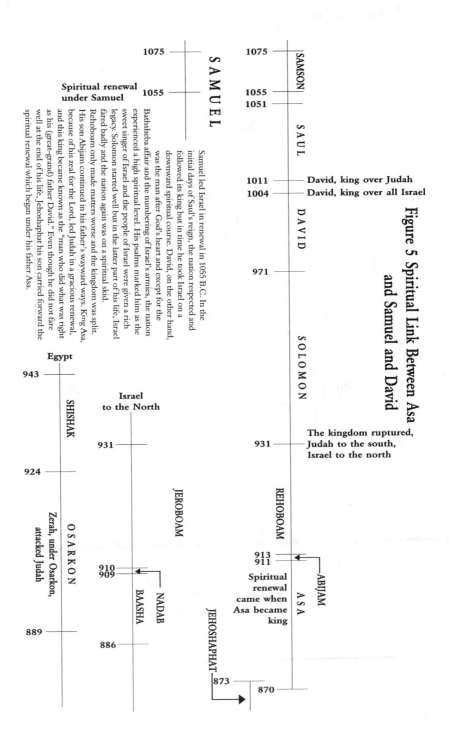

Figure 5 Spiritual Link Between Asa and Samuel and David

Samuel led Israel in renewal in 1055 B.C. In the initial days of Saul's reign, the nation respected and followed its king but in time he took Israel on a downward spiritual course. David, on the other hand, was the man after God's heart and except for the Bathsheba affair and the numbering of Israel's armies, the nation experienced a high spiritual level. His psalms marked him as the sweet singer of Israel and the people of Israel were given a rich legacy. Solomon started well but in the latter part of his life, Israel fared badly and the nation again was on a spiritual skid. Rehoboam only made matters worse and the kingdom was split. His son Abijam continued in his father's wayward ways. King Asa, because of his zeal for the Lord, led Judah in a gracious renewal, and this king became known as the "man who did what was right as his (great-grand) father David." Even though he did not fare well at the end of his life, Jehoshaphat his son carried forward the spiritual renewal which began under his father Asa.

S A M U E L

SAMSON   SAUL   DAVID   SOLOMON   REHOBOAM   ASA   JEHOSHAPHAT

ABIJAM

1075
1055
1051
1011 David, king over Judah
1004 David, king over all Israel
971
931 The kingdom ruptured, Judah to the south, Israel to the north
913
911 Spiritual renewal came when Asa became king
870
873

Spiritual renewal under Samuel
1075
1055

Egypt
943
SHISHAK
924
OSARKON
Zerah, under Osarkon, attacked Judah
889

Israel to the North
JEROBOAM
931
910
909
NADAB
BAASHA
886

Knocking out idols in our lives also has a modern application. Believers have to be able to recognize them and comprehend their deadly controlling influence. Practically speaking, idols are a barrier to genuine worship. Only a few of these idols will be mentioned and should suffice as a warning as to how dangerous they are:

1. *Self-will*—Where one goes his or own way, seeking to please the ego.
2. *Failure to trust God and his provision*—When believers become destitute because of adverse economic conditions or illness, the tendency is to become fearful about whether needs ever will be supplied. The old adage is true that when God guides, he will also provide. But after living so long in an affluent society, one finds it easy to forget how to trust God for simple needs.
3. *Misuse of time*—Many activities are not wrong in themselves, but they may not be profitable spiritually. Even Rav Sha'ul (Paul) recognized that while he was free to choose his activities, not every one of them was beneficial (see 1 Cor. 6:12). Certainly, there is nothing wrong in watching a football game, but if it hinders spiritual growth and attendance at local congregation services or involvement with some phase of ministry, then the game is no longer profitable.

Asa insisted that people who accepted God's atonement had a corresponding responsibility to come against false worship. So, as this king sought the Lord, he also called on the believers to stand with him, and together they would ask unbelievers in Judah to seek the Lord and turn away from foreign paganism.

The positive affirmations—King Asa also affirmed a positive emphasis: "He ordered Y'hudah to seek *ADONAI*, the God of their ancestors, and to obey the *Torah* and the *mitzvah*" (2 Chron.

14:4). As already noted, God's Word must be the guideline by which a nation finds its spiritual and moral pursuits. When the Word is no longer a guide, the nation will go astray. It is as simple as that.

A. AFFIRMING SPIRITUAL GOALS

Israel is supposed to be "the people of the book." And while good religious books are on the market that affirm the Torah, in a majority of instances, "the people" have become purveyors of books, many of which take their lifestyle cues from today's relativism. Moral absolutes are, therefore, lacking, and are replaced by religious tradition. Is it any wonder that many in Israel as well as among the nations have lost their spiritual and moral moorings?

God gave the Torah to be the guide for all peoples; but believers in particular need to order our lives by what it declares and not deviate from it, even when it cuts across our personal ambitions and desires. Therefore, faithful spiritual leaders must teach what God provided in his Word, and all believers must live accordingly.

B. AFFIRMING A GOOD DEFENSE

Asa further affirmed his faith in God when he built up the fortified cities of Judah (see 2 Chron. 14:6, 7). Building military fortifications and walls around Judean towns while trusting the Lord God solely for help may seem curious. However, Asa also knew that God expected him to exercise human responsibility. Judah still had enemies, and Asa felt obligated to build, strengthen, and maintain these military bases in order for Judah to be continually on guard. In other words, human responsibility and divine trust must be seen in perfect balance.

A human element also exists in our relationship with the Lord. Asa built fortifications in order to keep Judah safe. Believers today likewise need spiritual protection against the onslaughts of Satan. James reminds us, "Submit to God" (James 4:7), which becomes a pointed warning that in every sphere of activity we must submit to the King of our lives. At the same time, Rav Sha'ul (Paul) warns believers that we face intense spiritual warfare every day; so, to protect ourselves, each of us must put on the whole armor of God in order to do battle with the enemy of our souls. The two actions are to be in perfect balance. We should not overbalance the divine dimension of submission so that the tendency is to overlook or do very little with human responsibility.

The man who led me to Yeshua the Messiah was like this. He affirmed his faith, but not only through his words. He also had a love for me, even while I was an unbeliever. He demonstrated God's love, day by day and month by month for six months, until I made a decision. And even if I had not made a decision, he still would have remained undaunted as he affirmed his faith by what he said and how he expressed his love.

Spiritual renewal tarries because most of God's people, unlike Asa, are not willing to give their all in their human responsibility for service to the Holy One. As a result, we are not fully committed to reach the unbelievers in our communities.

Ask for God's Help

A second means of encouragement for renewal is simply to ask for God's help amid life's trials and pressures. Believers surely can cry to God for his help in times of great emergency. Sometimes we seem to do our loudest screaming when we are in the worst of circumstances. However, long before a believer finds himself in dire conditions, he or she needs to be consistent in prayer, asking God for his help day by day amid life's details. Asa began to do so almost as soon as he became king of Judah, even before he faced one of his greatest emergencies.

Judah outnumbered two to one—Asa and the people did not have to wait long for pressures. Zerah the Cushite marched against Judah with a vast army (literally, an army of thousands and thousands). Such numbers would have been overwhelming to any nation under attack. I once preached a message about Asa in one of the congregations of Israel, and upon mentioning the great numbers marching against Judah in Asa's day, I saw the meaningful look on the faces of Israeli believers. They immediately related this past experience to the current struggle, facing a constant barrage in warfare and terrorism in order to exist in their land today.

Zerah seems to have been a military officer under Osarkon (of Libya, in 914–874 B.C.E.) and perhaps was called an Ethiopian because of his residence in Upper Egypt.[21] The invasion probably was made much easier because of an Egyptian garrison left in Southern Judah by the former Egyptian King Shishak, who had invaded the country in the days of Rehoboam.[22]

Judah obviously faced a very serious and formidable army. In a spiritual sense, Satan did not like God's man Asa laying the groundwork for spiritual renewal. It would seem the nation's Adversary stirred up this military attack against Judah. Asa, however, had to recognize the military challenge. He was not afraid to meet it because he knew the Lord God of Israel was greater than any challenger, no matter whether it was a physical attack, a spiritual onslaught, or a combination of the two. The king's spiritual vision was 20/20! Courageously, he moved his army, even though outnumbered two to one. He took up his battle positions in the Valley of Zephathah near Mareshah (see 2 Chron. 14:10). This Valley of Zephathah was, perhaps, a site somewhere in the southwest part of Judea, coming down off the plateau into the foothills leading to the coastal plain. The area is generally east of the modern Ashkelon on the Mediterranean seacoast.

Asa's battle tactic—The test of the Lord's sufficiency, after the restoration of many Judeans, called for a confident response that he is supreme. In his moment of extreme urgency Asa cried, "ADONAI," thereby invoking the name of Israel's God. Does it sound like he is reminding God of who he is? Perhaps, but it was necessary for the king to do so; the Lord delights in being held accountable for Israel's protection!

The king continued on, however, with his plea: "ADONAI, there is no one besides yourself, strong or weak, who can help. Help us, ADONAI our God, because we are relying on you, and we are coming against this throng in your name" (2 Chron. 14:11). God positively delights to do for us beyond what we can even ask for or think. After all, what is a mere army of thousands of thousands to him? Asa sensed this great truth, and he is a wonderful Torah example of a believer coming boldly to God to make petition. And God was more than willing to answer.

Asa also reminded God, "You are ADONAI our God; don't let human beings stop you!" We are reminded that he very carefully stated the connection between the Lord and his people. An attack on Israel was actually an attack on the Lord!

The king also expected God to work a miracle. With the advance of perhaps a million-man army against only 300,000 men from Judah and 280,000 from Benjamin, Judah seemed to be helplessly outnumbered. No wonder Asa desperately called on the Lord; he needed more than mere human strength to triumph over the numbers arrayed against him and his people. The size of armies means nothing to the God of Israel; after all, he has at his disposal the armies of the heavens; what can mere man mount against him? The ancient world understood this matter of spiritual warfare and always wanted their gods to protect them; but they never understood that the God who protected his people Israel was really the God of the entire earth. What can man and his idols do against him?

Victory—The outcome was that God gave complete victory to Asa and Judah as the invaders were utterly routed. Victory or defeat had been placed at God's doorstep, and with a king's strong faith in what God can do, the Lord himself drove out a million people. Nothing in the records described what God did to chase the enemy out of Judah, but flee they did, leaving behind mountains of plunder for the people of Judah.

What are our tests today when we must lay either defeat or victory on God? In a sense, believers can throw the ball into God's court and expect him to give victory. What are the million crises we face? Of course, those who have walked with the Lord for a long time know that his resources are greater than all their difficulties as they see their trials through God's eyes. Those new in the faith are encouraged to allow God to work and demonstrate what he can do, far beyond what they can even think possible. Let God intervene and allow him the opportunity to demonstrate that he indeed is who he claims to be!

Always Remain Faithful to the Lord

The third means of encouragement for spiritual renewal is that, in exalting God for his great victories in our lives, we are encouraged to remain faithful to him. As noted already, worship follows as a natural course after renewal has come. And with hearts made aglow because of the Lord's intense inner presence, great victories can be accomplished through him. But King Asa soon discovered that God's call is not to rest on our laurels.

The call to ever seek the Lord—When Asa returned from the battlefield, a prophet of God, Azariah, met the king, declaring, "Listen to me, Asa, and all Y'hudah and Binyamin!" (2 Chron. 15:2) The emphasis was now placed on God's Word as the prophet proclaimed it. Vital spiritual renewal, which is sustained by worship, requires listening to and obeying God's Word.

The prophet continued with his challenge: "If you seek him, you will find him." The call was for Asa and his people to grasp for more and more of what God has to offer. Even after a great victory, these people had the privilege to realize he always was available to them, and that they could learn more of him. Rav Sha'ul expressed this same truth when he cried, "I want to know [the Messiah] and the power of his resurrection and the fellowship of sharing in his sufferings, becoming like him in his death" (Phil. 3:10, NIV). And yet, when he uttered these words, he had known the Lord for years. His desire to know him only underscored the truth that a believer must continually seek the Lord's face. Spiritual renewal can only be sustained as we ever seek the Lord.

This pursuit of God's presence reveals a curious paradox. The more a believer knows of him, the more he or she will have a comprehension of him and his work. But the more one's understanding of God is widened and deepened so as to live what we know, the possibility is ever present to learn even more. Even when believers exit from this world, the paradox will continue. Everyone always will have the capacity to learn more about him who loves us, and to live a godly lifestyle during the interim between physical death and the kingdom, during the kingdom age, and finally in the eternal state in the new heavens and new earth. The only difference between the believer's status now and in eternity is that the presence of sin and a sin nature no longer will threaten and thwart anyone in the grand adventure of becoming more and more like him.

On staying faithful—While this prophet encouraged the king and his soldiers—and believers in particular—with the great possibility of continually seeking God, he also said, ominously, "If you abandon him, he will abandon you!" (2 Chron. 15:2) Why would a prophet of God also warn king and people as they were coming back, riding the crest of a great victory over their enemies? On just such occasions people must be on guard against the enemy of our souls. The word from the Lord served notice for people not to live on yesterday's victories but rather to keep on "keeping on."

The prophet's warning to Judah was that they never forsake the Lord; but if ever the time came when people would run after pagan worship, they would fail miserably. God did not want a repeat of the experience of the period of the Judges (see 2 Chron. 15:3–6), with outright apostasy, when only a few priests actually taught the Torah. Moral values were compromised, rampant crime ruled the streets in the cities, and travel on the roads was precarious. Different parts of the nation at various times were under foreign rule, and everyone suffered distress. The time of the Judges was a deplorable period in the history of Israel, and the prophet used it as an example of what would happen in Asa's day if he or his people ever became unfaithful to the Lord. Not only would the people suffer, but also God himself would bring down his wrath to trouble the people of the nation if they ever turned their backs on him.

The prophet's words are also a warning for every generation of believers. When a believer backslides, he is in a position where God cannot reach him until he realizes that the ways of sin are bitter. The mystery of these tragic choices is that God can permit a backslidden believer to wander about in misery until he comes back to the occasion where he had gone astray. After many years of observation, I have concluded that I have never met a happy backslider. Remorse only accentuates the unhappy position. When the Holy Spirit is grieved with wrong behavior, he certainly has his ways of plaguing the believer so as to return such a person to the Lord (see Eph. 4:30).

Taking courage—The aim of the prophet's word to the people was to be strong and not to give up, literally, "Do not let your hands drop," which was an apt way to tell the people not to lose courage.

A. LISTENING TO THE WORD

The continual search for God's presence will be rewarded (see 2 Chron. 15:7). When the king heard these words of God from the prophet's lips, he took courage and sought to be an example of a true believer, with his heart tender before the Lord. Asa is a constant reminder that every believer can take courage. Ours is a noble experience to walk like princes and princesses of the King, no matter the circumstances.

I once went to visit Dr. Walter Wilson in the hospital after he had begun to recover from a heart attack. Earlier in life, he had practiced medicine, but for many years he was also on the preaching circuit, serving in many conferences and pulpits in the United States. I had intended to go and offer words of encouragement for and have prayer with him. But, frankly, I was not quite prepared for his response to my greeting. Quietly, he asked, "What did the Lord give you today?" I had come to encourage him, but he was reminding me that I was the one who had to continually seek God's face! It so happened that I did have the opportunity that day to share what the prophet Azariah had to say to king Asa. We spent some time discussing this portion of the Word, and then we had a precious time of worship and prayer. As I walked out of the room and started down the hall I thought to myself, *I thought I was going to encourage Dr. Wilson, but it ended up with both of us rejoicing before the Lord!*

B. REMOVING THE IDOLS, AGAIN

Asa continued on with what God already had begun in his heart regarding spiritual renewal; and his example had an effect on those who chose to stand with him. With their aid, the king renewed his efforts to remove the terrible idols from Judah. To worship the true God meant that no rival worship could be present. As noted already, he removed his grandmother from her position as queen mother because of her detestable example as an idol worshiper. Likewise, in the cause of doing God's will, he will sustain us as we are fearless in our service, even though it might upset the unbelievers in our own families.

c. Dedicating one's life

In a positive sense, he also restored the altar of burnt offering, which stood in front of the Temple. On this altar Israel was to offer the two major dedicatory offerings every day, morning and mid-afternoon, as a symbol and sign of total dedication to God (see Exod. 29:38b). Spiritual renewal always includes the commitment to dedicate oneself to God's will and ways.

d. Impacting the unbelievers

What was the result of this impressive movement of the Lord? When the people of Judah, Benjamin, and Simeon, along with those from Ephraim and Manasseh (the Northern Kingdom), gathered in Jerusalem to take their oath of allegiance before God (see 2 Chron. 15:14–15; Deut. 28), they did so with loud acclamation, with shouting, and with trumpets and horns. Because the believers sought God eagerly, they found him, and Judah enjoyed peace. When people are right with God, he knows how to make them live at peace even with their enemies. There is every reason to believe that multitudes came to the Lord because of the movement of God in the midst of the nation's leaders.

Many people today are constantly trying to find answers to life. When I was standing on a street corner at one time with a friend, a man said to us, "If I only had a million dollars, then I would have the answer to all of my problems." How many times have we heard such a statement, as if money and materialism are the panacea for all our problems? But then my friend and I walked three blocks to the upper class of town and ran into a man who had the million dollars but was still looking for peace. Where do people today find life's answers? We reminded this wealthy man as we share with everyone: Life, peace, rest, and hope can be genuine experiences, but only as we have forgiveness for our sins through the Messiah Yeshua and then as we constantly seek God's face and enjoy his presence. The outcome will then be visible to everyone when they see this joy and peace written on our faces. And we don't even need the million dollars!

The Warning against Alienation from the Lord

No guarantee is possible for the continuity of spiritual renewal unless believers continually seek to trust and serve him. The spiritual renewal at Sinai in the days of Moses did not preclude a complete breakdown at Kadesh Barnea. The renewal in Samuel's day did not provide any assurance that Israel's leaders eventually would demand a king to rule over them and insist they be like all the other nations. In fact, by so doing, these very leaders committed a grave sin (see 1 Sam. 10:19). Any number of examples can be cited, but Asa now becomes the focus of what alienation means.

Exhibiting a breakdown in faith—Five years before the end of the king's reign, Baasha, king of Israel, moved his armies toward Ramah at Judah's border, and proceeded to fortify Samuel's old hometown, which was near the border between the divided kingdoms. The northern king's idea was to completely cut off Israel from Judah, thereby preventing any more defectors from leaving and migrating south.

Asa regarded Baasha's actions as a war-like act, which was a correct assessment. But his solution to the problem revealed a complete breakdown in his trust in what the Lord could do. Possibly because of his old age, the Judean king had become fearful; but instead of looking to God, he sought aid by resorting to human schemes. Taking gold and silver from the Lord's treasuries, Asa sent these inducements to the king of Syria in Damascus. His plan was for the Syrian king and his troops to attack Baasha and his people in the north, draw off the soldiers from Ramah, and thereby relieve the pressure on Judah.

Tragically, this decision meant that the Southern Kingdom had placed itself in league with a pagan nation that had a
record of hatred for Israel.[23] Of course, Ben-Hadad in Damascus was only too glad to switch his alliances from Baasha to
Asa in exchange for gold and silver, so he attacked the towns
in Naphtali, Dan, and other areas in northern Israel. After all
the Lord had accomplished for Asa, how could the Judean
king think he could get away with his brash trust in a worldly,
pagan king? And yet, when one turns away from the Lord, Satan clouds that person's vision, and his decisions and actions
go far astray.

Asa's response to God's prodding—As a consequence, the prophet
Hanani came to Asa and raised some searching questions as to
the king's decisions and behavior: "The army of the Ethiopi-
ans and Luvim was huge, wasn't it? . . . Yet because you relied
on *ADONAI*, he handed them over to you" (2 Chron. 16:8).
The Lord obviously is greater than all human kings; but how
painful it is to listen to a tragic rebuke by a prophet who reasons with an old king who had alienated himself from the
Holy One and from one of the greatest spiritual renewals God
had given to Judah. With a heavy heart the prophet had to declare, "You acted foolishly in this regard; from now on, you
will have war" (2 Chron. 16:9). Of course, his actions were
foolish from God's point of view. Did he think that he could
have protection by buying it from a pagan king who would so
easily switch alliances for mere money?

How did King Asa respond? Instead of listening with care
and humbling himself before the Lord, he flew into a rage and
ordered the prophet imprisoned. How could the prophet dare
to rebuke him publicly, making him feel as a fool? But his anger also could have been directed against God for exposing his
spiritual lapse. After Judah had enjoyed such a tremendous
spiritual renewal, his response is amazing in that it reflected
outwardly for all people to see how he had turned so decisively

away from the Lord. The lesson is clear: Every believer has to stay close to the Lord for spiritual strength at all times. Otherwise, one can alienate himself from the Lord's presence, as Asa did when he lapsed and then hardened his heart and set his mind so as not to listen to the Lord.

Judgment and physical affliction—God had no other recourse but to physically afflict the king with severely diseased feet in order to get his attention. But it was to no avail. Even then Asa did not repent. Instead, he sought help from the physicians for his malady (see 2 Chron. 16:12). (By no means, however, should one conclude that the account prohibits the help of medical doctors; healing always comes from the Lord, either through his direct intervention or through the physicians' aid.) Because he did not return to the Lord, Asa no longer could function as king. So, during the illness of his last days, Jehoshaphat, his son, became his regent, ruling jointly with him.

At the end of his life, good King Asa was completely out of God's will; he had become rebellious and stubborn. Every believer can well ponder the old adage: *To begin well in one's experiences with the Lord is a good start indeed, but far more important is the challenge to finish triumphantly at the end of life's pilgrimage.* Therefore, God's call is to be ever vigilant with our spiritual experience, continually ask the Lord for his help, and seek his face and encouragement. The dreadful warning is always before us that we should never alienate ourselves from God's will as Asa did.

And yet, God was merciful. The opening statement regarding Asa, servant of the Most High God, is, "Asa did what was good and right from the perspective of *ADONAI* his God" (2 Chron. 14:2). Even though the Lord knew full well what would happen to this king at the end of his life, he chose to mention the good he did. The record includes it all, but in the one-line epitaph, God focused on Asa's accomplishments. He can be gracious with every one of us when necessary.

In her book *The Hiding Place*, Corrie ten Boom described her harrowing experiences in the concentration camp at Ravensbruck. During the day, the guards were continually present, at the place of work, and even when the camp inmates were lined up for whatever food there was. But in the barracks, when the women finally had retired for the night, the guards did not dare enter for fear of being contaminated by the vermin. That was when Corrie and her sister Betsy, along with some of the other women, had their Bible readings and worship.

As she pictured it for her readers, a little bit of heaven shone from the rays of the feeble glow of a small electric light. But God encouraged all of them, pouring out his Spirit even in such conditions. Corrie described the worship experiences and the keen presence of the Lord, declaring that, even in the darkest of nights, the light shone ever so brightly. Only God knows how many came to him in faith because of the way the Spirit worked in the hearts of all the women in those indescribably difficult situations.

In a similar way, God is merciful and even encourages believers today, wherever we are. He wants to work powerfully in each of us, individually and in our congregations. He wants to encourage us to affirm our faith, to ask for his help, and to remain faithful always. Perhaps spiritual renewal will touch our hearts and lives so that in an ever-widening circle others will find him. Ours is the joy of continually seeking his face.

CHAPTER FIVE

Elijah at Carmel
The Man Who Heard God's Gentle Whisper

(1 Kings 17:1–19:18; Matt. 17:1–13; James 5:17, 18)

"How long are you going to jump back and forth between two positions? If *ADONAI* is God, follow him; but if it is Ba'al, follow him!"

(1 Kings 18:21)

"Then when it came time for offering the evening offering, Eliyahu [Elijah] the prophet approached and said, '*ADONAI*, God of Avraham, Yitz'chak and Isra'el, let it be known today that you are God in Isra'el, and that I am your servant, and that I have done all these things at your word. Hear me, *ADONAI*, hear me, so that this people may know that you, *ADONAI*, are God, and that you are turning their hearts back to you."

(1 Kings 18:36, 37)

"After the earthquake, fire broke out; but *ADONAI* was not in the fire. And after the fire came a quiet, subdued voice. When Eliyahu heard it, he covered his face with his cloak, stepped out and stood at the entrance to the cave. Then a voice came to him and said, 'What are you doing here, Eliyahu?'"

(1 Kings 19:12, 13)

As we already saw, after Solomon died the kingdom split into two parts, the North under Jeroboam and the South under Rehoboam. The north pursued a policy of pagan worship, while God continued to work among the people of the south, "so that David my servant will always have a light burning before me in Yerushalayim [Jerusalem], the city I chose for myself as the place to put my name" (1 Kings 11:36).

The spiritual course pursued by the leaders in the nation of the North, beginning with Jeroboam, was a downward spiral, from one king to the next, each one in turn doing evil in the Lord's sight. God often gave victory to the leaders of Israel in their battles with Ammon, Moab, and Syria; in so doing, mercifully attempting to appeal to Israel that they might repent and turn back from destruction. At the same time, however, in his providential purposes, God judged these pagan nations for the perpetration of their evil.

In the last chapter we saw how God protected Judah and gave it a gracious renewal under good King Asa. We could focus exclusively on God's gracious care of the people of the south, but the Lord also was concerned about people of the north. He sought to reach out to the northern tribes, speaking to them through the prophets Elijah, Jonah, and others. Jonah's ministry, in particular, was to Nineveh, and many there did come to the Lord. As a result, Assyria had no military designs on the nations of the Middle East, especially Israel.

This temporary spiritual awakening in Assyria—along with its effects on Israel—was a testimony to the Northern Kingdom that they, too, needed to listen to the Lord as he spoke through the prophets. God was merciful to Israel, delaying for a long time his judgment, which eventually came upon a wayward people. But for now, we note some of the events leading up to the prophet Elijah's ministry.

Historical Background

Jeroboam (1 Kings 12:25–14:20)

Pagan worship—When Jeroboam (931–910 B.C.E.) became king of the northern tribes, one of his major policies was to insulate his kingdom from Judah by establishing a substitute worship system, attempting, thereby, to keep his people from returning to Jerusalem to worship in the Temple. He had two altars built, one in Dan in the north and one in Bethel, near

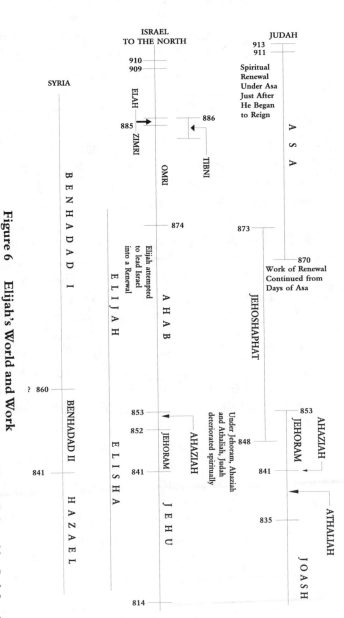

Figure 6   Elijah's World and Work

While Judah, after the rupture of the kingdom of all twelve tribes, had at least eight of its nineteen kings called good by God, Israel's nineteen kings of the North were all called evil. Yet God was gracious with Israel of the North and He sent Elijah to try and lead Ahab and his people to renewal in spite of the presence of wicked Queen Jezebel. The work failed. Elijah ran away when threatened by the queen, and at least 1,500 of Israel's leaders were put to death, those who had possibly come to the Lord because of the challenge by Elijah on Mt. Carmel. Recommissioned by God on Mt. Horeb, Elijah continued his ministry in the North to people and kings, anointing prophets (Elisha) and Kings (Jehu of Israel and Hazael of Syria).

ISRAEL
TO THE NORTH

JUDAH
913
911

Spiritual
Renewal
Under Asa
Just After
He Began
to Reign

SYRIA

910
909

ELAH

886

885   ZIMRI

TIBNI

OMRI

A S A

874

873

JEHOSHAPHAT

870
Work of Renewal
Continued from
Days of Asa

Elijah attempted
to lead Israel
into a Renewal

A H A B

E L I J A H

B E N H A D A D   I

? 860

BENHADAD II

848

853
852

AHAZIAH

853
JEHORAM

AHAZIAH

Under Jehoram, Ahaziah
and Athaliah, Judah
deteriorated spiritually

AHAZIAH
JEHORAM

841

841   JEHORAM

J E H U

E L I S H A

H A Z A E L

841

814

835

ATHALIAH

J O A S H

the border in the south. At each center, the symbols of this new worship program were two gold images of calves reminiscent of Egypt's bull worship. The king's deliberate attempt was to mimic the Jerusalem worship, building also a temple to house the calf-idol in Bethel. He even instituted a festival on the fifteenth day of the eighth month, apparently as a substitute for the feast of Tabernacles of the seventh month. Obviously, this was a rival system, with a pagan emphasis at its very heart, and the Lord could only conclude that this defiance was a flagrant violation of his Word regarding acceptable worship.

God's rebuke came quickly through his special unnamed "man of God" who came from Judah to Bethel (see 1 Kings 13:1) to issue a prophecy of condemnation of this false worship. The message: Someday, a future king from the House of David—Josiah[24]—would burn the bones of Jeroboam's priests (see 1 Kings 13:1–3; 2 Kings 23:15, 16). But instead of listening to this bona fide message, Israel's king became furious with this prophet and his message of challenge and, pointing to him with his finger, he called for his guards to seize him.

But God preserved his servant, thereby lending credence to his message, and when Jeroboam stretched out his hand, pointing with his finger and shouting to his guards, "Seize him," his hand shriveled up on the spot and he could not pull it back! The altar also was split apart and its ashes were poured out on the ground, exactly in accordance as a sign, confirming what was proclaimed as the word of the Lord through the prophet. Only then did Jeroboam change his countenance and tone of voice, and with great respect, asked the man of God to intercede for him that his hand should be restored. The man of God complied and then left, intending to return to Judah, leaving Jeroboam with plenty to think about. Yet, as is so often true with human nature, which refuses to bow to God's will, this king never manifested any evidence that he would change his original purposes for a rival worship. Even today men spurn the preaching of God's Word, and drastic are the consequences.

Jeroboam's son fell ill—Again, God jabbed at Jeroboam's conscience when his son fell ill (see 1 Kings 14:1–18). He greatly desired to know what would happen to the boy, and so he sent his wife in disguise to Ahijah, the prophet of the Lord in Shiloh. But God warned Ahijah that the king's wife was coming to seek for a word of well-being for her son. Exactly because Ahijah had once announced that Jeroboam would become the king (see 1 Kings 11:29–31), the latter assumed that the prophet would have some word of encouragement for his own son.

But there was to be no good news. God's prophets do not preach for man's favor or for monetary gain. Ahijah instead sent a message back to Jeroboam through his wife, chiding the king for his sin of leading Israel astray, and predicting that his successors would be cut off and that his services as well as those of any of his family were concluded. The prophet also predicted the child was going to die. Is this judgment harsh? People today might shudder at the words of such a "cruel prophet," but the man of God had no other choice if he was to honestly reflect God's holiness and righteousness as the contrast to Jeroboam's sin. One of the problems today's society has with such difficult words is that many people no longer have any fear of God before their eyes, and so they no longer see wrongdoing as God sees it!

Nadab—Another of Jeroboam's sons, Nadab (910–909 B.C.E.), succeeded his father, but his course was no different than the already-accepted policy for pagan worship. *The apple did not fall too far from the tree*: "He did what was evil from ADONAI's perspective, following the example of his father and the sin through which he made Isra'el sin" (1 Kings 15:26).

God gave him an opportunity to change his ways, but Nadab spurned that chance. So, after reigning for only two years in Tirzah (see 1 Kings 15:25–31), Nadab was assassinated by Baasha, who, in accordance with Ahijah's prediction, proceeded to destroy the house of Jeroboam. What is horrifying is that this description of Nadab is repeated across the years until this Northern Kingdom fell. In many different ways, Jeroboam's eighteen successors all came to an inglorious end, because once the ungodly example of Jeroboam I was established, the Northern Kingdom never was able to shake free from the golden-calf worship established at the centers in Bethel and Dan. Such false worship also made it easier at a later date for Jezebel, wife of Ahab, to also introduce Phoenician worship—to be described later in the chapter.

Baasha (1 Kings 15:25–32)

Baasha (909–886 B.C.E.) ruled for 23 years, fortifying Ramah in the days of Asa in order to keep people in the north from further migrating south to Judah. Asa, however, in his latter years, had persuaded the Syrian king Ben Hadad I to attack Israel so that the northern king never completed the Ramah fortifications.

Elah (1 Kings 16:8–14)

Elah, Baasha's son, came next, and he also ruled for only two years (886–885 B.C.E.). While Elah's general Omri was involved in an assault on Gibbethon, a Philistine stronghold, another military officer, Zimri (see 1 Kings 16:15–20), assassinated the king, putting to death all of the house of Baasha. This occurred exactly as prophesied by the prophet Jehu (see 1 Kings 16:1).

Omri (1 Kings 16:21–28)

Stabilizing Israel—When Omri (885–874 B.C.E.) heard this report, he proclaimed himself king and returned to the Israelite capital of Tirzah to put down the insurrection. After ruling only seven days, Zimri went into the citadel of the palace and committed suicide, burning down the palace around him. But Omri had another challenger, Tibni, who would not be dislodged. So a divided rule existed in Israel for four years. Eventually, Omri was able to take full control, and with him a new dynasty was established, lasting forty-four years (885–841 B.C.E.).

For the Northern Kingdom, this was a phenomenal record, considering the leadership of this kingdom had descended to the level of chicanery, duplicity, falsehood, fraud, and murder (exactly as one finds among other nations of the Middle East at the time). No integrity existed among the supposed people of God, again pointing to the tragic situation in which a people no longer feared the God who had brought them into existence. But at least Omri was able to stabilize the country politically, creating a new capital in Samaria and also subduing Moab.

Phoenician worship and an ungodly queen—Omri then took another step that ultimately would bring untold ruin upon Israel, and even indirectly upon Judah, when he made an alliance with the Phoenicians. Upon the ratification of this pact, Jezebel, the daughter of King Ethbaal of Phoenicia, was married to Omri's son, Ahab. Such marriages were quite common in the Middle East, but an alliance of this nature for Israel would only be an invitation to disaster. Not only did Omri follow the policy set down by Jeroboam, he also added to the evil when Jezebel was allowed to import the religious system of Ba'al-Malqart, a worship closely related to the older Ba'al worship of Canaan.

Through the order given by Moses and Joshua on behalf of the Lord, united Israel had one directive regarding the Canaanites of the Promised Land: These people were to be killed. But most important of all, their worship was to be completely obliterated so it would not become a trap for God's people. Omri's detestable relationship with the Phoenicians officially reintroduced the Ba'al worship system to the tribes of the north. What Joshua had fought against and what David had done in cleansing the land from this horrible pagan Ba'alism now became one of the pagan worship experiences of Omri and his followers.

Jezebel had carte blanche to bring in her pagan prophets of Ba'al, taking responsibility for their welfare as well as ensuring that Ba'al worship was to be the object of the devotion of the people in Israel (see 1 Kings 18:19). So as to guarantee the successful implementation of her religious preference, she ordered the slaughter of the Lord's prophets. And when Ahab succeeded his father as king, Jezebel became the real power behind the throne (see 1 Kings 18:4). Only through the faithfulness and support of Obadiah, one of the Lord's prophets, was it possible to hide at least 100 of his fellow prophets from Jezebel's executioners.

In the midst of these deplorable circumstances, God called Elijah to be his witness to Ahab and the people of Israel. Though the spiritual level of the nation was low, God was compassionate and always had his witness, even as he does in our day. No one from that time or from our era will be able to claim at the time of judgment that he never heard or had an opportunity to turn to the Lord.

The Man Elijah

Who was Elijah? He appeared suddenly, from Tishbe in Gilead (see 1 Kings 17:1), but we have no idea where this town was located. In many ways he was a man of mystery. At the end of his life, this prophet was caught up to heaven (see 2 Kings 2:11–12). But while his entry into the scene in Israel was a mystery, and his translation in the end bordered on mysticism, he was an earthy man, a person with feeling and passion and a great heart.

A Pronouncement and a Disappearance

In his first appearance, Elijah strode into the palace in Samaria, proclaiming to the king that no rain will fall for "the years ahead," and then he disappeared from sight. The record states he fled to the wilderness, living in a ravine called Kerith east of the Jordan (see 1 Kings 17:2). When the water supply there ran out, God directed the prophet to leave the kingdom of Israel, go to Zarephath of Sidon and there reside with a very humble and poor woman.

What did he do for more than three years? How did he spend his time? He had to remain hidden since King Ahab's agents were searching feverishly for him—even in foreign lands—as the water supply began to run out in Israel (see 1 Kings 18:10). But the prophet, no doubt, had the opportunity to wait upon God and do a lot of reflecting as he searched the Scriptures.

He was fearless under certain situations, not afraid to face King Ahab and warn him that the rain would fail. While confronting the prophets of Ba'al on Mt. Carmel, he was courageous in his challenge to the king, the leaders, and the people to choose whether they would serve Ba'al or the Lord.

Why Did Elijah Run?

As to why Elijah seemed fainthearted and even ran away after Jezebel threatened him, the record says, "He was afraid." However, the Hebrew text also can read, "He saw and arose and ran. . . ." Because of this possibility of textual translation, one should not be quick to find fault with the prophet.

When Jezebel found out that her priests had been executed after the fire of God fell on Elijah's sacrifice; she then sent word to the prophet that he was as good as dead within twenty-four hours. So, he had three options: 1) Face Jezebel and her state police and trust God to somehow protect him through some miraculous intervention. 2) Realize that it would be more expedient to leave as quickly as possible, expecting that at another time and on another occasion, Jezebel would be dethroned and killed. 3) To save his life, run eighty miles from Samaria to a hideout a day's journey south of Beersheba.

But before we second-guess what the prophet should have done, we had better be advised that facing up to Jezebel was no light matter. We know that when Elijah met with God, the Lord never rebuked his servant. Instead, God encouraged him to return and carry on the work he originally had been called to do.

The prophet may have spent about two days somewhere south of Beersheba and, fed by the angel, he fell into a deep sleep from nervous exhaustion. His strength was spent; he already had run from Carmel to Samaria, and then, within a day, another eighty miles. Then, after resting, he continued for another forty days farther at a more leisurely pace into the Sinai wilderness to Mt. Horeb, at the base of Mt. Sinai. This distance amounted to about 160 more miles as the crow flies but much longer if one takes the twisting and winding road through the desert. Elijah was eager to get to the place where God had met Israel hundreds of years before, apparently trying to clutch at some assurance for his ministry where his faith would be vindicated.

God's power was evident: A strong gale shattered the rocks, then the entire mountain shook from a sharp, jolting earthquake; and, finally, the fire of God fell, perhaps through some kind of violent storm. Elijah had told God he wanted to die, and he gave as his excuse that he was the only real believer left in Israel. Yet, just as God was not present in the violent wind, the earthquake, or the crash of thunder and the crackle of lightning, neither should anyone take seriously the first words that came forth from Elijah's mouth. It may be easy for a preacher to wax eloquent and accuse the prophet: "You shouldn't act that way, you have no right to act so childish!" But through the caress of a gentle whisper, God re-commissioned Elijah to continue on in the work he had been assigned to do. The original call and task for the prophet had not changed. Instead, he was encouraged in his challenge to the Northern Kingdom. Humanly speaking, the ministry appeared to be a thankless task, but Elijah would discover that God knows how to judge and to do away with all the Jezebels of this world and also how to discipline his people. He values the measure of a man's faithfulness in obedience to his call.

Elijah, a Respected Servant of the Lord

God honored his prophet, giving him the privilege of anointing kings: Hazael over Aram, and Jehu over Israel. Elijah also anointed his successor, Elisha, who served with him for many years. Elijah was a man of prayer and faith, announcing to King Ahab that it would not rain for three and a half years. He also showed his faith in praying for his food during the time of famine when he was by the brook, and by diligently trusting God to have an everlasting supply of flour and oil when he stayed with the woman of Sidon. Finally, after the contest with the false prophets was over, he prayed earnestly that it would rain in abundance and, as a consequence, many in Israel came to know the Lord.

In spite of Elijah's seeming failures, God highly respected him, and at the end of his life, God translated him directly into heaven, instead of permitting him to die as any other man or woman. And then, hundreds of years later, Elijah appeared again, standing with Moses on the Mount of Transfiguration, conversing with the Messiah during the dazzling display of his glory (see Luke 9:30–31). Elijah was a many-dimensioned figure, a man unique for his calling but also extremely human in his passions. No wonder Alexander Whyte described him with these choice words:

> Elijah was a man, indeed, of passions all compact. We never see Elijah that he is not subject to some passion or other. A passion of scorn and contempt; a passion of anger and revenge; a passion of sadness and dejection and despair; a passion of preaching; a passion of prayer. Elijah

was a great man. There was a great mass of manhood in
Elijah. He was a Mount-Sinai of a man, with a heart like
a thunderstorm. That man among ourselves who has the
most human nature in him and the most heart; the most
heart and the most passion in his heart; the most love and
the most hate; the most anger and the most meekness;
the most scorn and the most sympathy; the most sun-
shine and the most melancholy; the most agony in
prayer, and the most victorious assurance that, all the
time, his prayer is already answered.[25]

No wonder we sing songs about him at the close of the Sabbath service and also, during the course of the Passover Seder,
call for him to announce the Messiah's coming.

Possibilities for Spiritual Renewal

The days of Ahab and Jezebel in the Northern Kingdom were
a spiritual abyss, and the nation was on the skids, moving toward destruction. God never could approve of what the kings
of these breakaway tribes had done. But he could have let the
nation go its way to destruction, because he already had predicted through his prophets that Judah was his favored people
(see 1 Kings 11:36). Only the Southern Kingdom was to be
preserved and Jerusalem protected because of promises to and
consideration for David, his servant.

Yet the Lord is also the God of love, mercy, and compassion, not willing that any should perish; and all day long
he waits patiently for people to turn to him, no matter how
small their faith might be. In his unique design, God sent
Elijah with his message to Ahab and Israel, holding out the
possibility for people to respond to his overtures of compassion. When we understand the context in which Elijah had
to minister, we have a better understanding of what it means
when we hear the words, "For God so loved the world that
he gave . . ." (Yochanan [John] 3:16)

Confidence

The first possibility for spiritual renewal, even in Israel, was the confidence of the prophet Elijah, who had full knowledge of what God can do, and also that many in Israel would respond to his message. Elijah could not afford to have any false trust when he set out to announce to King Ahab that no rain would fall in the Northern Kingdom for three and a half years! Every agent of the king and his wife, Jezebel, was searching meticulously for the prophet, and there was no question what would happen to him if the queen ever laid hands on him.

An assurance in the Word—Elijah's confidence was based on God's Word, which does not lie. When God's man strode into the king's palace in Samaria, having come from the "boonies" of Gilead, he had God's message, which reflected his full assurance in the Lord, the real God of Israel. The covenant with Israel declares God's judgment very plainly.

> But be careful not to let yourselves be seduced, so that you turn aside, serving other gods and worshipping them. If you do, the anger of *ADONAI* will blaze up against you. He will shut up the sky, so that there will be no rain. The ground will not yield its produce, and you will quickly pass away from the good land *ADONAI* is giving you. (Deut. 11:16, 17)

Other passages likewise were quite clear about what God would do if his people became disobedient and turned from him to serve the false gods of the pagan nations (see Lev. 26:14ff; Deut. 28:20ff). But God was gracious to Israel in a time of great apostasy, and for the sake of his people he worked through his prophet so as to enter into a contest with the imported pagan god, Ba'al-Melqart, who was supposed to be the god of storms and good crops. So, the prophet was fully assured of the accuracy of the Scriptures and in the God of grace and love who sincerely desired the best interests of his people.

An anticipation of provision—After his bold pronouncement in the palace, Elijah went into hiding. Actually, walking into the palace to deliver such a devastating message to the king was far easier than waiting quietly out of everyone's sight for the appointed time in order to prove definitely to the people that God's word was true.

The prophet's confidence, however, also was in anticipation that God would provide for him during the time of testing. So he crossed the Jordan to an obscure ravine of Kerith, and there he waited upon the Lord. There was water enough from the brook, and inasmuch as the Lord guided the prophet, he also provided for his sustenance. One can only marvel how the ravens—God's waiters—brought their "trays" of bread and meat to the prophet exactly on time twice a day (see 1 Kings 17:2–6).

As the drought continued in the land, the brook soon dried out, and the word of the Lord then directed Elijah to leave the borders of Israel and go to Zarephath, a village between Tyre and Sidon. Once again we see the prophet's confidence in God's leadership: He was willing to leave his own country and go to a clearly pagan land. The Lord had an interesting plan in mind; so he sent his servant to a certain widow who was to care for Elijah until the time would come when he was to appear again before King Ahab. The prophet would remain there for three and one-half years from the time he originally issued his proclamation to King Ahab. The identity of the woman is not revealed. Perhaps she could have been a transplanted Israelite, there because of the famine. But her communication with the Lord and his word to her of Elijah's impending appearance indicates that she knew the Lord (see 1 Kings 17:9).

Because of the prophet's confidence in God's care for him, another miracle of sustenance was provided, not for the prophet alone, but for the widow and her son as well. The latter were so poor that all their food consisted of only a handful of flour in a jar and a little oil in a jug. The poor woman had no other income, and her only sure prospect for the future was that she and her son would soon die of starvation. Her faith was sorely tested when Elijah told her not to fear but rather to prepare food from everything left of the flour and oil in the jar and jug—not only for herself and her son but also for her guest. From a strictly human point of view, one might say he certainly had his *chutzpah!*

But Elijah also prophesied in God's name: "For this is what *ADONAI*, the God of Isra'el says: 'The pot of meal will not get used up, nor will there fail to be oil in the jug, until the day *ADONAI* sends rain down on the land'"(1 Kings 17:14). And so it happened. What must this widow have thought every time she went to use the flour and oil? She must have marveled and praised God, because as many times as she took from each of the containers, their remaining levels always stayed the same! Many believers have drawn from the story of the miracles in this woman's life an example for anticipating what God can do to provide for their needs.

An expectation of restoration of life—We also note the confidence of the prophet, fully expecting God to restore life to the widow's son, who had become so ill that he actually stopped breathing and then died. But the miracle took place when, as Elijah prayed over the boy and stretched himself out over him three times, God brought him back to life (see 1 Kings 17:22, 23). The widow then could take comfort in that she would not be tried beyond what she could bear. She also was assured, without any question or doubt, that she had entertained a man who had complete confidence in God and that whatever the prophet spoke was the truth (see 1 Kings 17:24).

Every morning, religious Jewish people, in their prayers of devotion, recite Maimonides' thirteen principles of faith, articulating his trust in God and his Word. Each principle begins with the statement: "I believe with perfect faith that God, blessed be his name . . ." Then the specific principle in each of the areas is mentioned. With the written Torah and New Covenant, God's full revelation to man is fully available, and believers have the high privilege to trust God in the midst of every problem. And, when he directs any believer for a particular service, he or she can we have full confidence as Elijah had, and say, "I believe with perfect faith!"

Courage

A determined prophet—The second possibility for spiritual renewal was the courage displayed by this prophet. After some three and one-half years had gone by, the Word of the Lord came again to Elijah (see 1 Kings 18:1; Luke 4:25; James 5:17). His long wait in obscurity finally was over; he was to present himself once more to King Ahab. The time was ripe to execute a plan God had in mind; but it would take a determined courage for the prophet to appear before this king. The famine was so severe that the people had no crops, and with no water and food the animals had to be slaughtered. King Ahab also lost much in taxes because the people had nothing to give. No doubt he was furious over how the country had been paralyzed by this upstart, unknown prophet. Any ordinary person would have quailed at the prospect of seeing this enraged king, because it might mean certain death. But the prophet's fear was in the Lord and not in mere man—even if that man was the king. Elijah's courage came from his trust in the God of Israel.

The presence of brave believers—Before Elijah encountered Ahab, God permitted him to meet other believers present in the Northern Kingdom. While Jezebel systematically killed the Lord's prophets, Obadiah, who was in charge of the palace and was a devoted follower of the Lord, bravely hid 100 of them in caves, and at great risk to his own life, provided them with food and water (see 1 Kings 18:3–4). No doubt Elijah was greatly encouraged to meet him and to know that here was another man who knew the Lord and had not denied his faith. As a distinctive mark of honor, Obadiah was asked to announce to King Ahab that Elijah had arrived out of obscurity and wanted an audience.

But this godly believer, who had bravely put his neck on the line by saving 100 prophets, was frightened at the prospects of what could happen when Ahab and Jezebel discovered his connection with Elijah. He had good reason to fear: If Jezebel ever discovered his "treachery" of saving the Lord's prophets, his life would not be worth even the hundredth part of a shekel. Nevertheless, Elijah encouraged him to bravely do what had been requested.

Elijah's bold approach—The encounter between Elijah and King Ahab bristled as the king exclaimed, "Is it really you, you troubler of Isra'el?" (1 Kings 18:17) Despite all of Ahab's emissaries' frantic and futile efforts to find the prophet, there he stood—boldly! But who was the real "troubler of Israel"?

Elijah fearlessly declared that the fault lay with Ahab and his father's family. They were the real troublemakers for the nation. The house of Omri and those who preceded him were the ones who had abandoned "*ADONAI's mitzvot* [commandments] and follow[ed] the *ba'alim*" (1 Kings 18:18). God's man now stood fearless before this king and had the courage to deliver the Lord's message to him.

Centuries later, Rav Sha'ul (Paul), bound in his chains, stood before Felix, the Roman procurator, and discussed the great themes of "righteousness, self-control and the coming judgment" with such conviction that Felix became afraid (see Acts 24:25). The people of this world often see governmental issues, sociological concerns, and morality in a topsy-turvy way. But who are the ones who really make the trouble? None other than the Ahabs and the Felixes who are shackled in their souls and spirits and are the most miserable of creatures. God's men and women come to bring Messiah's peace, contentment, and atonement for sin to the people of this world. When we understand the topsy-turvy sense of values of the unbelievers of our day, it should give us courage to be determined, brave, and bold in our courage for the Lord.

Challenge

The prophet issued his summons—The third possibility for spiritual renewal was Elijah's challenge to King Ahab, summoning to Mt. Carmel, no doubt, government leaders of the palace who cared for the everyday affairs of the nation, and also calling for as many people as possible from Israel. "Oh," the prophet added, "Bring the four hundred and fifty prophets of Baal and the four hundred prophets of Asherah, who eat at Jezebel's table" (1 Kings 18:19, NIV).

It would take Ahab's word to get these false prophets out from under the queen's thumb. But we can well wonder what the 850 false prophets would have thought if they knew their summons to appear on Carmel had been issued by a backwoods preacher dressed in camel's hair, representing the Lord God of Israel?

Testing the will of the people of Israel—When everyone had arrived at the designated spot on the Carmel range, Elijah then challenged all present to the test: *Who is the real God, the Lord, or Ba'al-Melqart?* In particular, King Ahab of Israel faced the supreme test of his life to make the right choice. Elijah then set forth the conditions of the contest: Elijah was to have a bull to sacrifice in the name of the Lord, while the 450 prophets of Ba'al could also have one to sacrifice to Ba'al-Melqart. The integrity of God's prophet was on the line when he issued his proposal, ". . . Call on the name of your god; and I will call on the name of *ADONAI*; and the God who answers with fire, let him be God" (1 Kings 18:24). Everyone agreed to the challenge.

What took place among the prophets of Ba'al was pathetic and amusing. The prophets of Ba'al prepared their bull, put its parts on the altar, and from morning until noon, they cried, "Ba'al! Answer us!" (v. 26) At noon, Elijah began to taunt these false prophets, calling to them to shout louder; perhaps Ba'al was traveling about somewhere and was not able to hear his prophets, or maybe he was sound asleep and needed even louder shouting in order to awaken him! Elijah's taunts not only goaded the false prophets; they caused them to become even more frantic to make their god answer their pleas. According to their pagan customs, they even cut themselves with their spears and swords, allowing their blood to run everywhere on their sacrifice.

Elijah's invitation for Israel to acknowledge the Lord—By the time of the evening sacrifice, it was obvious to King Ahab and the people of Israel that the prophets of Ba'al were no more than a sham. In spite of all the frantic efforts of the representatives of Ba'al-Melqart, no fire had fallen from heaven to ignite their bull. Elijah challenged his people, demanding they call on the Lord who is the only God Israel ever knew, and reminding them that he alone should be the object of their devotion.

The prophet then built an altar of twelve stones, one for each of Israel's tribes (including the tribes to the south). He dug a trench around the altar, then chopped wood and set it in the proper place on the altar, and the bull was cut into pieces and lain on the wood. Then, in order to make sure that the test would be as difficult as possible for the Lord to answer, proving that he is indeed the true God, Elijah also ordered that the bull sacrifice, the wood, and the stones be drenched with water—three times no less. As precious and as scarce as water was, this was the ultimate proof to the people that if the Lord answered by fire, then he indeed is the God of Israel.

When all had been prepared, God's man then prayed:

ADONAI, God of Avraham, Yitz'chak and Isra'el, let it be known today that you are God in Isra'el, and that I am your servant, and that I have done all these things at your

word. Hear me, ADONAI, hear me so that this people will
know that you, ADONAI, are God, and that you are turning their hearts back to you (1 Kings 18:36).

Elijah's plea to God was that when the answer would come,
the people would know the difference between Ba'al and the
Lord, choose the very one who had established his people—
and then serve him.

In response to his prophet—and as a confirmation of his
position in the eyes of the people—God sent down fire that
consumed the sacrifice and ignited the wood. So intense was
the heat that it burned the soil, cracked the stones of the altar,
and licked up every bit of water present. Elijah the prophet
was vindicated in the eyes of everyone present: King Ahab,
perhaps some 1,500 leaders in the government,[26] and, no
doubt, many of the common people of Israel, as well as the
850 false prophets who saw the miracle. The Israelites present
bowed low and worshiped, crying out that the Lord indeed is
the God of Israel.

What followed was the only logical conclusion to the
challenge. The 1,500 of King Ahab's court and the other
people of Israel rounded up the 850 prophets, brought them
down to the Valley of Kishon at the base of the Carmel range,
and slaughtered them there. While this behavior sounds horrible and gory, and our sensitivities may be violated with what
is nothing less than a massacre, the possession of Canaan relied on the premise that Israel must not have any rival pagan
religion present in the land. God alone was to be worshiped.
God directed Joshua and the people to slaughter the immoral
Canaanites and destroy their pagan gods. But for Ahab to permit the return of this horrible religion into the land of Israel
through the auspices of his wife, Jezebel, was a sin that left
God no other choice but to judge the nation. Therefore, the
rains were withheld, causing distress for Israelis in their loss
of food and bringing the country to the brink of disaster. The
only way to cleanse the land was to destroy any vestige of pagan worship and to slaughter the priests of Ba'al.

Elijah's final trial—After the representatives of the nation had acknowledged the Lord as their only God, Elijah then instructed Ahab and all the rest to take some nourishment before returning to Samaria. The prophet, however, remained behind and went farther up on the mountain range and began to pray to God that rain would come. The ultimate challenge by the prophet was now apparent. After three and one-half years of no rain, the real God of Israel was the only one who could bring the much-needed rain. After praying seven times in earnest, clouds began to appear over the Mediterranean Sea, so Elijah instructed Ahab and the rest to return to Jezreel. The rain overtook them on their journey, and the last view of Elijah on this occasion was of him running ahead of Ahab's chariot, from Carmel to Samaria, a distance of some twenty-five miles! (See 1 Kings 18:46)

Elijah's contest for Israel in his day raises questions for us: How do we handle our tests? Do we offer people around us the choice between the claims of God or mammon? Sometimes these challenges come to us without our asking for them. Ernest Gordon was a British soldier who survived the horrors of the Japanese prisoner of war camp by the River Kwai in Thailand. He describes some of his experiences:

> When Good Friday came we wanted to bow our heads and bend our knees before the Lord who had died for all of us. In my contemplation, I recognized that it was no easy thing to call that figure on the cross "Lord." I heard His words: "Father, forgive them, for they know not what they do."
>
> This He had said for His enemies but what was I to say for mine (the Japanese who had brutally overworked the British and had caused many to die)? I could not say what He had said, but He was innocent whereas I was not. Humbly I had to ask, "Forgive me and mine enemies for we know not what we do . . ."
>
> He asked us to believe in Him, but it was much easier for us to believe in a president or dictator, a scientist,

scholar, news commentator, movie actress, or baseball
star. Any of these was more acceptable than a Jewish car-
penter, condemned as a criminal, hanging on a bloody
cross.

I confessed, "It is hard to be a disciple, Lord."

At dawn on Easter some of us slipped out of our huts
to make our communion in the open at the edge of the
camp . . .

When we finished, the sun was up, the darkness was
still here but it was being overcome by light. Darkness
was here but it was being redeemed by life, God's life.[27]

As a prisoner of war in detestable conditions, held by cap-
tors who made life a hell, Ernest Gordon faced his challenge
with courage that could come only from God. Every believer,
likewise, with whatever task God has given, be it ever so
humble or great, needs to have the courage to challenge the
world.

God's Comfort

The final possibility for spiritual renewal was the experience of God's precious comfort. Israel stood on the threshold
of tremendous national renewal after such an auspicious beginning on Mt. Carmel. What could have happened to the nation if renewal had been given the opportunity to reach its
climax under God's guiding hand?

What happened subsequently, however, is disheartening.
When Jezebel found out that her favorite prophets had been
killed, she sent word to Elijah, saying, "May the gods do terrible things to me and worse ones besides if by this time tomorrow I haven't taken your life, just as you took theirs!" (1
Kings 19:2) Elijah had good reason to believe that this wicked
queen was capable of her word. When confronted with such
an enemy of the Lord, what should any believer do?

What did the 1,500 government leaders do, faced now
with Jezebel's threats, especially after they had so boldly ac-

cepted the challenge by the prophet and confessed their faith in the God of Israel? Quite possibly these prominent people did not have time to digest their true feelings, because when Jezebel did not find Elijah, it appears that she vented her full fury on these hapless leaders with orders for their execution.

Where was God in this carnage? The element of mystery in the providential rule of God at this point in Israel's history is difficult to understand, but certainly from a human point of view, it was a tragedy. Speculations abound. What if Elijah had remained? Perhaps, he, too, would have been killed. Had it occurred, perhaps the news of the prophet's death would have spread throughout the Northern Kingdom and people would have revolted and put Jezebel to death. But these are only speculations on a strange state of affairs.

Seeking solace—The prophet sought solace in leaving Jezebel and Samaria, running south to Beersheba and then farther into the wilderness (see 1 Kings 19:3). There, he sat down under a tree and prayed that he might die, declaring to God that he was no different from his fathers. Then, exhausted from the journey, he fell asleep.

After being comforted and cared for, he went on to Mt. Horeb, at the base of Mt. Sinai. What consolation was he looking for in the Mount Sinai region? Did he feel that he needed to return to the place where God had originally revealed himself to Israel? Was he really looking for a new message from that very same God to encourage him in his ministry? All we know is that Elijah was a man who had lost his grip on his commission and, perhaps, hoping against hope, he wanted to hear some additional word of encouragement.

We might criticize Elijah for abandoning his commission. How easy it is to censure when not standing in the sandals of the person who is wavering under an attack by the enemy. On the other hand, some believers can also relate to Elijah and ruefully confess that they too have fumbled their commissions. How great, however, are the mercies and the comfort of God, who knows our every difficulty and who stands ready to encourage and even to send us forth again to do his task, renewed and reinvigorated.

Peace of mind and heart—God finally revealed himself to Elijah and asked what he was doing at Mount Horeb instead of being in Israel (see 1 Kings 19:9). The prophet's reply reflected his shaken confidence in the commission that God had given him, because the renewal at Mt. Carmel had been aborted. Indeed, the Northern Kingdom had rejected the covenant and Jezebel had just killed many in the administration who had acknowledged the Lord as their God. He now felt that he was the only one left and was in danger of being killed. God did not rebuke his servant. Instead, he directed Elijah to stand on the mountain, declaring that he would pass by him even as he had done for Moses centuries before.

What followed was a powerful display of God's might in the stormy gale, no doubt intended for the prophet to learn that God is sovereign, and, therefore, even greater than Jezebel and her gods—and, yes, even greater than all of the prophet's problems. After the wind, came the sharp jolt of a great and powerful earthquake, which made the ground twist violently. This show of force was designed to help Elijah to realize that God was greater than anything Elijah faced from people.

Following the earthquake was the fury of a storm, with its crashing thunder and jagged displays of flashing lightning, setting on fire anything the bolts struck. The fire and smoke of burning brush accompanied the storm, perhaps something of the same fire and smoke that once had terrified the people of Israel at Sinai when they were confronted by God's holiness.

While the Lord used these lessons to teach Elijah that he (*ADONAI*) is holy, sovereign, and has all power, nevertheless, this was not the way he would re-commission his prophet. Instead, the gentle caress of a soft wind on Elijah's cheek accompanied by a soft voice spoke quietly to the prophet so that he understood that he was standing in the very presence of God—the one who sought to give his servant peace of mind and heart. That experience was no less real than it was for Moses when he saw the back parts of God as his glory passed by (see 1 Kings 19:11–13).

God consoled his prophet—After God asked him again what he was doing at Mount Horeb, Elijah repeated his complaints about his ministry in Israel (see 1 Kings 19:14). Did he speak with the same tone of voice that he had prior to the dazzling display of God's power? No doubt the prophet's voice was softer. And even as he thought to himself, his words of excuse sounded hollow. God consoled his prophet. However, he re-commissioned him, and told him to return to his task of being a witness to Israel and to anoint kings and prophets (see 1 Kings 19:15, 16). God's call had not changed. He sent Elijah back to continue to share his love with his people. But what a testimony to the great comfort of God, who—even as he took the time to care for his prophet—also can take away our fears, give us courage once more, and enable us to continue on in his work.

Then the Lord informed Elijah that he was not the only believer in Israel. There were 7,000 others among the northern tribes who were faithful to the Lord and had not bowed their knees to Ba'al (see 1 Kings 19:18). Seven thousand might sound paltry among a total of two million, but God is not impressed with numbers. One man with the Lord is always a majority, and 7,000 make it an even greater majority! These believers also needed Elijah's encouragement to maintain their witness and share their faith so that others could turn to the Lord and find atonement for their souls.

David sought to console us with his words: "Taste, and see that *Adonai* is good. How blessed are those who take refuge in him!" (Ps. 34:8) and "How sweet to my tongue is your promise, truly sweeter than honey in my mouth!" (Ps. 119:103) May those who have been beaten down by problems, disappointments, sagging health, defeated spirit, or whatever makes one run away from what God has called us to do take God's comfort and consolation to heart. Let him speak to you in his gentle whisper and encourage you, re-commission you, and help you realize the sacred ideals you had when you began your work.

We are grateful to the Spirit of God, who has given us his Word, through which we see the tremendous possibilities for spiritual renewal in Elijah's days, even though it did not come to fruition. They were difficult days, but God's gracious comfort also re-anointed his servant to continue with his work.

When Elijah was taken up in the whirlwind, he cried out, "My father! My father! The chariots and horsemen of Isra'el!" (2 Kings 2:12) We cannot even begin to grasp the tearing asunder of the veil that separates believers here from the other world and view the presence of the angelic hosts in their chariots who had come to translate the prophet from earth to heaven. But his experience is a reminder of inexpressibly glorious experiences that await each one who will arrive one day on the other side of the curtain of eternity! Even as God's visible presence in the translation of Elijah was starkly real, so his presence also can be genuine in the lives of believers now. He stands ready to empower every servant of God in his or her ministry to the congregations and to the unsaved around us.

Some of that visible display of his presence that caught away Elijah also empowered Elisha as he began his ministry. And when he turned and came to the banks of the Jordan, carrying Elijah's cloak in his hands, he struck the water with it and cried, "Where is ADONAI, the God of Eliyahu [Elijah]?" (2 Kings 2:14) As he did so, the water parted and he walked across on dry ground.

The God of Elijah is here today as well, and living in our hearts. He is not the God of the dead but of the living. As we are filled with his presence to capacity, as much as anyone can even dare to take, perhaps the possibilities for spiritual renewal can become a reality in our congregations and in our nation.

CHAPTER SIX

Jonah at Nineveh

The Man Who Ran Away From the Lord

"But Yonah [Jonah], in order to get away from ADONAI, prepared to escape to Tarshish. He went down to Yafo, found a ship headed for Tarshish, paid the fare and went aboard, intending to travel with them to Tarshish and get away from ADONAI."

(Jon. 1:3)

"But this was very displeasing to Yonah, and he became angry. He prayed to ADONAI, 'Now, ADONAI, didn't I say this would happen, when I was still in my country? That's why I tried to get away to Tarshish ahead of time! I knew you were a God who is merciful and compassionate, slow to anger and rich in grace, and that you relent from inflicting punishment. Therefore, ADONAI, please just take my life away from me; it's better for me to be dead than alive!' ADONAI asked, 'Is it right for you to be so angry?'"

(Jon. 4:1–4)

The spiritual renewals seen in the Old Testament are intriguing because of the way God chose to work during the worst of spiritual circumstances within Israel. But God also is interested in pagan peoples, even those who are excessively immoral and cruel. To reach one such group, the people of Nineveh in Assyria, the Lord tried to send the prophet Jonah. But God had to go to drastic measures to convince the reluctant prophet to do his bidding.

A study of this period demonstrates how God chose the specific historical periods through which he worked in order to accomplish even greater purposes, not only for Israel, but for a pagan nation as well. This demonstrates not only that God is interested in Israel as a people, but also that he desires to reach others.

Jonah, a Shaliach (a Sent One) to the Gentiles

Historical Background

Advantages for Israel

Jonah was the son of Amittai, the prophet from Gath Hepher (see 2 Kings 14:25; Josh. 19:13), a town in the territory of Zebulun, located on a hill about five miles north of Nazareth. He lived during the "golden age" days of Jeroboam II of Israel (793–753 B.C.E., see 2 Kings 14:23–29), under whose leadership the territory of the North—apart from the southern boundary—was extended to approximately the same boundaries that David was able to conquer in his days. Damascus also was recovered, which means that other powers in the area were too weak to oppose the military thrust of this Israeli king (see 2 Kings 14:28).

There are two reasons why Jeroboam II was able to lead his country to be the most influential nation in the region: First, Syria's capital, Damascus, had previously been weakened by the attack of Assyrian king Adad-Nirari III (810–783 B.C.E.) just before Jeroboam came to the throne. Second, after Assyria's former peak of power, it entered into a period of weakness, possibly because of the danger of enemy attack on its own northern border as well as internal dissension and feeble rulers.

Nevertheless, the geo-political situation in the Middle East was such that God gave the Northern Kingdom an opportunity again, not only to enjoy some political, military, and economic success, but also to turn to him who alone made possible all these advantages. Unfortunately, material prosperity and a false optimism because of the weakness of Israel's enemies, as well as a low spiritual ebb, all combined to be a danger to the nation. And yet, God was gracious to these northern tribes, giving them ample opportunity for repentance before they would cease to be a political unit in 721 B.C.E. No one could accuse the Lord of not being merciful.

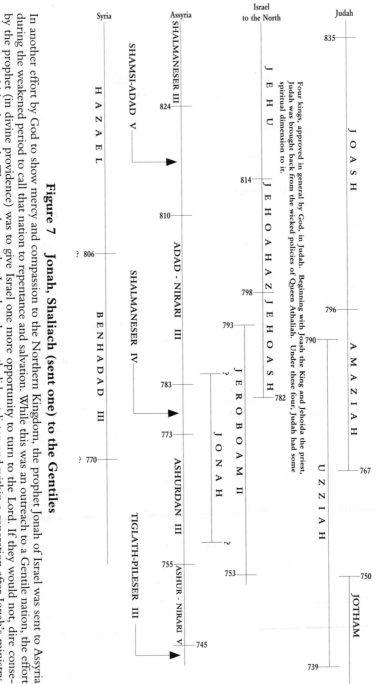

Figure 7   Jonah, Shaliach (sent one) to the Gentiles

In another effort by God to show mercy and compassion to the Northern Kingdom, the prophet Jonah of Israel was sent to Assyria during the weakened period to call that nation to repentance and salvation. While this was an outreach to a Gentile nation, the effort by the prophet (in divine providence) was to give Israel one more opportunity to turn to the Lord. If they would not, dire consequences would be the result. The tragedy was that Israel to the north did not listen and within a generation after Jonah's ministry, Assyria was on the march again under Tiglath-pileser III and eventually Israel ceased to exist as a political entity in 722/21 B.C.

Advantages for Assyria

But God was also interested in Assyria, at a time when that nation would be in a position to listen to his words through one of his prophets. Assyria had been a strong nation. Shalmaneser III was a powerful leader who, along with other nations, fought against Ahab of Israel and Ben-Hadad of Syria in the battle of Qarqar (853 B.C.E.).

In the Assyrian records, Shalmaneser claimed a great victory, but, evidently, it was not so. It seems that the Assyrian leader did not consummate his control by invading lower Syria. But in 841 B.C.E., Shalmaneser came again, fought against Syria, and then forced Jehu in Israel to pay heavy tribute.[28] In 783 B.C.E. Shalmaneser attacked Syria again, although nothing is known of this venture. But later on, as we have already mentioned concerning Adad-Nirari III, another attack further weakened Syria.

In the midst of this historical background, we can see why God wanted Jonah to enter Assyria at a time when it was politically weak and while Israel was militarily and politically strong. Three of the Assyrian kings during this period were Shalmaneser IV (783–773 B.C.E.), Ashurdan III (773–755 B.C.E.), and Ashur-Nirari V (755–745 B.C.E.). In addition, according to the Assyrian records, during the period of these weak kings, the country suffered a series of deadly epidemics. A total eclipse of the sun also occurred in 863 B.C.E., which certainly would bring about an atmosphere of fear among the people and provide good reason why Jonah could arrive and preach a message of judgment.

Jonah probably arrived in Assyria no later than 760 B.C.E., but any time during the period of that nation's weakness would be the context in which the prophet issued his word to bring these warlike peoples to repent before God. But the Lord's interest in Assyria's repentance—and that he knew that these people would respond to Jonah's preaching—may be regarded as a sign that God also was encouraging the people of Israel to turn back to him in faith and repudiate their idol worship as well.

Nineveh was a great city; the record indicates that it took three days to pass through all of it (see Jon. 3:3). Records indicate that the city was approximately 25 miles long by 15 miles wide. God also mentioned a group of 120,000 who didn't know the difference between their right and left hands (see Jon. 4:11). If this is a reference to the infants in Nineveh, then, along with their parents and older siblings, this could add up to a population of one million or more.

The Man Jonah

In Hebrew, Jonah means "dove." We have no idea why this name was assigned to him, and it is useless to speculate.[29] The fact that the record tells us something about where he came from, the name of his father, and his prophecies concerning the success of Jeroboam II, indicates that he was a genuine historical figure and possibly quite well known in the Northern Kingdom. Yeshua's reference to him in the New Covenant further establishes him as a historical figure.

Even as God genuinely cared for the people of Nineveh and wanted them to hear the message of life, so God is interested today that his good-news message be brought to unreached peoples, regardless of the cost. But what does it take to bring together the Lord's messenger and the people to be reached? Some of the people God called did respond with, "Here am I. Send me!" Of all people, however, God called Jonah, who never said, "Send me." Indeed, he was the least likely candidate to reach a people who had a special reputation for brutality. Strange indeed are God's ways.

God's Involvement in the Life of His Prophet

How many of God's people today will go out of their way to share with a homeless person, sit where he or she sits and extend a hand of love to demonstrate their care? How many will share God's love with people who are unlovely? And, let's face it, if such a needy person showed up in our congregations, would he or she really be made to feel welcome?

Behind the outward actions and words, what is the state of the heart that makes a person uncaring toward one who does not live within our carefully marked lines of social preferences?

Yet, not all believers fall prey to an indulgent life. I remember when the Lord worked in quite different circumstances in the early 1950s. Along the river border of their territory in Ecuador, an Auca tribe martyred five dedicated young missionaries. The five young men had come from a lifestyle that afforded them a good education; if they had stayed in their country of plenty, they could have accumulated more and more goods. Instead, these five left their easy life and gave their all to bring Messiah's message of salvation to that underprivileged people.

Some might say this loss was a total waste. Was it? Through the deaths of his servants as a dedicatory burnt offering, as it were, God's Spirit began to touch the hearts of many young people in North America for the cause of taking the gospel around the world. The whole body of believers was shaken out of its complacency and made to realize that everyone must ever be sensitive to God's will and purposes for the peoples of the world.

So we need now to consider how God was involved in guiding Jonah to be obedient to his call. But as this prophet's life was made into a public spectacle, perhaps we might learn the lessons of what it means to climb out of ourselves and pay attention to the needs of people all around us and be involved in what God calls us to do.

Emotional Response of the Petty Prophet

Often, the war for spiritual renewal occurs at the emotional level. People have likes and dislikes deep within their hearts. Believers can attend congregational gatherings, be enthralled with the worship and liturgy, and listen dutifully to the message, but within an hour after leaving the service, the old nature works through their emotions. Any believer who takes an honest look within will discover that the "gut level" of the emotions seriously blocks the effort God desires. A closer look at some of Jonah's emotional levels should prove helpful.

Partial obedience—The prophet was, first of all, characterized by obedience to God that was only partial at best. As long as Jonah could have remained in Israel, he would have been content to do what God asked him to do. His dedication to ministry was based on what he wanted to do; so when God asked him to go to the great city of Nineveh, Jonah ran away and headed to Tarshish—about as far away from Assyria as Jonah could think of.

The Lord now had to work patiently in the prophet's life—even though he had to use drastic means to finally turn Jonah in the right direction. Perhaps he assured himself, once having obtained passage on the ship for Tarshish, this must be the Lord's will. But while on the ship bound for Tarshish, a great storm came up, obviously providentially arranged. The sailors were thoroughly frightened by the unexpected tempest; they realized that the ship might go down and they would be lost at sea. After tossing overboard the ship's entire cargo and gear and still not making any headway—and with the situation becoming ever grimmer—the captain and his crew cast lots to see who was responsible for this great calamity.

When the lot fell to Jonah, they asked him where he came from and to which people he belonged. His reply was forthright: "I am a Hebrew; and I fear *ADONAI*, the God of heaven, who made both the sea and the dry land" (Jon. 1:9). Even though he had insisted on the area where he wanted to serve, he still acknowledged the Lord God of Israel and bore testimony to him before these pagan sailors.

Many of the men of the Old Testament did exactly as Jonah did. When God called Abram to leave behind his family in Ur and go to a land where he had never been before, Abram packed up, took his father as well as his nephew Lot, and moved north in the general direction of Canaan. But he stopped short of his goal, in Haran (see Gen. 11:31), and tragically spent up to fifteen years there before God took his father, Terah, out of this world. Then God called a second time for Abram to go where he should have gone when God first spoke to him (see Gen. 11:31–32; 12:1; Acts 7:2–4).[30]

Believers today are much like Abraham and Jonah. No, the problem is not with an outright unfaithfulness to attend the meetings of the congregation, or with giving resources. Often, however, when God puts his finger on specific areas in order to correct believers or move people from complacency, emotions can get in the way and believers can even become angry with God, who is trying to move them beyond the stage of partial obedience.

Apathy—Jonah's lethargy also was a problem. He had paid his fare for a voyage in the opposite direction of where God wanted him to be. Then, safely on board when the ship pulled out for Tarshish, he fell into a deep sleep below deck (see Jon. 1:5). Did he somehow feel he was safe and secure just because he had found space on this ship? But what was Jonah doing when the storm began to rise on the sea, the wind started to howl, and the swirling waters of the high waves tossed the ship like a matchstick? He was sound asleep! "Jonah, what about Nineveh?" was God's cry, trying to get through to his prophet. No one could sleep so soundly as apathetic Jonah, even though the angry waves were crashing onto the ship. Apathy in the spiritual realm can be death to the Lord's work.

Some time ago I went to the post office to mail a letter, and at the window I asked the clerk for the necessary stamps. She gave me six stamps so slowly that I wondered if she was really ill. When I exclaimed, "I can't put all six stamps on this small envelope," she very slowly went through her book and finally found two stamps of equal value that would fit. When I put the stamps on the envelope and handed it back to her, she took the envelope very slowly. With her other hand she had the marker that would postmark the stamps, but it was only the weight of her hand that finally brought the marker down on the stamps! I looked at her in amazement because her work was the perfect picture of slow-motion apathy.

That postal clerk is a demonstration of where many believers are spiritually, unaware of the times and the opportunities. Congregation members barely say hello to visitors who come into the assembly. Rarely do we follow through to visit newcomers in their homes. Hardly ever do people go with enthusiasm, again and again to new contacts, alive to the possibility of reaching those people so as to befriend them and win them for the Lord. Apathy is a monster of an emotional problem, and it can pull down a congregation spiritually and bring its outreach to a screeching halt.

Prejudice—Racism is still another serious emotional difficulty. When God told Jonah to go to Nineveh, all the prophet could think was how these vile people had a history of causing so much suffering to the nations in the Middle East, including his own people in the days of Jehu. He felt they did not deserve the opportunity to hear the message of grace.

At a later date, Nahum described how a resurgent and vicious Assyria waged war: "The chariots rush madly about in the streets, jostling each other in the open places; their appearance is like torches, they run here and there like lightning" (Nah. 2:4). The Assyrians were notorious for the way they used their chariots. They attached blades to the axles, and as they drove the chariots through the roads they cut down anyone who got in the way. The Assyrians also often attached torches to the axles so that when they ran their chariots through the wheat fields, everything was scorched and burned to the ground. It isn't difficult to see why Jonah was prejudiced against these enemies of Israel. But, in effect, his reply to God's call was, "Me, go to the Assyrians? Count me out! I am not going to my enemies; I don't want to even get near those people!"

Smallness—Still another emotional level exhibited by this prophet was his pettiness. The prophet's world was a small one: "Me, myself, and I; what a nice trio to go around with." God's view of the world goes beyond the needs of our areas where we live and minister. God's love and concern extends to people throughout this world. Electronic communication devices, such as the Internet, allow us the opportunity to become more knowledgeable of people groups and their needs beyond our own, and to develop empathy for what other peoples have to face. On a deeper level, we have to sense spiritual needs of internationals who live in different cultures, trapped in various religious systems and suffering under alien ideologies. We simply cannot be small and look at our ministries only. God, therefore, took drastic action with his prophet's emotions. God often has to act likewise with believers today.

An emotional ride

God's answer for Jonah's lethargy jolted the prophet awake to spiritual realities. The Lord prepared a great fish to be in the vicinity of the struggling ship. As soon as the frightened sailors, with great misgiving, threw Jonah overboard, the big fish was there to swallow him. With Jonah off the ship, the winds died down and the seas calmed—but Jonah ended up as fish food.

Quite frankly, that fish would never be the same again. What a ride with this emotional Jonah on board. What a trauma it must have been for the prophet. What a place to learn—at the point of death—that one is never safe when out of God's will. How much easier it is when believers listen intently to what God wants in our lives and seek to serve him for the greatest possible blessings.

Some years back, a *sh'lachah* (a woman messenger [missionary]) sent to Japan related how God had to work drastically with her emotions. She had boarded a train in Japan which, as usual, was packed full of people, with only a little place to stand along the side, where she had an opportunity to face the Japanese people sitting in their seats and crowded in the aisles. As she leaned against the sidewall of the train, she began to observe closely the facial characteristics of the people to whom she had been sent. From the depths of her heart arose revulsion for these Japanese faces, because they seemed so odd and strange to her.

She sensed immediately that God had dredged this emotional attitude out of the depths of her heart, where the root of prejudice existed toward the very ones to whom she had gone to minister. She vowed then and there, on a fast-moving, crowded train, to confess and put away this sinful attitude, seek God's forgiveness, and ask for a new sense of love for the people whom she was called to serve.

Only after her confession to the Lord, when she had peace in her heart, could she again look at the Japanese with love and compassion. God's Spirit also brought to her mind that her own facial characteristics might seem just as odd to the Japanese. But this dear woman had to open up completely before the Lord, let him deal drastically with her, and allow him to exhibit more of the new nature within her and take away some of the ugly emotions of the old nature. Only then could God minister through this missionary with a new emotional outlook toward people who did not know the Lord.

Repentance and Evangelism that reaches a City

God had to deal drastically with Jonah to move him in the right direction to reach a people who were in desperate spiritual need.

Deep in the stomach of this big fish—with other fish, seaweed, and debris brushing against him, weakened from the heat, with skin and hair being discolored by the digestive juices—the prophet finally took the first step in spiritual renewal. It was a bizarre place to finally yield his life, repent, and pray to the Lord and worship him in the beauty of holiness. He began to pray to God for direction and guidance. If only he had prayed in the beginning, when God first approached him. If he only had gone into his secluded closet, or walked out on the hills by himself so as to seek guidance on how to put God's will into action and take that journey to Nineveh.

Even today, the Lord's people can find themselves in strange places when they finally begin to worship the Lord meaningfully, with a repentant attitude. It might happen in a hospital room with nothing left to do but look up, or at the graveside of a departed loved one who had prayed for those left behind.

The prophet dedicated himself to the Lord, even though he was in the fish, in a sense banished from God's "sight" (see Jon. 2:4). But even in the depths of the sea, in the stomach of a sea monster, he expressed his faith: "But I will look again at your holy temple" (Jon. 2:4). As he felt his life ebbing away, he still remembered the Lord and directed his prayer to the holy Temple—not to any temple in Israel, but in Jerusalem (see Jon. 2:7). He knew that the idols his countrymen worshipped, as well as the idols in Nineveh, were all worthless and that no grace or mercy was forthcoming from these pagan gods. Jonah's deliverance finally came when the Lord commanded the fish to vomit him out onto dry ground (see Jon. 2:10).

Any question as to where Jonah was headed after he disembarked? Right where God wanted him to go in the first place—to Nineveh! And wasn't that fish happy to be rid of one huge stomachache from a passenger who could not be digested? So Jonah was re-commissioned to do the task he had been asked to do in the beginning (see Jon. 3:1, 2).

An Evangelism Empowered by God's Presence

A simple message—As Jonah walked a day's journey into Nineveh, he preached his message of only five words in Hebrew (eight words in English): "Yet forty days and Nineveh will be overthrown" (Jon. 3:4). Was it a profound message? Not at all. In fact, many of the men God has used through the years are not, humanly speaking, great speakers. Often the message is a very simple witness, but it comes from a heart of love and concern and with the Lord's support.

Jonah's message was succinct. Proverbs 15:23 says, "But a word at the right time, how good it is!" Jonah did not have to go into a long discourse; instead, a few well-chosen words were enough to bring a nation to repentance.

God's presence—God empowered the simple message, which served as a warning to the people of Nineveh. Jonah had been called to share with the people of Nineveh that above the multitude of idols in the city is the true God of all the earth. And, their well-being was at stake if they would not listen to God's call to them at this strategic moment. The danger of destruction was a dread reality if they chose to snub and turn away from this God. So, when Jonah talked about Nineveh's destruction, they were chilled with fear as the Spirit worked his power of conviction in their hearts.

Many people find this appeal to fear unsettling, and they might ask indignantly, "Is it fair to put such an emphasis on a message of warning? Why speak or preach the fear of God and try to scare people into the kingdom, or to accept Yeshua?" Surveys show that two-thirds of young people accept Messiah's offer of salvation because of a fear of God's wrath. After all, "The fear of *ADONAI*," said the wisdom writer, "is the beginning of wisdom" (Prov. 9:10). Wisdom calls for a humble attitude to listen to God's full counsel and then accept Yeshua the Messiah and be born into God's family.

The crucible of crisis—Jonah preached his message in the context of crisis. A lot is said today about having a warm, loving relationship with God, and that he desires to reach out and embrace people and call each his own. The content of so many messages in the pulpit has a strong emphasis on God's love; and, no doubt, these words reflect a great and precious truth.

However, God's love without the sense of his holiness as it confronts human need, is in reality a defective view of his love. The importance of holiness in the midst of a person's or a nation's crises is what causes people to face their insufficiencies and sins, as well as their needs. But, as we turn to the Lord and comprehend his grace, we can then have a sense of reverence for him, as well as of his love for us.

Years ago, my wife and I met an art teacher in Israel whose constant claim was that she saw beauty everywhere. She sensed we loved her, but whenever we initiated any conversation concerning humanity's sin nature, she became very upset. Yet she had to learn of God's holiness, which convicts of righteousness, self-control, and judgment to come. This dear woman needed to recognize the fear of the Lord so that she could respond to his love, which has been sent forth to save us from our hopelessness, even from our sins. Merely telling her about God's love would be an insufficient message. At the end, however, just before she died, she raised up on her bed and spat out Isaiah's words at me: "My thoughts are not your thoughts, and my ways are not your ways" (Isa. 55:8). Tragically, God will use these very words as she stands before him and realizes that he is holy and we are sinful. She had rejected the Messiah, the one who could have taken away her sin.

The People of Nineveh Repent

Through the conviction of sin and the judgment to come, God wanted Jonah to call Nineveh to repentance, to have the people of that nation turn to him with a change of heart and the Holy Spirit's presence worked in their lives. The word repentance itself is not mentioned specifically, but the action is strongly implied when the king of Nineveh declared: "No person or animal, herd or flock, is to put anything in his mouth; they are neither to eat nor drink water. They must be covered with sackcloth, both people and animals; and they are to cry out to God with all their might—let each one turn from his evil way and from the violence they practice" (Jon. 3:7, 8).

The spiritual renewal in Jonah's heart, occurring during a traumatic ride in the fish's stomach, was designed eventually to call Nineveh to repentance.

Jonah's message also implied that if the people of Nineveh turned to this God, his salvation of them was a distinct possibility. But which Lord? Which God? He was not one of the idols in the city. Rather, he is the God of the whole earth, who, incidentally, is Israel's God. Jonah was his representative. Even though the Ninevite leaders did not know this God, it was to him they cried out in order that he should relent and, with compassion, turn from his fierce anger (see Jon. 3:9). Even though the Assyrians had a history of thinking their gods were greater because of their military strength, these people had been brought so low in that generation that they were ready to consider Israel's Lord as their God.

Times have not changed; we need to preach the message of repentance today. But how can the call to unbelievers take place without believers also turning away from a self-serving kind of life? Even we who have accepted Yeshua into our lives can be so locked within ourselves for our own self-gratification or so caught up in all the social activities within the congregation that we have little or no heart to sit with unbelievers and feel their needs. Even as Jonah had to turn to God before he ended up in Nineveh to call them to repentance, so do we need to repent, turn to God, and get in step with his concerns in order to reach out to unbelievers.

In 1980 I visited Cambodian refugee camps in Thailand. It was a pitiful sight, as we viewed these people who had lost so much, and who, in many instances, even lost their will to live. They had run away from unspeakable horrors where entire families were killed by the Communist regime that had taken control over their native country.

Our highlight in that camp was the talk we had with a Cambodian pastor. Some eight months previous, he and his congregation of about 200 were able to get away from Phnom Phem and escape into the relative safety of a refugee camp in Thailand. But this pastor, his elders, and their people felt overwhelmed. The camp housed some 140,000 people, most of whom were Buddhists. What could these Christians do? No recourse was left them but to turn to God and seek his face, spending whole days and nights in prayer and fasting that he would work on their behalf. As we looked intently into the faces of this care-worn pastor and some of his elders who had aged beyond their years because of all their privations, we heard with amazement how, in eight months, this congregation had grown to 26,000 believers! His testimony sounded incredible but was nevertheless true. Even as God worked with power in Jonah's efforts, he did the same with these Cambodian believers. Who knows but that he might do the same with believers today in a needy and fearful world?

The Results of Evangelism among the People of Nineveh

Thanks to Jonah's spiritual renewal, the Ninevites believed God (see Jon. 3:5), and many came to know the Lord.

Or did they? Many will challenge the sincerity of the faith of these Assyrians. They might ask, "Were many of these people really saved, as the record seems to indicate?" It is quite possible that some had only an intellectual confession of belief. But, no doubt, many people had been born again. The Scriptures declare, "So trust comes from what is heard, and what is heard comes through a word proclaimed about the Messiah" (Rom. 10:17). The spiritual renewal that came as God became involved with Jonah the prophet was for the purpose that unbelievers be saved. The Ninevites cried mightily (urgently) to the Lord (see Jon. 3:8). They realized they were on the brink of disaster and, therefore, forsook their evil ways and trusted God for his deliverance. Through a few words from Jonah in the streets and squares of Nineveh, we gain an insight as to how God's Spirit made it possible for many to trust God and receive the truth. Who can tell, even today, what would happen if believers in a congregation desire urgently to do God's will and become involved with neighbors and people in our communities?

God also forgave the Assyrians. When the Lord "saw by their deeds that they had turned from their evil way, he relented and did not bring on them the punishment he had threatened" (Jon. 3:10). God changed his attitude when Ninevites' hearts changed. Here is a great truth: God changes as we change. We might say that he changes so as to remain unchangeable—so as to be true to himself. When a people are far from God, he can act only in judgment and discipline; but when they turn to him, then he also changes accordingly.

What was the effect on Old Testament history? Assyria was quiet for almost an entire generation before Tiglath-Pileser III (745–727 B.C.E.) marched out with a great army, bent on military conquest of many parts of the Middle East. Until the beginning of this Assyrian king's rule, God gave Israel time and opportunity to listen to his Word as he arranged the circumstances among the nations of the Middle East, keeping them within their own boundaries. That peace and quiet was why the lack of repentance of many in the Northern Kingdom was even more serious. But, instead of turning to him as did the Assyrians, the people of northern Israel sought after their own economic prosperity and flouted God's wishes, thereby treasuring up for themselves greater judgment than the Assyrians of Jonah's day.

Centuries later, Yeshua declared to some of the religious leaders of his day that Jonah was a sign to Nineveh, because they repented when he preached to them his message of challenge (see Luke 11:30, 32). Jonah's ministry was also a sign to Jeroboam II and to all Israel as well, because, while the pagans responded to Jonah's message, the Northern Kingdom practically ignored it. But even as the people of Nineveh will condemn the northern tribes at the judgment, so, Yeshua declared, those in his day who seek signs merely to play with them also will be condemned by the Ninevites. Jonah's message was calculated to impress the Assyrians, but it became a sign to the unbelievers in Israel in his day as well as for those in generations to come. Little did Jonah realize the effects God desired, not only in his day but also in days yet ahead.

Conclusion

The spiritual renewal wrought through Jonah's experience was for an outreach far beyond what he anticipated. Many in Assyria heard the message and responded. Such good news was glorious, but then came the bad news.

Why, why, why did Jonah sit on the edge of the town to see what would happen to Nineveh? (See Jon. 4:1–3) In his heart, the prophet knew that God was going to spare the Assyrians and bring them to himself. But the unsettling response to the question of Jonah's behavior is that, knowing the sense of God's plan, he sat on the edge of the town and insisted that judgment come upon Nineveh!

God then had to get further involved in Jonah's life. Believers have to realize that a great work of God in our hearts and in outreach does not mean complete freedom from difficulties with our commitment to the Lord. This prophet still had elements of prejudice in his heart, and they needed to be rooted out.

So the Lord prepared a vine that grew rapidly, providing comfort and shade to the prophet as he sat and waited for the worst to happen to Nineveh. How the prophet enjoyed the plant that gave him a measure of relief from the sun. But God also prepared a worm to chew away at the vine, causing it to wither and die; so Jonah was left without protection from the heat of the sun. Would this prophet, after being involved in one of the greatest outreach miracles in history, figure out the lesson God was trying to teach him regarding the plant and the worm? Apparently not, because all he could do was pout and feel sorry for himself. The Lord then had to plead with him to at least have sympathy for 120,000 infants in the city who could not comprehend the difference between their right and left hands. Jonah took delight in a quick-growing and yet worthless plant, but he seemed unable to rejoice at the Lord's mercy to the people of Nineveh.

God wants to work with all of us as he did with the people of Nineveh. Jewish people need to be reached and loved into the Kingdom, but our interests need not stop there. Black people need to be reached and loved, and so do Native Americans, Hispanics, Asians, and everyone around us. The fact that we do not pray and witness or even change our feelings about peoples different from ourselves points to a great spiritual lack in our own lives.

I love Jewish short stories. One of my favorites is "The Zaida and the Zulu," a short story by Dan Jacobson.[31] The word "Zaida" is Yiddish for grandfather. Zulu provides the clue as to the locale of the story—in South Africa.

The grandfather was old and senile, and his son felt he was unable to care for the old man. So the son hired a Zulu man to take care of his father. The black man took great honor in caring for this elderly man, and soon the two became inseparable. The grandfather had a companion with whom he could share, and the Zulu man cared for the old man's every need.

One day the Zulu man had to return to the country for a couple of days for some urgent business, and his absence left the grandfather completely devastated. Finally the old man became so agitated that he ran out of the house, into the street, and was run down by a car.

After the funeral, the son stood at the grandfather's door, watching the Zulu man lovingly pack up the old man's belongings. The son realized the Zulu loved the grandfather more than he had. The son had disliked his father, and had even resented the relationship the black man had with him. Now, however, as he stood watching the Zulu man, whose heart was overcome with grief, he had a deep sense of remorse. He asked the loving caretaker, "What else could I have done? I did my best," and then the tears flowed. The son had missed his opportunity.

May God speak to our hearts, and may we be filled with his Spirit to have a genuine compassion for people who do not know the Lord. May we not miss the opportunities God gives us to share his love.

CHAPTER SEVEN

Hezekiah and the Temple of the Lord

The Man Who Opened the Temple Doors

(2 Kings 18:1–20:21; 2 Chron. 29:1–32:33; Isa. 36:1–39:8)

"Besides the abundance of burnt offerings, there was the fat of the peace offering and drink offerings for each burnt offering."

(2 Chron. 29:35, 36)

"For a large number of people, especially from Efrayim, Yissakhar and Z'vulun, had not cleansed themselves but ate the *Pesach* [Passover] lamb anyway, despite what is written. For Hizkiyahu [Hezekiah] had prayed for them, 'May ADONAI, who is good, pardon.'"

(2 Chron. 30:18–20)

God works in many different ways in the lives of believers to bring about spiritual renewal. Here are two examples.

Only after Geof Bull had spent time in a communist prison in Tibet in the early 1950s for trying to witness for the Messiah was he able to write the following words in his book *When Iron Gates Yield.* "How the Spirit of God worked in power in his heart as he lived for the Lord under such drastic conditions."

Jim Elliott and his four colleagues, already mentioned, were martyred by a riverbank in Ecuador in the early 1950s. Although they had their hearts set on reaching the Auca Indians, God had other ways of continuing their efforts: The entire worldwide outreach was strengthened as many young people gave their lives for the Lord's work throughout the world when they heard of the selfless service of the martyred five.

The testimony of the five is encapsulated in a statement written by Jim Elliott in his diary before all of them were offered in death as a dedicatory burnt offering: "He is no fool who gives up what he cannot keep in order to gain what he cannot lose." No wonder many young people responded to these martyrs' sacrifice by giving themselves to the Lord's service.

Joseph Rabinowitz moved to Israel from Czarist Russia in 1882 because he wanted to throw in his lot with the early settlers during the first *aliyah* (immigration wave) in modern times. Then, as he sat down on the Mount of Olives, overlooking the old city of Jerusalem, God spoke to his heart. Perhaps this was when he became a believer in Yeshua the Messiah. He had carried a copy of the New Testament with him and had become aware of Yeshua's claims.

A short while after the Mount of Olives experience, God directed him to return to Russia. How could he leave when he was already in the land and had fully expected to share in its rebuilding? Yet, he was obedient to the Lord's call and returned to what today is the Ukraine. He was instrumental in leading many Jewish people to the Lord and establishing congregations of Jewish believers during the last decade of the nineteenth century and up until the First World War.[32] The peculiar leadership of the Holy Spirit is amazing as he works in the hearts of God's people who are open to his leadership. When the Holy Spirit can work freely and unhindered, many will come to know the Lord as a result.

So it was with Hezekiah, called a good king who "did what was right from *ADONAI*'s perspective, following the example of everything David his ancestor had done" (2 Chron. 29:2). The ninth king from Asa, Hezekiah was one of Judah's eight good kings (see Figure 1, page xii). Before discussing Hezekiah further, however, we need to consider how his background had a significant bearing on the great outpouring of the Spirit in the days of this king.

Figure 8 God's Gracious Renewal Under Hezekiah

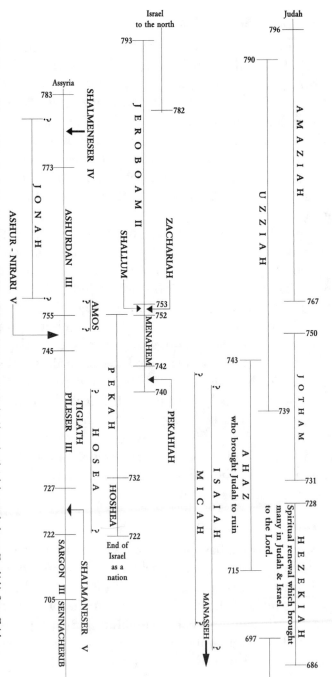

After the reigns of the good kings, Joash, Amaziah, Uzziah, and Jotham, Judah sank into apostasy under Ahaz who closed the temple doors. Hezekiah's first official act of opening the temple doors and restoring worship led to a tremendous renewal. The Spirit of God poured out His blessings so that in a Passover they celebrated, there was nothing like it since the days of Solomon, a period of more than 200 years. The times were especially rich with the ministry of four great prophets, Isaiah, Micah, Amos, and Hosea, who also laid the groundwork for renewal for many in Judah and even in Israel to the north. Although Israel had failed in the north as a nation, it was still possible to hear the message in the south in Jerusalem, go there and share with the Judeans God's salvation and live for Him.

Jehoshaphat, Son of Asa

After the interlude of noting how God attempted to work through Elijah and Jonah to turn people in the Northern Kingdom to him, we look again at the kings of Judah (the Southern Kingdom), and in particular at Asa (911–870 B.C.E.). His son, Jehoshaphat, was also a good king and continued much of what his father had started. The record declares of him, "he lived according to the first ways of his ancestor David, not seeking the ba'alim, but seeking the God of his father and living by his *mitzvot*, not by what Isra'el did" (2 Chron. 17:3, 4).

Time, however, has a way of testing character. After a blessed ministry of teaching his people the right and good way, Jehoshaphat pursued a course that led to tragedy, not only for himself, but also for his people Judah. He allied himself—and, consequently, David's royal line—with King Ahab of Israel (see 2 Chron. 18:1) when his son Jehoram was married to Athaliah, the daughter of Ahab and Jezebel (see 2 Chron. 21:6). Another misguided decision almost ended in disaster: Jehoshaphat joined Ahab on the battlefield against the Arameans in a fight over Ramoth Gilead. Even after being warned by God's faithful prophet Micaiah (see 1 Kings 22:19–28), the Judean king still fought with Ahab against Ben-Hadad and was almost killed for his efforts (see 2 Chron. 18:29–34). Any contact with the kings of the Northern Kingdom always led to humiliating consequences.

Jehoram and Ahaziah

After Jehoshaphat died, Judah's spiritual level degenerated. In succession, Jehoshaphat's son Jehoram, who should have learned from a godly father and grandfather, became rebellious against the Lord. He did evil, no doubt influenced by his wife Athaliah, Jezebel's daughter. Perhaps Jehoshaphat thought that his aligning with the people of the Northern Kingdom would help draw them back to the Lord. But alliance with evil always boomerangs, and through Athaliah,

Jezebel impacted Judah for evil and brought about a spiritual decline because of the introduction into the south of pagan Ba'al-Melqart worship from Phoenicia.

The next king, Ahaziah (841 B.C.E., see 2 Chron. 22:1–9), reigned for only one year, but, because of his mother, Athaliah, he too was involved in spiritual wickedness. When Ahaziah died at the hands of the men of Jehu of the North, Athaliah became queen, and Judah sank into one of its worst spiritual lows (see 2 Chron. 22:10–23:15). To insure her right to the throne of Judah as the queen, she ordered the death of all her son's children; in the process, she almost succeeded in snuffing out David's royal line. But God intervened through Jehosheba, a sister of Ahaziah, who managed to hide one baby son, Joash. In these dastardly circumstances, however, Athaliah ruled, and it seemed that no one dared withstand her. Yet, God always has people he can trust, people who will take a stand against the forces of evil.

When Joash reached the age of seven, during the sixth year of Athaliah's reign, the young king was brought into the Temple. With careful pre-arrangements by Jehoiada, the godly high priest, many of the military and religious leaders were present so that the real heir to the throne could be crowned king. With great relief and joy, all present in the Temple clapped their hands and shouted loudly, "Long live the king." Upon hearing the roar of the acclamation for Joash, Athaliah cried, "Treason! Treason!" But the high priest ordered her execution, which was carried out gladly because of Judah's hatred for such an evil leader.

Joash, Amaziah, Uzziah, Jotham

Four kings followed in succession: Joash (835–796 B.C.E.), Amaziah (796–767 B.C.E.), Uzziah (also known as Azariah) (791–739 B.C.E.), and Jotham (750–731 B.C.E.). None of these kings were commended in the record as "good," as Hezekiah and Josiah were. Yet, in a general sense, for more than 100 years, Judah had some kind of sensitivity to the things of God. These four leaders may have started out well and had good intentions to achieve the ideal, but, because of the pressures of power and self-seeking as the kings grew older, they manifested less and less desire for the Lord's wishes.

Ahaz

The next king, Ahaz (743–715; see 2 Kings 16; 2 Chron. 28), ruled for twenty-eight years, but a good many of these years were in co-regencies, first with his father, Jotham, and then with his son Hezekiah.

One significant statement describes Ahaz: "He did not do what was right from the perspective of *Adonai*" (2 Chron. 28:1). Instead, he chose to follow the worst of the pagan practices of the nations of the Middle East. Furthermore, the record states that this king "sealed the doors of the house of *Adonai*" (2 Chron. 28:24), thereby cutting the very nerve center of Judah's worship. Temple life was central to the nation; leaders and people met the Lord there in daily worship as well as in observances of specified holidays of the covenant. No wonder Ahaz led a troubled life; God had no recourse but to judge him severely for his evil deeds.

This decision to shut the Temple doors must have had a profound impact on Hezekiah, who was in his teen years at the time. As a believer, he could have known already that his father's policy of shutting down the Temple would have disastrous consequences for the nation.

The Man Hezekiah

Hezekiah became king when he was twenty-five years old, ruling for a total of forty-two years. Through the first thirteen, however, he appeared to serve as co-regent with Ahaz.[33]

Hezekiah's first official decision, in the first month of the first year of his reign, was to reopen the Temple doors (see 2 Chron. 29:3). The correlation between Ahaz's closing the

Temple doors and Hezekiah's opening them is not to be taken lightly. Ahaz's drastic policy of shutting down the Temple led the nation into paganism and ruin. His son Hezekiah, as Judah's new king, reversed his father's apostate decision and, in a dramatic gesture, gave the orders to reopen the Temple doors. In so doing, he became the instrument for the nation's spiritual renewal.

A Pro-*Adonai* Policy

No information is provided as to when Hezekiah came to know the Lord. Evidently, however, this simple but profound matter of reopening the Temple's closed doors was something special in his appreciation for the things of God.

Hezekiah was one of Judah's choice kings as well as a man whom God trusted explicitly. He took a stand that was at cross-purposes with his father's pro-Assyrian policies, exchanging them instead for a pact that favored the Lord. He was a man of courage and purpose, leading Judah to a higher spiritual level. When he became king, he challenged the priests and other religious leadership to begin again their service at the Temple, sensing no doubt their frustration while they sat idle, unable to do anything while Ahaz was in power.[34]

When God finally brought precious renewal to the nation, this king encouraged the believers to carry its message far and wide. Their testimony was so powerful that many, even from the Northern Kingdom, came to the Temple in Jerusalem to worship with their brethren in Judah. Inspiration from God's Spirit was necessary to bring about such a change of affairs from the horror of Ahaz's policies, and Hezekiah became the man God chose to use on this occasion.

Facing Up To an Imposing Military Threat

This new king was not afraid to face the Assyrians when some of their advance units were at the gates of Jerusalem, engaging in psychological warfare with the city's inhabitants who were looking down from the city walls. The Assyrian commanders mocked and insulted the Lord God of Israel and declared that their gods were greater. Did Hezekiah think he could reverse Ahaz's policies and stop paying tribute to Assyria?

Didn't Hezekiah know he was up against the most powerful military machine in the Middle East at the time? Of course he did. But the king did not falter in his reliance in the Lord. Instead, he went up to the Temple of the Lord and spread out the letter from the Assyrian king before Judah's God, the King over all the earth, and pled his country's case. With no hesitation, Hezekiah knew that the God who controlled the nations of the entire world was entirely able to reckon with even the most powerful of them all. To God's glory and to Hezekiah's testimony as God's man, the Angel of the Lord severely judged Assyria, striking down 185,000 troops, probably through a fast-acting plague (see 2 Chron. 32:21; Isa. 37:36).

A Man of Faith

Hezekiah also demonstrated his deep faith. When he contracted the infection that led to his mortal illness, Hezekiah pleaded for more time in order to continue to lead the nation in its renewal. God was pleased to hear his prayer, adding fifteen years to his life. A record of his prayer exposes the wellsprings of his soul when he thanked the Lord for what he was able to do for him. He was grateful that he could continue to live; he gave praise to God's goodness, blessing, and mercy, saying, "The living, the living—they can thank you, as I do today" (Isa. 38:19).

A major clue as to why Hezekiah was so distressed at his point of death was that, at the time of his illness, he apparently had no children whereby the line of David could continue. Careful note should be taken that when his son Manasseh became king as a possible co-regent, the boy was twelve years old, which meant that he was born three years into the fifteen years of grace after Hezekiah's recovery from his illness. Without being dogmatic on this point, one can understand why Hezekiah pleaded so urgently with God. Although he made no mention of it in his prayer, his faith was that David's line had to continue through him because of a promise in the covenant with David (see 2 Sam. 7:12–16). God was pleased to hear his cry so that Hezekiah could have a successor.

Toward the end of Hezekiah's life, the record describes his self-sufficiency in what he had accumulated (see Isa. 39). When Babylon's envoys came to congratulate him on his recovery, the Judean king showed them everything he had—his storehouses, his treasures, and his armory. The prophet Isaiah then had to rebuke him for his indiscretion, stating that the time would come when everything the Babylonians were able to observe would be carried off by the armies of that nation. Although Hezekiah's common sense and faith failed momentarily, his heart was tender and he confessed his weakness and managed to retain a good spiritual sensitivity to the day of his death.

The Influences in Spiritual Renewal

Symbol of Nation's Rebellion

Note carefully the inner moral and spiritual choices of Judah's leaders that led to the outward decisions of closing and opening the Temple doors. We open and close doors all day long without giving it any thought whatsoever, but the choices to close and open the doors to the Temple reflect morally and spiritually on the person giving the orders.

Despicable decisions—Ahaz's moral and spiritual inner choices became the symbol of a nation's rebellion. Political leaders often have it in their power to lead their people to greatness or to ruin, but the direction a country takes can depend greatly on motivations, attitudes, and priorities that guide its ruler's choices. Closing the Temple doors reflected rebellion in Ahaz's heart toward the Lord God of Israel, and the consequences were drastic. The Temple doors were closed because Ahaz had determined to give honor and devotion to the Assyrian pantheon of gods and goddesses. Therefore, this king's rebellion in his heart and his subsequent outward decisions and actions led to rejecting the Lord and choosing a false worship. The tragedy was compounded as he led Judah astray and, consequently, everything else went wrong.

Ahaz's decision for idolatry was detestable for the following reasons—as seen in 2 Chronicles 28:

1. He cast idols for worshiping the Ba'alim (v. 2).
2. He burned sacrifices in the Valley of Ben Hinnom (v. 3).
3. He sacrificed his sons in the fire, as was practiced by the nations of the Middle East before Israel drove them out from the land hundreds of years before (v. 3).
4. He offered sacrifices and burned incense at the high places (v. 4).
5. He sacrificed to the gods of the kings of Aram, attempting to enlist their help as well (v. 23).

What a terrible price to pay for a leader's bad choices.

What are our idols as a nation? Do we think that if we have a lot of material things, we will have all that we need? Do we think that because this nation is important among the rest of the nations of the world that we alone will be able to solve all our country's ills? Whatever are our idols (whatever comes between God and us), they become a curse to us—individually and corporately. God help this nation, and particularly the believers, that we not follow the ways of Ahaz.

The nation was militarily weak—For all of these abominations, God judged Ahaz and his people terribly. He permitted Syria, Israel, Assyria, Edom, and the Philistines to attack Judah. In particular, his kingdom was humiliated when the Northern

Kingdom killed many Judeans and took 200,000 women and children into their land. As terrible as moral and spiritual conditions were in the north, a few believers there, nonetheless, warned their fellow Israelites that they must not keep their brethren as slaves. Instead, their kinsmen must be sent back to Judah. The testimony of these few believers in Israel reflected that God is never without his witness, even in the worst of darkness. But the point was that more spiritual light existed in darkened Israel than was present in Ahaz's darkened heart or even in supposedly enlightened Judah (see 2 Chron. 28:9–15).

Ahaz's choice to close the Temple doors also became the symbol of how low Judah had sunk spiritually compared to the rest of the nations (see 2 Chron. 28:5, 8, 17, 18). How can a nation have any military strength if its leadership has no sense of the Lord's presence? When leaders and people question God's existence, they become insensitive to the presence of a morality in the universe that cannot be flouted without dire consequences.

I remember well when my wife, Claire, and I were in Israel during the 1973 war. The conflict was disastrous for Israel in the first three or four days. Many lives were lost, and the nation was in profound shock, even though eventually Israel did win a tactical victory, pushing to within forty kilometers of Damascus and seventy kilometers of Cairo. A few days after the war, we visited with a librarian on a kibbutz, and we will never forget how meaningfully she analyzed the reason why Israel lost so much in the first few days. "If a nation knows it has the strength and then makes adjustments for specific needs, there can be victory. But if a nation thinks they will have victory when they really do not know if they are prepared, something is drastically wrong." She put her finger on the specific problem, "Many of our leaders in 1973 were just *too proud*," she said. The librarian aptly described how the leadership's motivation by the idol of pride had colored so many of their choices, which led to such loss in the beginning of that war.

Do we in the United States trust in more and more so-
phisticated weaponry for our defense, without at the same
time realizing who is the Lord of heaven's armies? Have
people forgotten that God alone is our genuine support? For-
getting the Lord, the one who rules among the nations, has
devastating consequences. The danger is that we can put too
much trust in our strength and not realize how the Lord of
Hosts can line up against us. And then what strength will we
have?

The nation was diplomatically weak—Still another tragic consequence of Ahaz's moral and spiritual choices was other nations' lack of respect for Judah. When God's leaders and
people were right with God, all the nations highly honored
them. But when they failed to acknowledge that he alone is
the God of the nations, the surrounding countries mocked
and sneered at Judah.

Ahaz turned from one nation to another, trying to engage
in successful diplomacy, but nothing seemed to help (see 2
Chron. 28:16–18). The king even took huge sums of money
from the treasuries of the Temple of the Lord and his royal
palace and presented them to the king of Assyria in an effort
to buy that country's help. Instead, the record indicates, "It
didn't help him at all" (2 Chron. 28:21). God continued to
trouble the people of Judah because their moral and spiritual
values were topsy-turvy. Why, then, should the pagan nations
show any respect for Ahaz and his policymakers? Everything
about Judah had gone wrong.

The Watergate affair in the United States in the 1970s,
with its involvement by key people and government leaders is
tragic to contemplate. One piece of evidence in the matter is
amazing. A security guard with a sharp eye discovered that a
door lock leading to the Democratic headquarters was unfas-
tened. Eventually, careful examination of why that little lock
had been tampered with led to the initiation of a massive in-

vestigation of wrongdoing and to uncovering crookedness in high places in government circles. That little lock became a symbol to the American people that, in order to further their own selfish interests, some of their leaders had made wrong moral choices.

One major consequence of the inner examination of leaders and people regarding the Watergate affair was that once more they had to take a vital interest in the choice of a moral standard. Even more, the very basis for living such a moral standard is related to a personal relationship and warm experience with a Holy God. Interestingly, many of the key players who ended up in prison eventually became believers, and are active in ministry today.

The Shaping of the Revivalist Used in Renewal

Ahaz's inner moral and spiritual choices, which led to closing the Temple doors, also shaped God's revivalist. Hezekiah was young—twenty-five years old—when he came to the throne, but already he had the testimony that "He did what was right from *ADONAI*'s perspective" (2 Chron. 29:2). He was not officially of the priestly class, nor was he a prophet. He was a lay person, a civil ruler, and yet, regardless of whom God calls, the characteristics of what motivates his men are almost always the same.

A man of purpose—Judah's king was a man of purpose. He said, "Now it is in my heart to make a covenant with *ADONAI*" (2 Chron. 29:10). This is what Moses had called on Israel to do whenever a new king came to the throne—or on other special occasions (see Deut. 28; Joshua 8:30–35). In one sense the Mosaic covenant was ratified at Mt. Sinai (see Exod. 24), yet the people of every generation were to accept in their hearts the covenant between Israel and the Lord (as did the second generation that came out of Egypt). God wanted a warm-hearted relationship with his people; but the tragedy was that many in Israel rejected the covenant and turned to other gods. On the other hand, Hezekiah's moral and spiritual choices were guided by a sincere motivation to serve the Lord and, consequently, his desire for his people was for them to think seriously of their covenant relationship.

A man with good motives—Hezekiah's desire was, literally, ". . . in my heart" (see 2 Chron. 29:10), expressing a radically different set of inner motives from that of his father. Because he feared the Lord his God, he was determined to remove from the nation the cause of the Lord's hand of judgment. The call to believers today, likewise, is to be people with correct motives and priorities so as to sincerely do God's will as revealed in his Word. Many believers can talk a good talk about the things of God, mouthing it almost like a parrot, but society cannot really see any corresponding spiritual dimension in their lives or that of their families. In many instances, the world does not see anything genuine in what is supposed to be godly.

A man with godly wisdom—Hezekiah demonstrated wisdom and tact in the way he talked to people, in contrast to what Rehoboam said when many in the nation cried for tax relief (see 1 Kings 12:12–15). Instead of listening to the wise men, Rehoboam took his counsel from his playboy companions. Rather than sensing and responding to the people's needs, he was rude and insulting to those who desperately needed relief from the heavy load they were carrying. Hezekiah, however, with the priests and the Levites, reasoned wisely, explaining that the nation had turned its back on God and was in danger of further judgment.

A man of righteousness—Hezekiah served God with a righteous zeal. His sole desire was to do what was right, even as his father David had done. No one could miss the moral and spiritual intensity of this young man whose heart was set on serving the Lord God of Israel. Hezekiah served his generation, insisting that a biblical faith must touch every area of life, calling for all to be responsible to a holy God. In the same way, with a genuine hunger in the hearts of modern-day Hezekiahs, God might be gracious to give us spiritual renewal that will impact our nation.

A Call for the Realities of Renewal

Ahaz's moral and spiritual choice of closing the Temple doors became the goad to his son to call for the nation's renewal. No doubt Hezekiah had thought long and hard about the closing of the door under his father's reign; and as he grew physically and matured spiritually, under God's leadership, he reasoned what he would do as king. God was in the process of preparing his man, guiding his thinking, deepening his spiritual understanding, and grounding him in Scriptural principles that would all be a part of the spiritual renewal of the nation.

The Negative Realities

Before a new high-rise building is ever put in place, workers have to destroy any old edifice on the site. Then they must dig down to bedrock, hauling out tons of dirt and rock that may have to be blasted before any concrete is ever laid on the bedrock for the supports of the new building. Before Hezekiah could direct the leaders of the nation concerning a spiritual edifice of renewal, he had to point out what was so drastically wrong with Judah's relationship with the Lord.

Leaders and people had turned away from the covenant—The new king began his assessment of the nation's ills, speaking first to the priests and Levites. He said, "our ancestors acted treacherously, they did what is evil from the perspective of *ADONAI* our God, they abandoned him, they turned their faces away from where *ADONAI* lives and turned their backs on him" (2 Chron. 29:6).

Hezekiah used the first-person plural when he referred to "our fathers," and perhaps with sadness of heart he had to confess that it was his own earthly father who had brought most of the disaster on Judah. His description of a nation that had turned its back on God painted a precise word picture of how his own people had become so proud they found it difficult to respond to their redeemer and benefactor.

Confession of sin—Before any renewal can occur, believers must confess wrongdoing between themselves and the Lord, as well their relationships with other believers, or with any acquaintances in the community. How many are willing to say, "I did wrong! I am sorry"? How many will cry in intercessory prayer, "We did wrong," even though the one praying may never have been involved in the sins about which he is praying?

Hezekiah confessed in intercession, identifying himself with the nation's sins, as many godly leaders had done in the past. Confession of sin, however, cannot be general only, but must be *specific* as well. The king had to point out the particular wrongs that left Judah in such a mess, and why the nation had been judged so severely; and this revelation led to the next drastic specific charge by the king.

Public worship of the Lord had ceased—Hezekiah declared, "They . . . stopped burning incense and offering burnt offerings in the Holy Place to the God of Isra'el" (2 Chron. 29:7). Incense was the symbol of communion and prayer. When it was a certain priest's turn to offer incense at the altar of incense, which stood at the entrance into the holy of holies, then all the priests and people standing outside joined together in prayer to God. Furthermore, no burnt offerings, which were the symbol of Judah's total dedication, had been offered to the Lord. In a clear focus on the Torah, Hezekiah named those very factors of worship that established the nation's right to exist before the Lord who is their only king. When the doors to the only God-given place to worship were shut, Ahaz had led his people away from public worship. When the *menorah* (the lamp in the holy place) was put out, this king and many of his subjects had in effect turned way from the light of God's presence.

In the same way, we also need to discover the serious errors in our own spiritual lives in order for our hearts to be in a state of renewal before the Lord. In counseling sessions, one of the first questions I ask backslidden believers is if they are daily, consistently reading God's Word and praying. When believers no longer live in God's Word—which reveals his character and his will—they really are turning away from the light of his presence. If God's people have little or no communion with the Lord in prayer, is it any wonder they are spiritually weak, with no sense of the Lord's presence in fellowship? How then can we have a life-transforming message for unbelievers?

Hezekiah had to be honest and forthright as he faced the sickness of the nation, reminding believers to do likewise if Judah ever was going to experience a spiritual renewal. In the same way, if we believers really want God's presence with power in our lives, so, too, must we face up to areas of sin and confess them to the Lord.

Positive Action

Hezekiah now turned to the decisions and deeds that must be accomplished in a nation's renewal.

Cleansing the Temple—His first instruction to the priests, after proclaiming his intention to make a covenant with the Lord God of Israel, was to call for cleansing and purifying the Temple (see 2 Chron. 29:15). The record indicates that the priests went into the sanctuary to clean it and brought out from there all that was unclean, no doubt including many idols. The Levites then carried the filth down to the Kidron Valley. We can well wonder how any king of Judah could have called for closing the Temple building and allowing it to become filthy—and even worse, to have placed idols in it. No wonder Judah's position with the Lord was in danger.

The priests and Levites took eight days to clean the courtyard in front of the Temple and an additional eight days to finally consecrate the Temple itself as well as the entire area (see 2 Chron. 29:17). The cleansing was a sign to God that the new leaders of the nation were willing to do what was right, symbolizing that their repentance as well as Hezekiah's was genuine. What was accomplished in the Temple courtyard and in the Temple itself also was to be the incentive to believers in the nation to remove all uncleanness in their lives. Hezekiah's decisions and call for action also would be used by the Lord as a testimony to unbelievers in Judah and even to those in the Northern Kingdom.

Worship in accordance with what Moses had prescribed—The king encouraged the priests to begin the stated and prescribed order of worship in accordance with Moses' instructions. The order was 1) the offering for sin, 2) the offering for dedication, 3) the emphasis on communion (see Exod. 25:22; 29:42; 30:36). In so doing, Hezekiah demonstrated an awareness of what Moses had taught Israel, and that he was eager to follow these procedures.

The priests offered the prescribed animals used for the sin offering *for the kingdom, for the sanctuary and for Judah* (see 2 Chron. 29:21–24). The sin offering pointed to the need for forgiveness of sin; and while the offering in itself never took away sin, the priests once more explained the principles attached to this offering. In the sacrificial system of the Mosaic covenant, Israelite offerers had atonement for their sins when they accepted by faith these four principles.[35] Hezekiah understood well these principles as a believer and appropriated them for himself in faith, and surely others did as well.

The next step in the prescribed worship was to offer the sacrifices of the *burnt* offering on the altar, the symbol of total dedication on the part of the nation. Israel had been instructed to offer two burnt offerings every day, one in the morning after sunup and one in mid-afternoon (see Exod. 29:38–44).[36] Once again, the nation had its symbol of commitment and dedication on its altar before the Lord.

The record also indicates that, "The moment the burnt offering began, the song of ADONAI also began" (2 Chron. 29:27). Such was the practice already in place by the Temple choir in Hezekiah's day. At the moment when there is total commitment and dedication on the part of the nation as well as individuals, believers surely can begin to sing. How can there be genuine joy and singing before the Lord unless there is total commitment to do God's will?

What were the results after the offerings for atonement and dedication had been presented to the Lord? The king and everyone present with him knelt down and worshiped their God; the entire company bowed their heads to their sovereign (2 Chron. 29:29, 30). What a sight that must have been. The leadership of a nation, and many of the people, who no doubt longed for this closeness to the God of Judah, actually experienced his outpouring of blessings. No wonder the choirs sang praises with gladness in their souls. No doubt also, although not mentioned, they also offered incense at the altar of incense before the curtain leading into the Holy of Holies.

Once all the prescribed sin and dedication sacrifices had been offered, the king called for the *thanksgiving* offering (see 2 Chron. 29:31). Hezekiah himself led in this act of worship, declaring, "You have consecrated yourselves to ADONAI." After the appropriate parts of animals had been offered to the Lord on the altar, the priests, the king, other officials, and the people sat down to celebrate God's goodness at a grand fellowship meal.

Because there was a shortage of priests to help in the work of offering the animals, the Levites lent their aid until the task was completed. During the former apostasy of the nation under Ahaz, many of the priests had drifted off to their respective dwellings in many parts of the country. But Hezekiah's call for setting Judah on a right course came about so quickly that many priests had not the opportunity to return to Jerusalem, be cleansed, and then become involved with the newly established worship in the Temple.

The progress of Temple worship that led to spiritual renewal is both enlightening and challenging as it points to the lack of understanding among many believers today of how to genuinely approach and worship the Lord. While believers understand the biblical atonement in Yeshua the Messiah, very few understand how the other sacrifices are also present in the death of Yeshua.

These sacrifices relate to

1. The dedication of *life* in the burnt offering (see Rom. 12:1, 2);
2. The dedication to the *work* God calls us to do (see Heb. 6:9–12);
3. Genuine *thanksgiving* to the Lord (as in the experience of the communion table, or the Lord's table).

This same progression also is reflected in the New Covenant and can, therefore, be appropriated today so that the walk as a believer can be biblically normal. Otherwise, the approach to God becomes subnormal and lacking in every respect.

What would happen in our congregations if there was a genuine desire to worship God, even as Hezekiah had, and willingness to commit ourselves to prayer and fasting in order that God can graciously work in our hearts, our congregations, and even in our nation? May our God enable us to really seek his face.

Measuring the Results of Renewal

Hezekiah's honorable moral and spiritual choice behind the little effort required in opening the Temple doors had a potential that led to desirable spiritual results. The prescribed worship had been reestablished.

The presence of joy—One of the immediate results of the renewal was the experience of great joy for Hezekiah, the other leaders, and the people. The record states that, "Hizkiyahu and all the people rejoiced over what God had prepared for the people, since it had all happened so suddenly" (2 Chron. 29:36). Everyone felt it keenly in the depths of their being; after all, a believer's life should always be joyful, otherwise, he is living a subnormal life.

Too many times, because we are so taken up with our own pressures and the materialistic influences of our day, we have lost the capacity to be surprised by joy, to be thankful for the triumphs God can provide—and we forget to praise God for victories in his name. When this experience is not visible, what does the world really see? Does it see people who are supposed to be believers, who give testimony that God is our all and all but who then live a lie? God grant that our hearts can be filled with joy for everything that happens, for the ill as well as for the good.

Pre-eminence of holiday worship—Spiritual renewal also brought about a meaningful worship at the prescribed holidays, as well as an appreciation for the precious experiences one can have with them. According to the record, the first holiday after the great spiritual renewal was the Passover, and King Hezekiah called for its celebration (see 2 Chron. 30:1).

The king and his officials decided to celebrate this great event in the second month of the year. Normally, the prescribed time was in the first month of the religious calendar in the springtime, beginning on the fourteenth day, when the animals were sacrificed. Then the Passover dinner (*seder*) took place on the evening of the fifteenth of the month.

The explanation for observing the Passover during the second month was that "They had not been able to observe it at the proper time because the *cohanim* [priests] had not consecrated themselves in sufficient number; also the people had not assembled in Yerushalayim" (2 Chron. 30:3). Does this mean that the great renewal broke out during the first month on the religious calendar? The Scripture had stated already that during the re-establishment of worship, not enough priests were present to minister, and the Levites had to help their brethren who were present already (see 2 Chron. 29:34). So, the decision was made to have it in the second month, exactly according to Moses' directives that already had provided for such a possibility (see Num. 9:10, 11). Because Hezekiah knew Moses' instructions, and since he and the leaders were sensitive to them, the Lord honored their decisions.

The call for all Israel to celebrate the Passover—The king not only felt a responsibility to Judah, Simeon, and Benjamin, but to the people of all Israel. If we establish the beginning of Hezekiah's sole reign as occurring in 716/15,[37] then the Northern Kingdom already had ceased to be a political entity. Israel's end came when Assyria destroyed Samaria in 721 B.C.E. But in God's merciful timing, he sought to reach a defeated people, making possible an evangelistic outreach through a spiritual renewal in the Southern Kingdom. So Hezekiah issued the proclamation to send messengers, from "Beersheba to Dan," from the south to the far north of Israel, asking everyone to come to Jerusalem and celebrate the Passover (see 2 Chron. 30:5).

This invitation by Judah's king to all the people, including those in the north, was an appeal not to be stiffnecked like their fathers who had been so unfaithful. Rather, the offer was for people to have a new spiritual beginning by returning to the Lord who had a great compassion for them. Couriers were then sent into Ephraim and Manasseh, and as far north as Zebulun.

Unfortunately, many spurned the gracious invitation, and their decision only heaped condemnation on their own heads when they scoffed at the messengers who came with the good news that God had visited his people in the south. But, some will always listen and respond, and the record indicates that "some of Asher, M'nasheh and Z'vulun were humble to come to Yerushalayim" (2 Chron. 30:11). Likewise, a great number of people in Judah had a God-given unity of mind and heart to carry out what the king had requested.

God's blessings upon willing hearts—Those who came—even though they had been so far removed from any Mosaic worship and were strangers to the things of God and consequently were ceremonially unclean—were still permitted to take part in the Passover worship. They had even brought animals that were not entirely consecrated. And though many of the priests themselves were not entirely purified to be able to minister in the Temple, Hezekiah prayed to God. He said, "May *ADONAI*, who is good, pardon everyone who sets his heart on seeking God" (2 Chron. 30:18, 19). The guidelines for Temple worship were important, but God does not stand on ritual, and to him be the glory because he heard the king's prayer and healed his people. A genuine return naturally followed the great outbreak of spiritual renewal among his believers, and the Lord himself cleansed the hearts of unbelievers because they sought him for salvation and to enjoy his presence.

Sometimes we tend to look on outward appearances and condemn people because they do not measure up to our expectations of what is right. We tend to condemn quickly and easily. Nevertheless, the Lord knows the heart, and he is the one who can cleanse it, regardless of whether our appearance suits society's standards. We need to take this lesson seriously, so as to be ever sensitive to people's needs and their inner longings. Our desire needs to be as Hezekiah's was—to be a blessing. In time, the outward appearances can be adjusted after the inner being has been cleansed.

A sudden movement of the Spirit—During the Passover celebration in Jerusalem the people experienced a marvelous joy—a joy unlike anything since the days of Solomon some 200 years before (see 2 Chron. 30:26). The spiritual renewal was so intense, and people's hearts were so stirred within them, that when the priests and the Levites blessed the people, God was pleased to hear.

The results can also be seen when many of the peoples of Israel and Judah "smashed the standing-stones, chopped down the sacred poles, and broke down the high places and altars throughout Y'hudah, Binyamin, Efrayim and M'nasheh" (2 Chron. 31:1). The destruction of the images of the false gods was the final sign that genuine repentance had occurred, even among many in the Northern Kingdom. We always have to remember that God will work in power when his people's hearts of are right and they seek to be a good witness, sometimes even in the most unlikely places. Hezekiah's moral and spiritual choice to open the Temple doors not only turned Judah around from Ahaz's disastrous course. This decision also brought about one of the greatest spiritual renewals in Judah's history, one in which the outreach was such that many people in Judah and Israel came to the Lord for salvation and to worship him.

What is the true Check of our Hearts?

Sholom Aleichem once wrote a short story titled, "The Yom Kippur Day Scandal,"[38] describing how a wealthy man, while traveling on business, realized that he would not be able to make it home for the high holidays—the New Year and the Day of Atonement. He came to a small town while en-route, and decided to take lodging within the Jewish community there to observe in their synagogue the Day of Atonement, which is the most holy of all days.

Because he carried what was considered a large sum of money at the time—1,800 rubles—and feeling that he did not want it on his person during the holidays, he slipped the rubles into the prayer stand he would use while he prayed to God. So he felt secure and free from worldly things during this sacred time.

As the Day of Atonement was finally drawing to a close, he reached into the stand to check for his money, but discovered it was gone. He was so devastated that he fainted, and only when the people of the synagogue revived him did they then discover that his money was missing.

The rabbi ordered the synagogue doors closed, and everyone had to be searched, beginning first with himself. As they went through each person's clothes, it became apparent to all that the most sainted person in the congregation was becoming more and more nervous. So pious was this man that, along with others who were extremely devout, a place was reserved for him at the eastern wall of the building. Finally, there came the moment when this man had to be searched; he put up a tremendous struggle, resisting any effort to touch him.

A number of men finally pinned this fellow to the floor and went through his pockets, expecting to find the money; instead they found two well-gnawed chicken bones and six plum pits!

Yom Kippur, the Day of Atonement, is the most sacred day of the Jewish calendar, designated a fast day for twenty-five hours, when not even water is consumed. Here, however, was the most pious man in the synagogue with food remnants in his pockets. He had committed the unpardonable offense, breaking the fast, in the synagogue of all places, when no one was looking!

The last scene was that of a mortified Rabbi, going down the street, beside himself that such disobedience had occurred in his synagogue on the Day of Atonement.

Then someone asked about the 1,800 rubles. A bystander, after being pressed, offered the only response. "Oh," he drawled, "The eighteen hundred. They were gone."

"Gone?"

"Gone forever," the man stated as he watched the smoke exhaled from his cigarette.

Shalom Aleichem, of course, had focused on a point. Too many times, people make their own moral and spiritual choices for whatever reason; but then they strain at the smaller issues and overlook weightier matters. But in a positive sense, Hezekiah had made right choices, first in opening the Temple doors, and that in turn led him also to choose the greater deeds. Likewise, the moral or spiritual choices we make, first in the small issues, enable us to follow through on the weightier matters of spiritual truths that lead to renewal.

CHAPTER EIGHT

Josiah, Near the End of the First Temple Period

The Man Who Tore His Clothes When the Scriptures were Read

(2 Kings 22:1–23:30; 2 Chron. 34:1–35:27)

"Because your heart was tender, and you humbled yourself before God when you heard his words against this place and its inhabitants—you humbled yourself before me, tore your clothes and cried before me—I have also heard you, says *ADONAI*."

(2 Chron. 34:27)

"No Pesach [Passover] like that had been kept in Isra'el since the days of Sh'mu'el the prophet, and none of the kings of Isra'el observe a Pesach such as Yoshiyahu [Josiah] observed, with the *cohanim* [priests], *L'vi'im* [Levites], all Y'hudah, those of Isra'el who were present, and the inhabitants of Yerushalayim."

(2 Chron. 35:18)

Tragically, the great spiritual renewal that occurred in Hezekiah's reign began to ebb. We can assume, however, that as long as he remained on the throne, the nation's spiritual sensitivity remained high. But near the end of the king's life, as we have already seen, God graciously had to reason with him for his lack of spiritual grasp when he revealed the details of all his defenses to the envoys from Babylon.

Historical Background of Josiah and Middle Eastern Powers of the Day

Manasseh's evil deeds—Unfortunately, Hezekiah's son Manasseh turned the spiritual level of the nation for the worse. This rebellious son "did what was evil from ADONAI's perspective." Instead of following the example of his godly father, he pursued with a vengeance "the disgusting practices of the nations whom ADONAI had expelled ahead of the people of Isra'el" (2 Chron. 33:2).

We can ask ourselves again why godly parents cannot guide their children to be faithful to the Lord. Often parents are quite able, as were Hannah and Elkanah. Sometimes good parents do everything right, but still their children turn out to be rebels. Parents can be "nice people," but if they do not take the time to follow the biblically prescribed procedures to rear their children in the fear of the Lord, then the children will have little God consciousness. Then again, some parents do everything right, and still their children do not walk in the training and instruction of the Lord. Then their only hope is the son or daughter will come to the Lord later in life.

Instead of recognizing who gave Judah its greatness, evil king Manasseh's plans and deeds led the people to rebuild the high places, erect altars to the Ba'alim, make Asherah poles, and worship the starry hosts. He actually had the audacity to build altars to pagan gods and goddesses, even within the sacred confines of the Lord's Temple. He sacrificed his sons, literally making them "pass through the fire," which meant offering his sons to the pagan gods in the Valley of Ben Hinnon. He practiced the evil deeds of the pagans: sorcery, divination, witchcraft, consulting mediums and spiritists, etc. (see 2 Chron. 33:3–6) Tragically, Manasseh rejected the covenant of Moses and led astray the people of Judah and Jerusalem.

The profound truth is that man does have a free will; he can do right and be a blessing to his fellow man when he

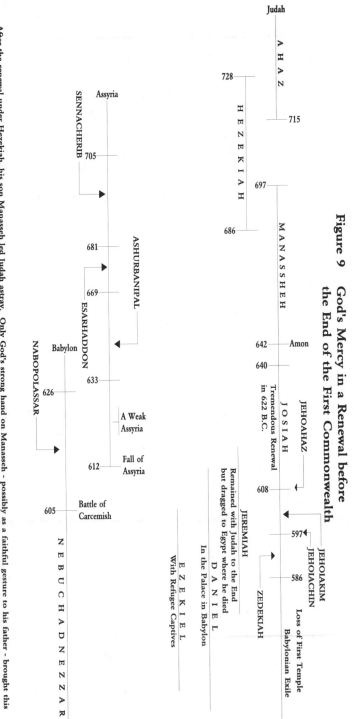

Figure 9   God's Mercy in a Renewal before the End of the First Commonwealth

After the renewal under Hezekiah, his son Manasseh led Judah astray. Only God's strong hand on Manasseh - possibly as a faithful gesture to his father - brought this king to repentance. But because of Manasseh's waywardness in the early days of his reign, the nation never recovered the keen spiritual level of Hezekiah's day. Amon was worse than his father Manasseh, but with Josiah a new day came for Judah amidst a great renewal. The joy of the Lord was so great that there was no comparison since in the days of Samuel, more than 400 years! But spiritual renewals are never self-sustaining and Josiah died tragically in a battle with an Egyptian king who did not want a fight with Judah. After Josiah, the nation plunged into apostasy and the end came in 586 B.C. Even then, God was gracious, giving Judah two opportunities to turn back to Him, in 605 and 597 B.C. Eventually, it took the exile to purify a remnant before a second commonwealth could begin.

makes the right choices and seeks the Lord's ways. But free will also leads some to choose evil, which is the dreadful price man pays for his freedom. Yet, while God allows people to make their decisions, he also is faithful, and many times he intervenes in order to persuade, or turn away a rebellious person from pursuing evil deeds.

So it was with Manasseh. Many times God tried to speak through his prophets to this wayward, wicked, and stubborn king. Even the older, trusted, and godly advisors to Hezekiah did their utmost to speak sense to the son. But Manasseh's heart was perverted and he did not listen. But at the right time, God knows what to do. The record indicates that a commander of the king of Assyria's army[39] took this wicked king prisoner, "put a hook in his nose, bound him with bronze shackles," and carted him off to a jail in Babylon (2 Chron. 33:11, NIV).

How dreadful it is when, in his perfect justice, God wreaks his vengeance and retribution on ungodly and detestable people. Yet Manasseh was not killed, probably because God respected his father Hezekiah, but perhaps he also saw the desperate need of Manasseh's heart and knew he would come to his senses and acknowledge his terrible deeds.

Manasseh turned back to the Lord—During his imprisonment, Manasseh turned to the Lord his God. As he came to his right mind and realized his distress, he "humbl[ed] himself before the God of his ancestors" (2 Chron. 33:12) and, moved with compassion at the sight of this pitiful, humiliated Manasseh, God responded. He also worked again through the political circumstances so that this king was permitted to return to Jerusalem and to his throne, where he then acknowledged what God had done in his life. Manasseh's testimony reflected his belated realization that the Lord is God of Israel. Sometimes we are so slow to listen to the Lord.

Manasseh's repentance was genuine and his salvation sure—his deeds as a believer reflected that a change had occurred in his heart. He removed the foreign gods and the sacrilegious idol from the Lord's Temple. He had the altars to the false gods destroyed and restored worship in the Temple as God had prescribed in his Word. Manasseh was not ignorant of the divinely revealed worship because, no doubt, he had observed his father's sacrifices and devotion to the one true Lord in the Temple. The tragedy of the situation was that Manasseh had to be severely disciplined before he would listen.

Amon

Manasseh's son, Amon, however, lasted only two years as king (642–40 B.C.E.). Amon pursued the early policies of his father, but there was a decided difference between the two of them: Amon set his heart against God and was not impressed with his father's later salvation and dedication to the Lord. So the Lord's judgment of Amon came swiftly. Amon's servants conspired against him and murdered him in his own house, possibly because they were so totally disgusted with him as a person. In turn, however, people loyal to the kingship of Judah put the conspirators to death. God can permit his retribution through the hands of evil people. Although God certainly did not approve of the servants' wicked deeds, in his permissive will, he did allow judgment to take place when Amon was killed. But then, in his timing and will, he also brought about the death of the murderers.

The testimony of Amon's son Josiah was that he "did what was right from A*DONAI*'s perspective, living entirely in the manner of David his ancestor" (2 Chron. 34:2). He was the last of the eight kings who were declared good, and through him God once again was gracious enough to bring about a national spiritual renewal.

The Crucial Movement of the Middle East Powers

Josiah came on the throne in 640 B.C.E. and reigned for thirty-one years, until 609 B.C.E. Part of his rule was during the last years of the Assyrian king Ashurbanipal, whose rule lasted until 633 B.C.E. After Ashurbanipal's death, Assyria went into decline until Nineveh fell in 612 B.C.E., and never again was Judah bothered by this nation.

At this time, the Middle East went through an international tilt of power. In 626 B.C.E. Naboplassar of Babylon embarked on a policy of expansionism in a period known as the Neo-Babylonian rule. This new power did not have much influence on Josiah at first, yet after Nineveh's fall and the end of Josiah's rule in 609 B.C.E., his successors became a part of the Babylonian Empire when Judah fell into its hands. Exactly as Isaiah had foreseen, Judah would suffer greatly under Babylon's rule (see 2 Kings 20:17–18). The times were strategic for Josiah, who came on the scene before Judah would cease to be a political entity; and once more God would bring about a spiritual renewal to prepare people for what was going to happen.

The Man Josiah

Josiah became king when he was only eight years old, in 640/639 B.C.E. (see 2 Chron. 34:1). The after-effects of Amon's reign were still being felt, but it is also quite possible that godly people who sought to offset the worst practices of Manasseh and Amon influenced Josiah.

Young People Can Be a Challenge for Good

The record declares that in the eighth year of Josiah's reign, at sixteen years of age (632 B.C.E.), "He began seeking after the God of David his father" (2 Chron. 34:3), which was probably the time when he came to the Lord. When Josiah was twenty, God worked profoundly in his heart, no doubt burdening him with the despicable presence of idolatry in Judea. So Josiah gave orders to cleanse Jerusalem and Judah of the sickening paganism and deplorable morality his grandfather and father had imported into the country. At the king's command, the altars to the Ba'alim were torn down, the Asherah poles were cut to pieces, and the idols and the images were destroyed. He even ordered the false priests killed and had their bones burned. We might shudder at such violent behavior, but this was a king bent on cleansing Jerusalem and Judah to avert God's judgment on the nation for its false worship.

He did not stop with Judah either, but also sent his emissaries into the towns of what was once the Northern Kingdom—in Manasseh, Ephraim, and as far as Naphtali—repeating what he had done in Judah. Josiah had freedom to accomplish his goals because Assyria's control in Israel was only nominal; no one opposed his zeal for the God of Israel. And Josiah was only twenty years old!

What are the interests of twenty-year-olds in our congregations? When our young believers are challenged to do God's work and given responsibility to minister, they can respond unselfishly and seek the Lord and serve him with all their hearts. However, in too many instances, youth programs are self-serving, and expect nothing difficult of our young people. But the God of Josiah is the same today; as the Lord worked in Josiah's heart, he can do the same for dedicated young believers.

The Word is Powerful When it is Read

When Josiah was twenty-six years old (633/621 B.C.E., see 2 Chron. 34:8), he realized that a greater and deeper work of God was necessary—although he appeared gratified with what had been accomplished so far. So he set about to further purify the Lord's Temple; he gave the orders to various leaders to repair it. Money was given, men were appointed to supervise the work, and many became involved with the repair and restoration of God's house. Not since the days of Hezekiah had anything been done to it, and the record indicates that in many places in the building, the stone and timber were falling into ruin (see 2 Chron. 34:11).

As the workers were involved in the Temple repairs, they came across a book of the law. We should not assume that God's Word had been lost altogether. In his early years, when Manasseh had reintroduced false worship into Judea, a zealous believer-priest could have hidden a copy somewhere in the Temple, thinking it would have its effect on some people in the future, but its location was subsequently forgotten.

Critics suggest that at this point Josiah and others brought out the so-called the "D" code, the book of Deuteronomy, and added it to the canon in order to bring about a centralization of worship.[40] However, the entire Torah of Moses was present; most of the prophets and even a good portion of the Writings had also been in place for a long time. The only exceptions were the books that came after the exile.[41] Evidence exists that, because of Josiah's zeal in doing what God wanted him to do with all of the reforms, many copies of the law were present in the land. However, something specific and special occurred on this occasion when this particular copy of the law was discovered and brought up before the king.

The Start of Spiritual Renewal

Josiah tore his robes as this copy was read in his presence (see 2 Chron. 34:19). His actions reflected the presence of God's Spirit deep in his heart. He realized then and there that many in Judah and Israel had an abysmal lack of the knowledge of God. Judah was far removed from its allegiance to the Mosaic covenant during Hezekiah's days. And yet, to Josiah's credit, he was stirred to action because he knew that God's judgment hand was going to fall if he did not guide the nation to return to the Lord.

After spiritual renewal came to Judah, God gave the king peace, rest, and quiet for a time. With believers revived, they shared with the unbelievers, and God's Word had great success as many were born again. Josiah had a great capacity for leadership, and his authority was felt far and wide, but what people recognized most of all was that their king was a man completely dedicated to do God's will.

The fact that he died later on the battlefield, possibly contrary to the wishes of Jeremiah and other godly people, is another indication that spiritual renewal is never self-sustaining. We shall explore this fact further when we consider what God wrought in Judah near the end of the first commonwealth.[42]

Josiah served as the last godly king before the end of the First Temple period and was, therefore, God's final envoy to reach a generation. Likewise, in our day we can question where we are going as a country, given our country's materialistic bent, lack of morals, trust in humanism, and all science can accomplish.

The precedent for spiritual renewal laid down by Josiah and Jeremiah can be the means whereby God can work in our lives with similar results—even as we enter a new millennium.

Obligations for a Spiritual Renewal

Willingness to Listen to God's Word

As already noted, God uses his Word to work in hearts. When God's wishes are proclaimed, his Spirit can draw believers to the Lord and bring about corresponding changes in lives.

Believers need to be revived—When Josiah heard the reading of God's Word, he tore his clothes as a sign of humility and repentance (see 2 Chron. 34:19). He had been zealous in tearing down pagan altars, smashing idols, images, and Asherah poles, but now he was aghast with how much more had to be accomplished for his people. He trembled at the power of God's Word and the necessity of yielding completely to its guidance and direction. He shook with fear because he had a new comprehension of God's holiness, and he realized how far Judah had to go to fully conform to God's wishes. His torn clothes were the sign of his willingness to bend his will before the truth and to walk with its obligations in mind (see 2 Chron. 34:27).

Neither can we evade the power of God's Word as it is preached. We cannot just sit in some kind of ritualistic pose and listen, glassy-eyed, to the Word when it is proclaimed in our congregations. Rather, we must always have the willingness to listen intently to God's living Word and also to realize that it is speaking to us personally. We must be personally involved!

Again, the effect of the Word—As already noted in the renewal in Moses' days, the Word of the Lord is living, active, sharp and is a judge or critic (see Heb. 4:12). Every time we listen intently to the Scriptures, we are confronted with its deep penetration into our very being. We cannot avoid it.

In many places in Scripture, we note the presence of the power in God's Word. It can wound the sinner, as in the confrontation between David and Nabal; even his wife called him a *nabal* (a fool), a description that became a part of the sacred record (see 1 Sam. 25:25). The Word was used to convict the hypocritical attitude of some of the religious leaders of the nation when Yeshua had to chide them for their lack of spiritual sensitivity (see Matt. 23).[43] The proclamation of the Word of power also rebuked King David; the prophet Nathan had to boldly point at the king and declare that David was wrong concerning the dastardly affair with Bathsheba and the murder of her husband. Nathan proclaimed, "You are the man!" (2 Sam. 12:7)

God's Word is no less powerful today than it was in the days of Josiah, Yeshua, or any other period. We need to ask ourselves, "Are we really carefully listening with our hearts as the Word is preached or taught, that it will have a meaningful effect, as it did with Josiah?

The Word from Huldah the Prophetess

A call for inward change—The king's immediate response was to seek further direction from the Lord; so he sent his chosen leaders to the prophetess Huldah. He sensed that Judah faced imminent judgment because many in the nation still had not come to a living and vital experience with the Lord. Until this point in Josiah's reign, most people conformed only outwardly to a zealous king's wishes (see 2 Chron. 34:21, 22). But God wanted inward change as well. The law was quite specific: The people of Judah were to fear the Lord their God, walk in all his ways, love him and serve him with their entire heart and soul. But how was Israel to live this lifestyle? Moses had called for hearts to be circumcised, and Josiah had this same message in his day. That is why he was so burdened for his people (see Deut. 10:12, 16). Jeremiah echoed this same call in his message (see Jer. 4:4). In New Testament language, the call to the nation was for repentance and a born-again experience.

Josiah and his people are equal before God—Huldah was faithful to her calling, warning that God was calling Judah to account. The nation had been privileged to have a Temple, priests who ministered, and a godly king such as Josiah. But what were people doing about their need of salvation? Again, we see how God was ever involved with believers, working in their hearts to bring about renewal, a deep commitment to him, and also to have a concern for people who are far from him.

Furthermore, all believers are equal before him. So when Huldah directed her message to the king, she proclaimed,

"Tell *the man* who sent you to me" (2 Chron. 34:23, emphasis added). The prophetess was bold; she was God's mouthpiece, and she spoke to Josiah as a mere man, even though he was the king. As mere human beings, all believers are alike before the Lord. When his children have the fear of the Lord and his holiness, the Spirit can then strive with them and bring them to renewal, and then the work can commence in reaching out to unbelievers.

Good reasons exist for comparing the situation of Judah then and many Western nations today. We, too, have been privileged. We have been able to build affluence unparalleled among the nations of the world. We have a freedom that is the envy of many other peoples.

But affluent nations also are challenged in many areas. Do we think that money is the answer to all our problems? Can Western societies get away with condoning abortion, which is an affront to the holy and righteous God? When will people take seriously their marriage vows? When will we realize God will not always overlook moral permissiveness and misuse of sex? God will hold us accountable for such disobedience. Can we not see that we are much like ancient Judah, standing on a brink, beyond which there is a downward slide?

God gave Josiah time for renewal to occur—Because Josiah humbled himself before the Lord, had a tender heart for God's wishes, greatly respected his holiness, righteousness, and justice, and wept before him, Huldah held out a promise: God's judgments would not take place during the lifetime of this king. He would delay his judgment for the time being (see 2 Chron. 34:27, 28).

Are believers such as Josiah the salt of the earth? Does it matter if we pray on behalf of our congregations and our nation? Will God hear and answer because he sees the tears of believers—the humility of his own people as they ᵖray on behalf of others who desperately need him? Judah was to have another opportunity to hear, respond, and once more experience a spiritual renewal. What happened in the king's heart was to be translated into an outreach unparalleled in the history of Israel and Judah to that date.

Believers today need to pray and wait upon God and allow his Word to speak to our hearts. We have to ask ourselves continually, "Is this Word of God the soup and salad of our lives? Is this Word meat for our souls? Are the Scriptures dessert for our inner being? Or is it a book we read for a few minutes a day? Are the Scriptures open only as we listen to the pastor or rabbi with one ear while the other ear is tuned in to all to all the experiences of the previous week?" It appears that believers have become like people who go to the cafeteria, picking and choosing what is exciting, easy, or convenient and skipping over the hard demands that call for drastic change. How can God speak to and visit such a people with a gracious renewal? We need to listen intently to God's Word as if our souls truly depend on it.

Work at This Change of Heart

When the king's officials brought back Huldah's reply, Josiah's immediate action was to call for a command presence of the elders of Judah and Jerusalem, along with the priests and Levites, in the Temple of the Lord. Judah's king then took decisive action, not merely to avert God's judgment on the nation, although that was the goad that produced such a quick response. But this king wanted something more; he wanted people to act decisively on what God's Word said.

A call for commitment—In front of the assembly in the Temple, Josiah "read in their hearing everything written in the scroll of the Covenant." Then he "stood in his place and made a covenant in the presence of *Adonai*" (2 Chron. 34:30, 31). Once again, he issued a call to yield allegiance to the Mosaic covenant, which is the basis of any relationship between Judah and the Lord. As the people listened to God's Word, Josiah also wanted them to give assent that the Word of the Covenant would occupy first place in their hearts and lives. He asked for their promise as a grand expression on the part of God's people, in particular the believers within his kingdom. He wanted them to promise God that they would indeed act on God's commands.

God's people today cannot be made to stand in front of a congregation and make a promise they will do what the Scriptures proclaim. But as we listen to God's Word, our supreme desire should be to do what God asks. His call is for a moral and spiritual commitment, for (re-)dedication of our lives. Only then will we have God's power to touch unbelieving hearts.

As the people from Jerusalem and Benjamin stood before God's presence, they were impressed by their king's earnest plea, and they took note of what had happened to him in his encounter with the living God. So they pledged themselves to be committed to the covenant and to service (see 2 Chron. 34:32). That decision became one of the chief ingredients that led to spiritual renewal.

Remembering the holiday cycle—After this tremendous outpouring of support, the people observed the Passover, as had a previous generation under King Hezekiah. Josiah gave instructions for an elaborate observance that the people of Judah—and Israel as well—would long remember (see 2 Chron. 35:10–14). The Scriptures indicate that, in addition to the people of Judah and Benjamin, many came from tribes in the north to celebrate the freedom festival of Passover and to observe the Feast of Unleavened bread for seven days (see 2 Chron. 35:17). The Judean king had previously carried out his reforms in the north in Manasseh, Ephraim, and as far as Naphtali (see 2 Chron. 34:7). No doubt, when the renewal broke in Judah, many of these people who had hungry hearts came to take part in what God was doing in Jerusalem. While Passover was a reminder of the great victory God gave Israel in its release from Egypt, for the people of Josiah's day it meant a fresh outpouring of God's Spirit on all Israel, giving the people cause to rejoice in a newly found freedom in the Spirit.

The record also testifies to this occasion: "No Pesach like that had been kept in Isra'el since the days of Sh'mu'el the prophet" (2 Chron. 35:18). This passage suggests a time span of some 434 years from the time of the renewal under Samuel at about 1055 B.C.E. until the renewal under Josiah in 622/621 B.C.E. The work in the king's heart, the renewal of the covenant, the removal of the idols, and the celebration of the Passover all took place during the eighteenth year of his reign, when God's Spirit *quickly brought about* the renewal (see 2 Chron. 34:8; 35:19). What joy is present when hearts are totally yielded to the Lord.

Along with the Sabbath day, the Passover, the Feast of Unleavened Bread, Pentecost, the Day of Atonement, and the Feast of Tabernacles, are special days of worship and service in Israel (see Lev. 23). The people of Israel were expected to attend and be wholly involved with these pilgrimage festivals (see Exod. 23:14–17). A clear parallel exists today for us likewise to attend the stated meetings in our congregations. Our involvement with worship should be an established habit in our lives by which we also teach our children what is most important to us. We assemble ourselves together for the privilege and opportunity to worship the living God, to expose ourselves and our children to God's Word, and for the challenge to make the decision to know the Lord as well as for the commitment to do his work.

The need is great today, and many of us in the Lord's work continually ask, "Where are the workers?" There is a need for specialized workers such as spiritual leaders, elders, and *sh'lichim* (special messengers who carry the Word, reach people, and plant congregations). Believers who can be involved in the social, educational and political arena with its needs also are necessary. How else are those far from God to be impacted unless by godly believers? Only as God's people are involved in the ministry to the total man will there be the opportunity for sharing a biblical message.

Service that leads to the unusual—A young man came to Moody Bible Institute during the early 1960s. He listened intently when God's Word was taught and preached. He also spent much time in prayer and invited other students to pray for lost peoples with him. Then he put shoes to his prayers and began to lead students to minister to people in the United States and Mexico, distributing literature and seeking to reach people with the message of life. God's Spirit continued to mold and prepare this young man for a special kind of work in the years ahead, while the constant renewal in his heart touched many students.

Across the years, through involving students on five continents as well as by using two ships loaded with literature, we have seen how God called this person for a worldwide outreach in literature distribution. And we have seen him encourage other believers to seek the lost and lead them to Yeshua the Messiah. Obviously, we are not all called to minister as George Verwer has in a worldwide ministry such as Operation Mobilization, but the principles remain the same as God seeks to speak to hearts and involve his people in an outreach where we live, work, and play.

But there is a wider goal of spiritual renewal that goes beyond reviving God's people and guiding them in outreach. Francis Schaeffer pointed out quite aptly, "The old revivals in Great Britain, in Scandinavia, and so on, and the old revivals in this country did call, without any question and with tremendous clarity, for personal salvation. But they also called for resulting social action. . . . The Wesley and Whitefield revivals were tremendous in calling for individual salvation, and thousands upon thousands were saved. Yet even secular historians acknowledge that it was the social results coming out of the Wesley revival that saved England from its own form of the French revolution."[44]

Working at this change of heart will spread to an ever-widening and ever-increasing range of people to be reached and of issues to be challenged.

What Do I Really Want for My Heart?

Once again, we have to be ever aware that spiritual renewals are not self-sustaining. Renewed believers always need to keep a constant watch over their lives, continually asking questions that guard against cooling off and becoming uninvolved in spiritual matters. While not every possible question can be suggested, and you might add a few of your own, four will be mentioned that should prove helpful.

Making progress?—To constantly keep a watch over our hearts means some self-analysis, asking first of all, "Am I making progress in spiritual growth?" For example, "What is my attitude toward wrongdoing and sin? Is it more keen today than it was a year ago?"

When I used to counsel students, they would mention concerns about their keen sensitivity toward wrongdoing. They were troubled about it, feeling that perhaps something had gone wrong in their personal spiritual lives. My counsel on many occasions was that these deep concerns for sin and this sensitivity might actually register progress in spiritual development. The more one listens to God's Word, taking it to heart and keeping involved with spiritual commitment, the more that person will mature spiritually and morally to have a keener sense of what is right and wrong.

Increasing in spiritual stature?—Another question we can ask is, "Do I have a tendency to cool off to the Spirit's prompting?" Ignoring the Holy Spirit's leadership can lead to spiritual lapse, and one needs to ever guard against such a danger.

Josiah enjoyed the blessing of a spiritual renewal after hearing God's Word in 621 B.C.E. But just a scant thirteen years later (609/608 B.C.E.), he went out to fight Pharaoh Necho of Egypt, who was leading his troops on the coastal highway along the Mediterranean Sea to join Assyria in the battle against the Babylonians. The Egyptian venture should have been none of Josiah's business. Even the Egyptian Pharaoh "sent envoys to him with this message: 'Do I have a conflict with you, king of Y'hudah? No, I am not coming to attack you, but to attack the dynasty with whom I am at war. God has ordered to speed me along; so don't meddle with God, who is with me; so that he won't destroy you" (2 Chron. 35:21).

A pagan king tried to reason with Josiah that he should not fight against God! Perhaps Jeremiah also had warned the Judean king not to get into this battle because it was no affair of his. The only conclusion that can be drawn is that with Josiah's refusal to listen, the indication was clear he had forgotten how God's Word had spoken to him. He had grown cold, and his apostasy led to his death and to Judah's eventual downfall. One jarring sign of his spiritual lapse was the attempt to disguise himself on the battlefield, thinking thereby that he would be safe. But an arrow, as from God, was shot indiscriminately, and it found its target in the king's body (see 2 Chron. 35:22, 23).

How vivid is this warning from Josiah's life that every believer must always guard against turning away from the Spirit's leading, because by turning away we grow insensitive to God's Word. How urgent is the appeal to be involved continually with the work God has called us to do rather than getting into worldly pursuits.

Increasing trust in God?—Another question is paramount in order to sustain spiritual renewal: "Do I have a greater trust today than I had when God spoke to my heart and I became a believer?" Do we worry about things such as how God will provide for our needs? The sign of maturity and the presence of spiritual renewal is to realize with even greater assurance that the Lord will provide. Perhaps the reply to the concern about the mounting pressure of bills is to learn to live more simply. We don't really need all the gadgets and things we think we do. We really don't improve our lives by getting more and more things. Our task as renewed believers is to get back to the basics of life and get on with the business of serving God and doing what he asks of us in his Word.

Growing in love?—A final question we could ask is, "Am I growing in my devotion to God as Yeshua's presence in my life increases?" The sign of continuing spiritual renewal is that we should ever be more deeply devout in our relationship with the Lord. I will never forget a German exchange student who came to our seminary in the United States after World War II. He had grown up in a home where a godly father and mother knew God's Word; his father was a pastor.

But, during his teens, this lad had turned away from anyone who tried to witness to him of Messiah's salvation. He became an ardent member of the Hitler youth movement. During the war, he was a captain in the Nazi army on the western front. Soon after the Battle of the Bulge in 1944 —after the German offensive began to wither—the American army went on the attack, and the former captain told us of what happened to him when many of the men under his command were killed. He dove into a foxhole and began to pray to the God he had heard about as a child. While a lot of foxhole prayers are soon forgotten after the danger passes, in this case his cry was sincere. Then and there he asked the Messiah to really live in his heart and promised God that he would serve him all the days of his life.

This German believer remained sincere in his convictions. Five years later in seminary he had a deep devotion for the Lord and for his war-torn people who had lost everything. His prayer and desire was to reach his people with the message from the Word. And his testimony became a goad, reminding us of the necessity to mature in our devotion to God, and to have a keen sensitivity to serve him and love people sincerely. Only then will we continue to sustain spiritual renewal in our hearts.

About a hundred years before Josiah, the prophet Isaiah internalized much of what has been said of the spiritual renewal that had occurred in the days of Josiah and Jeremiah. Isaiah listened keenly to the Word and sought always to be involved as he set his heart to serve the Lord. He described the conditions of his day:

> Thus justice is repelled,
> Righteousness stands apart, at a distance;
> For truth stumbles in the public court,
> And uprightness cannot enter.
> Honesty is lacking,
> He who leaves evil becomes a target.
> (Isa. 59:14–15)

As Isaiah described the desperate need for the one man to stand in the gap to intercede for a wayward people, he became that man for his generation (although the passage does have a prophetic intent that points to the coming ministry of the Messiah). As Isaiah constantly asked the questions of his heart, which kept him in continued touch with the Lord, he became a trusted instrument in God's hands.

God help us to be one he can rely on to be an interceder for our day—one whose prayers will help to bring a spiritual renewal in the lives of believers that will affect our congregations and even our nation.

CHAPTER NINE

Nehemiah At The Wall

The Man Who Said, "The Joy of the LORD is your strength"

(Neh. 1:1–13:31)

"When it was reported to Sanvalat, Toviah, Geshem the Arab and the rest of our enemies that I had rebuilt the wall and that not a single gap was left in it—although up to that time I hadn't yet set up the doors in the gateways—Sanvalat and Geshem sent me a message which said, 'Come, let's meet together in one of the villages of the Ono Valley." But they were planning to do me harm; so I sent them messengers with this message: 'I'm too busy with important work to come down. Why should the work stop while I leave it to come down to you?'"

(Neh. 6:1–3)

"Then he said to them, 'Go, eat rich food, drink sweet drinks, and send portions to those who can't provide for themselves; for today is consecrated to our Lord.'"

(Neh. 8:10)

The next spiritual renewal in Judah's history took place in Nehemiah's days, after the nation had gone through a startling transformation. From the days of Josiah (640–608 B.C.E.), who ruled an independent kingdom, the intervening years include a number of changing circumstances. Spiritually, Judah spiraled downward, culminating in the loss of the Temple, exile to Babylon (597 and 586 B.C.E.) and, finally, a Babylonian and then a Persian sovereignty over the territory of Judah. From the death of Josiah in 609 or 608 B.C.E. to the inception of Nehemiah's ministry in 444 B.C.E. was 164 years, but in that period the national language changed from Hebrew in Josiah's day to Aramaic in Nehemiah's time. Much indeed had happened in the political, military, and economic condition of the country. Nevertheless, the God who had led Josiah in spiritual renewal was the same one who also would lead Ezra and Nehemiah in the revitalization of Judea. Politics and economics can change, but God remains the same through the ages; and the principles of spiritual renewal are similar for a people who are free and for those who are under the sovereignty of a foreign power.

Historical Background

Pre-Exilic and Exile Periods

King Josiah was killed on the field of battle in 609 or 608 B.C.E., and what subsequently occurred was exactly what Huldah the prophetess had predicted (see 2 Chron. 34:24, 25, 28). While Josiah lived, he did not see God's judgment on Judah, but as soon as he was off the scene the course of the nation degenerated rapidly. However, God repeatedly spoke to his people—even during the downward slide—through the prophet Jeremiah and through others he had led to the Lord (see Jer. 26:20–24), as well as through Habakkuk.

Josiah's successor was the middle of his three sons, Jehoahaz,[45] who reigned in Jerusalem for only three months (608 B.C.E.). After Jehoahaz was in office for a mere three months, Pharaoh Necho deposed him and sent him as prisoner to Egypt, where Jehoahaz died, as had been predicted by Jeremiah (see Jer. 22:11, 12).

Egypt's pharaoh installed Jehoahaz's older brother, Eliakim, on the throne and ordered his name changed to Jehoiakim. But the Egyptians retained control of Judah for only three years. Nebuchadnezzar of Babylon became ruler following his victory in the final Battle of Carchemish in 605 B.C.E. against the Assyrians, Egyptians, and other allies.

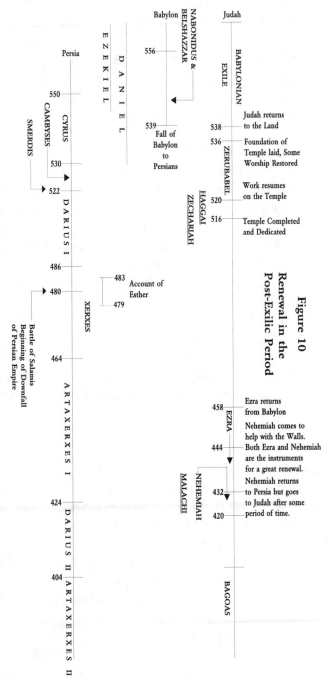

Figure 10
Renewal in the
Post-Exilic Period

Judah

Babylon

NABONIDUS &
BELSHAZZAR

Persia

E Z E K I E L

D A N I E L

BABYLONIAN

EXILE

556 —

Judah returns
538 — to the Land

536 — Foundation of
Temple laid, Some
Worship Restored

ZERUBBABEL

539 — Fall of
Babylon
to
Persians

550 —

CYRUS

CAMBYSES

SMERDIS

530 —

522 —

D A R I U S   I

HAGGAI
ZECHARIAH

520 — Work resumes
on the Temple

516 — Temple Completed
and Dedicated

486 —

483
480 —   Account of
479   Esther

XERXES

Battle of Salamis
Beginning of Downfall
of Persian Empire

464 —

458 — Ezra returns
from Babylon

EZRA

Nehemiah comes to
help with the Walls.
444 — Both Ezra and Nehemiah
are the instruments
for a great renewal.

Nehemiah returns
432 — to Persia but goes
to Judah after some
420 — period of time.

NEHEMIAH
MALACHI

BAGOAS

A R T A X E R X E S   I

424 —

D A R I U S   I I

404 —

A R T A X E R X E S   I I

After the Babylonian exile had accomplished its purpose of purifying a remnant of Judah, God overturned Babylon when Persia conquered it. Many refugees from many nations were permitted to return to the countries of their origin including Judah. Those returning to Judah laid the foundations for the second temple, marking the beginning of the second commonwealth. Because of a number of circumstances, the work on the temple was not completed and people sank into lethargy, and were only interested in themselves (Haggai 1:4–7). Haggai and Zachariah were used of God to encourage people to complete the temple. Afterwards, the spiritual life in Judah lagged and it took the work of Ezra who returned from Babylon in 458 B.C. to begin the foundation for a spiritual renewal. Ezra was a second Moses, establishing the religious life of Judah after the exile. Nehemiah was a strong political leader and led Judah in plugging up the broken sections of the city walls. Most important, he and Ezra guided the nation in a great renewal. While some of its effects had begun to wear off by 420 B.C. when Malachi ministered to the needs of the people, the work of Ezra had long lasting effects.

The Babylonians also confirmed Jehoiakim as king. But, unfortunately, Jehoiakim failed to follow his father Josiah's godly example, in spite of all the opportunities to do so with Jeremiah present to guide him. In the end, he rebelled against King Nebuchadnezzar and possibly died fighting army elements consisting of Babylonians, Syrians, Moabites, and Ammonites in 597 B.C.E. (see 2 Kings 24:1–4; Jeremiah 35:11).[46]

Jehoiachin, the son of Jehoiakim, then became king of Judah, but he too reigned only three months, doing "evil from *Adonai*'s perspective" (2 Chron. 36:9). When Nebuchadnezzar and his army laid siege to Jerusalem, the city finally had to surrender. The Babylonian monarch captured Jehoiachin, his mother, and many of the choice officers and leaders, taking them to Babylon. The Judean king was imprisoned for as long as Nebuchadnezzar lived, and was only released by Nebuchadnezzar's successor, Evil-Merodah in 560 B.C.E. (see Jer. 52:31). Jehoiachin had been a prisoner for thirty-seven long years, and even after he left prison, he still remained in custody of the Babylonian court. No doubt, as he thought wistfully of his home country, Judah, he could have remembered what Jeremiah had declared in his prophecies concerning the nation.

Nebuchadnezzar then made Josiah's other son, Zedekiah, king. Zedekiah reigned for eleven years, but he also "did evil from the perspective of *Adonai*" (2 Kings 24:19), in spite of the repeated opportunities he had to follow Jeremiah's advice. He too rebelled against Babylon, prompting Nebuchadnezzar to come for a third time to quell a Judean uprising (587/586 B.C.E.). In that battle, the city of Jerusalem was sacked, Solomon's Temple was destroyed, and for all practical purposes, Judah ceased to be a political entity. Everything Huldah said concerning Judah had come true; it would appear that Judah had come to a bitter end.

God, however, had other purposes. When I have asked students in schools and people in congregations the reason for the Babylonian exile, almost everyone declares that it occurred because of God's judgment on Judah's idolatry. But this assessment provides only the negative dimension. A positive view, however, reflects God's mercy and love for his people, as well as his righteousness in keeping his promise to Abraham to watch over his descendants throughout all their generations (see Gen. 17:7). God's care for his people through this exile was to purify a remnant who would eventually know him. When they finally returned to the homeland, Judeans would never again be caught up in worshiping idols. Ever since their return from Babylon, Jewish people have been a testimony to the one God who is sovereign over the entire earth and universe.

The People Return to the Land

After the Persians conquered Babylon in 539 B.C.E., Cyrus issued a proclamation that all refugee peoples could return to their homeland if they so desired. The edict also included the people of Judea, and a specific copy of the proclamation concerning their future is seen in Ezra 1:2–4. Forty-two thousand three hundred thirty-seven men and women returned. As the Temple foundations were laid in 538 B.C.E. and the leaders initiated some semblance of altar offerings to the Lord, this new day marked the beginning of the second commonwealth of Judea.

As the foundation was laid for this Temple, while people gathered around to watch such a significant event, human nature was on exhibit. The younger generation, born in Babylon, shouted because they had no experience with a Temple and looked forward with keen anticipation to its completion and to worshiping and glorifying the Lord in it. The older people who remembered the Temple and its glory wept, because it was evident from the Second Temple foundations that this building was to be much more modest than the original (see Ezra 3:8–12). Such responses are very similar today. Young people have a zeal and ideal to remake their world, while older people have a tendency to look back and talk about the "good old days." What is necessary, however, is balance. A backward look can be instructive for our work today, but all believers, young and old, should have the eager desire to look forward and be excited with what God can do in our day as well as in the future.

The Samaritans, comprised of those of the Northern Kingdom who had intermarried with non-Jews, sought to help the Judeans rebuild the Temple. The Samaritans still followed the Torah, having adapted it for their own needs. The Judeans, however, refused their help, feeling they had become a hybrid people, and were ritually unfit to have any part in the reconstruction. Once the people of the north were rebuffed, they stirred up opposition among the Persian leadership against Judea. Because the orders to rebuild the Temple were lost, the Persians ordered the Judeans to cease any further building activity. Meanwhile, the people of Samaria were permitted to build their own temple, so from then on the rivalry between the Samaritans and the Judeans intensified. However, in the second year of Darius (518 B.C.E.), the Persian orders that gave permission for rebuilding the Jerusalem Temple were found, and with the encouragement of the prophets Haggai and Zechariah, construction was resumed and the Second Temple was finally completed in 516 B.C.E. (see Ezra 6:15).

Ezra and His Work

Apathy—In the years between the dedication of the completed Temple in 516 B.C.E. and the time when Ezra returned to Jerusalem from Babylon, the spiritual level of the Judeans sagged. The people became self-seeking, building their own homes and farming their own plots of land. The zeal with which the people had finished the Temple under Haggai and Zechariah was greatly diminished; spiritual apathy had set in. Ezra also discovered that many of the people had transgressed by intermarrying with pagan peoples (see

Ezra 9:1–15). Furthermore, when Nehemiah came to Jerusalem twelve years later, in 444 B.C.E., a court order by the Persians enjoined the Judeans from plugging the gaps in the city walls and refurbishing the burned-out city gates (see Ezra 4:12–122; Neh. 1:1–3). Once more, we see that the spiritual encouragement under Haggai and Zechariah had not sustained itself, and a fresh work of God was necessary to revive Judea's believers.

Upon Ezra's return with many more people—including priests, Levites, and various others qualified to serve in the Temple—he established himself as a religious leader of Judea because, "He was a scribe, expert in the *Torah* of Moshe" (Ezra 7:6). God used this man to lay the groundwork for the renewal that was to follow.

Revitalizing the interest in Torah—The new leader had a monumental task ahead of him; he had to meet the deep needs of his people. And because he was especially equipped to do so, he was seen as the second Moses. Here are a few of his accomplishments:

1. He completed the book of 2 Chronicles, as well as being the author of his own book.
2. Because of the influence of the exile in Babylon and the subsequent Persian sovereignty, many of the younger generation of Judah spoke only Aramaic. So Ezra saw the necessity to provide the Hebrew Scriptures with Aramaic characters. The younger generation could no longer read the ancient Hebrew script that existed in Israel prior to the Babylonian exile. Therefore, Ezra transliterated the ancient script (the Tanakh) into the Aramaic script. The language they read was still Hebrew but, with this change, at least the younger generation of Judeans could read the new script. Ezra's legacy of transliteration is still with us to this very day in the form of the Aramaic script in the Hebrew Bible.

3. One of the functions of the priests and Levites was to teach the Word of God to the people. Because Ezra was numbered among the priests (see Neh. 8:2), he took on the responsibility of training a staff of selected religious leaders in the understanding of the Scriptures, so that in turn they would be able to teach others. Once more, we see the importance of the Word in the preparation for spiritual renewal. Long before Ezra mounted the pulpit to preach from the Scriptures (see Neh. 8:7), he already had prepared Levites who knew and understood the Word (see Neh. 8:8).

4. Finally, because the younger generation spoke Aramaic, a translation (*Targum*) of the Scriptures from Hebrew into Aramaic was necessary so that people would be able to understand the meaning of God's Word. This is one of the earliest references to such a Targum. Ezra trained men to translate the Word as it was read, and to provide an explanation of the Word in a language that could be understand.

Ezra was the key man God used to lay the groundwork for the spiritual renewal that was yet to take place. Before God visits his people in a special way, he has selected individuals behind the scenes whom he is preparing, through Scripture study or through learning, to wait upon him in prayer for the right time when the Spirit can commence his work. This has been true in every renewal that has occurred across the centuries. And when the backgrounds of renewals are researched, the evidence always indicates that a select few were vitally involved in the preparation.

Nehemiah's Return

Ezra laid the groundwork for renewal behind the scenes. Meanwhile, the Lord also used Nehemiah to unite the Judeans in repairing the walls and gates, in encouraging them to stand boldly against the enemies of Judah, and in calling leaders to account when they had sinned against their brethren by enslaving them (see Neh. 5). As a unified people dependent on God, they would be ready at the right moment when Ezra was ready to read God's Word—and they also would be prepared for the unusual work of God's Spirit.

The Man Nehemiah

A Man of Prayer

While Nehemiah has been mentioned already as a special instrument in God's hands, he bears additional consideration because of his special involvement in Judea's renewal. When he heard, in far off Persia, that the wall around Jerusalem in Judea was still in a state of neglect, he was concerned. He humbled himself and, over a period of some four months, he mourned, fasted, and prayed that the capital city could be restored.[47] Nehemiah was a unique person, a decisive and strong leader, but also a humble man of the Spirit. These characteristics made him the man eminently qualified to give Judea the political leadership it so desperately needed.

By no means did he have an easy task. Artaxerxes, the Persian king, granted him permission to rebuild Jerusalem's walls. The king also provided him an armed escort and papers of official permission for the necessary materials from the forests.[48] Soon after arriving in Jerusalem, Nehemiah took a few trusted men, went around the city walls, and assessed the damages. They considered what was needed—at the very least—to quickly plug the broken sections of the wall and then to provide plans in the future for a more extensive work.

The Man Who Led His People against Opposition

Nehemiah was a man with qualities that inspired people. The people in turn sensed that a godly governor was in their midst, to guide them in restructuring the leadership of Jerusalem and Judea. Very quickly, priests, civil authorities, and lay people were organized in their efforts of temporarily closing the breaks in the walls (see Neh. 3). Nehemiah faced opposition in many forms, among his own people (see Neh. 4:10, 12) as well as those from the pagans surrounding Judea. In particular, Sanballat the Horonite, Tobiah the Ammonite, and Geshem the Arab greatly opposed the new governor's efforts.

The list of difficulties appears formidable. Nehemiah had to face the following:

1. Ridicule and mockery by Sanballat, Tobiah, and Geshem (see Neh. 2:19; 4:1–2).
2. A plot by these three to come with armies to fight against Jerusalem (see Neh. 4:7–8).
3. His own anger against some of the Judean nobles who had enslaved fellow Judeans. Satan used this state of affairs to cause dissension *within* the ranks of Judea so that a complete breakdown would occur between leaders and people (see Neh. 5:1–13).
4. A call from Sanballat, Tobiah, and Geshem to go down to the coastal plain in Ono and discuss the building of the walls, taking him away from his task. In reality, this was a plot to harm him (see Neh. 6:1–2).
5. Slander through an unsealed letter circulated among the pagan peoples declaring that the Judeans were plotting a revolt against their Persian leaders. The scheme was designed to turn neighboring nations against Judea, with the intent of causing Nehemiah to fear for his life and to be greatly concerned for the welfare of his country (see Neh. 6:5–7).
6. A ploy by a physically disabled person, warning Nehemiah to flee to the Temple for safety and to close the Temple doors behind him because there was a plan to kill him. But Nehemiah saw through the sham suggestion to make him run away and hide from an imagined enemy (see Neh. 6:10–11).

In every case of opposition, Nehemiah leaned even harder on God and encouraged the people to continue on with their task of plugging the breaks in the wall. At the same time, he stood ready to fight when necessary and asked the people to do likewise in order to resist the attempts by God's enemies who were trying to stop the work. Again we see Nehemiah's qualities of courage, strength, and leadership, but he understood that his strength came only from the God of Israel.

. Finally, the Lord rewarded the people's efforts in rebuilding the wall—as well as Nehemiah's political leadership and Ezra's religious leadership—with a gracious spiritual renewal (see Neh. 8).

The Man Who Wanted His People to Honor the Lord

Nehemiah remained governor in Judea for twelve years, from 444 until 432 B.C.E. (see Neh. 13:6). Sometime later, he returned again to Jerusalem to encourage and continue the work that was so graciously begun. He guided the people to be honest and righteous before the Lord, giving them orders to evict Tobiah the Ammonite, the enemy of Judea, who had actually moved into a room of the Temple that had been used as a storage for peoples' tithes. He also provided instructions to honor the Sabbath Day, keeping it sacred (see Neh. 13:4–9, 15–22). He even had to speak out against repeated cases of mixed marriages, in spite of Ezra's earlier efforts to stamp out this practice (see Neh. 13:23–28). Some of these violations had gone on for twelve years after the spiritual renewal. He also encouraged the people to always stand guard, so that once having tasted the work of the Spirit, people should not forget and turn away to serve their own interests. God had his man on location in order to encourage Judea to live faithfully in accordance with his Word.

The Call for Spiritual Renewal

Internal and external opposition to spiritual renewal can be seen in spiritual apathy, lack of knowledge of the Word, prayerlessness, interest only in self and family, materialistic mindset, and so on. But Nehemiah's ministry demonstrates that the Lord does not want us to be spiritually dry and empty, to be enduring a subnormal walk. The normal experience of a Spirit-filled believer is to enjoy the Lord's presence and to have a spiritual life worth living, even when outward circumstances seem to prevail against us. The Lord desires that we know more of him and the power of his resurrection as we also seek to touch others' lives.

God does not want us to have a roller-coaster, up-and-down spiritual experience, high one day on some emotional kick and then in the depths the next day. The Spirit-filled believer is supposed to have an in-and-out lifestyle: into the congregation for fellowship, filling up with what God provides, and then out for service, relating to others who have desperate needs.

The spiritual renewal under Nehemiah and Ezra sets before us four calls for an earnest consideration.

Pray for It

Assessing the opportunities—The setting for spiritual renewal in Judea began in the heart of a young palace officer in the far-away city of Susa, in Persia. Nehemiah heard the news that parts of the walls around Jerusalem remained broken down, the city itself was an object of disgrace, and robbers could enter at will. Travelers in the Middle East would only sneer at the few Judeans for being so foolhardy as to live in their capital city, exposed to danger.

Evaluating the higher power—Was Nehemiah discouraged and disheartened when he heard the news about his people's city? Of course! But instead of merely talking about the tragic news and clucking his tongue in desperation, what did he do about it? Interestingly, Nehemiah did not immediately run to the king of Persia and ask him to rebuild the walls of Jerusalem. After all, why should a Persian king care about the city of the Jews, especially after the report that these people must be considered dangerous because of their long history of sedition and "revolt against kings" (see Ezra 4:19–23). In addition, Nehemiah rightly felt that if something tangible was to be accomplished for Jerusalem, he had to go to the highest power and authority, the God of Heaven, who also is the God of the nations. Nehemiah's faith was not in this world's kings and princes, because whether they realized it or not, they themselves were subject to the higher power.

Empathizing with his people—Nehemiah was a man of compassion. When he heard the report of his beloved city of Jerusalem, he sat down and wept, and for a number of days mourned and fasted. But this response does not mark him as a weakling. Years later, when he had to exercise his authority, the record says, "I disputed with the leaders, demanding, 'Why is the house of God abandoned'" (Neh. 13:11). When the occasion arose, he could assert strong leadership, which was already a dimension of his character. But, in the beginning, he waited humbly upon the Lord who, in time, gave him the guidance for the proper balance of compassion and strength.

Interceding for his people—Nehemiah also began to pray. He was a high court official, a servant of the Persian emperor himself. He may have been wealthy and had the means to help his brethren in a tangible way. Yet when he began to pray he was like a little child; his weeping and fasting demonstrated the character of a great man of God.

The elements of his prayer have been preserved for us (see Neh. 1:5–11). In his first words, he began to confess the sins of Israel, as well as his own. The use of the word *we* in this passage is indicative of the prayer of intercession.

Nehemiah was in exile because God had put his forefathers out of the land for their disobedience. Therefore, he confessed wrongdoing and evil: "I confess the sins of the people of Isra'el that we have committed against you. Yes, I and my father's house have sinned. We have deeply offended you. We haven't observed the *mitzvot*, laws or rulings you gave through your servant Moshe" (Neh. 1:6, 7). The Lord burdened Nehemiah's heart to intercede for his people, for the forgiveness of sin. But if he could ever do anything regarding Jerusalem's walls, the project would be connected with a concern even more important: the nation could really experience a spiritual renewal. Nehemiah took the first steps that eventually led to the change of heart among his people.

Once again, we are reminded of the necessity for confession of sin. Too many times there are barriers between the believers, even within the local congregation. It seems contradictory that a local body of believers—part of Messiah's present Body on earth—can also have within its membership brethren who have an intense dislike for one another. Such a state of affairs does not reflect Yeshua's love. We begin spiritual renewal by confessing our own sins, and in intercession, as Nehemiah, also confessing our corporate sins.

Reminding God of his promises—In his prayer, Nehemiah also reminded God of his promises in the covenant (see Neh. 1:8, 9). Does God need to be reminded of anything? No, but he certainly takes delight when his servants *think of* and *claim* what he promised for Israel. As his people pray and seek his face, his attitude of disapproval and discipline will change to approval, which will result in blessing. Therefore, God burdened his servant Nehemiah to pray for his people, and in time they experienced the Lord's blessing. Likewise, when we have God's promises on our hearts and on our lips, we also can make claims that God should honor them and bring blessing on our ministry.

Being tenacious in prayer—Nehemiah's prayer was not hit and miss; rather, his petition was strong and persistent, over a span of some four months. In this period he also mourned and ate very little, spending all his free time earnestly engaged in his intercession concerning Jerusalem. God delights in persistent prayer. Too many times believers stop short, give up, or feel that the task the Lord asks us to do is impossible to accomplish. Nevertheless, his desire is that whether his sons and daughters are praying for the small interests or major issues, he wants everyone to be faithful in prayer. The guideline is to: *Continue to ask, continue to seek,* and *continue to find* (see Matt. 7:7). While God hears the first time, often the answer does not come until later—at just the right moment.

Why should Nehemiah even care? He already had a good position, so why jeopardize it by going to what would be considered the "boondocks" of the Persian Empire? Because Nehemiah had set his heart on the things of God. So what would be God's response to this man who had become burdened about Jerusalem's walls? Obviously, the Lord had great respect for his servant and would be pleased to answer his plea when the timing was just right.

In God's timing—After some four months had gone by, while Nehemiah continued to pray, the Persian emperor recognized that something was transpiring in the mind and heart of his cupbearer, even though Nehemiah had not uttered a word about his concerns. When Artaxerxes asked why Nehemiah had such sadness of heart, the Jewish official explained that he was extremely burdened about the disrepair of the walls and gates of his people's city, the place where his fathers were buried. When the king further asked his servant what he would like to do about it, his reply was immediate: " . . . Send me to Y'hudah, to the city of my ancestors' tombs, so that I can rebuild it" (Neh. 2:5). The culmination of all Nehemiah's praying and fasting came when the king not only gave permission for his trusted servant to go to Jerusalem, but also provided him with authority and materials to make possible the rebuilding of the city. The king's reply was God's answer to Nehemiah's desires.

Often our spiritual welfare, and that of our families, our congregations, and even people far away hinges on whether or not we are ready to yield up our self-seeking, self-service, and self-gratification for the sake of God's will, which is by far the higher calling for our lives. It is no wonder that God was pleased to grant Nehemiah not only his request of repairing Jerusalem's walls, but also, through King Artaxerxes' permission, to be governor over Judea.

And why did all this come about? What was the first step on the way to rebuild Jerusalem and that eventually would lead Judea to spiritual renewal? It all began when one man became concerned about his people and had faith that God could accomplish what people consider impossible.

Prayer is a vital ingredient God uses to bring about changes in the hearts of individuals, congregations, and even whole communities. Illustrations abound concerning the power of prayer. David Brainerd believed in the power of persistent prayers of faith. Brainerd was responsible for reaching thousands of Native Americans for the Lord during the latter 1700s. His diary contains an incident of how, as he approached an Indian camp noted for savagery and fierceness he affirmed his need for God's intervention. He dropped to his knees in the forest, praying for his ministry there. He was not aware that some Indian scouts already had surrounded him as he was on his knees with face turned upward to heaven, praying for the people in the village. He did not know that the braves were slipping their arrows into their bows to cut him down.

At that very instant, however, a poisonous snake slithered out of the bushes and moved to a point just behind Brainerd and began to coil itself, ready to strike. The warriors silently put down their bows, expecting the snake to do their task for them. Just as the snake was about to strike the hapless Brainerd, before their very eyes, the reptile unloosed its coils, ceased its hissing, and slithered back into the bushes. All the while, David Brainerd continued to pray until early morning, completely oblivious to what had transpired around him!

Later in the morning when Brainerd entered the Indian camp, he was dumbfounded by the tremendous reception of the people. The braves told him what they had seen and addressed him with great honor, exclaiming, "The Great Spirit is with the paleface!"[49] God worked mightily in that camp all because one person, oblivious to all his surroundings and not caring for himself, had waited upon God. Even though Brainerd's ministry was short, it is no wonder that his incident-packed diary, with testimonies of God's answers to prayer, became the catalyst for William Carey and Henry Martyn to go to India, as well as others who were likewise challenged for the Lord's work.

Pursue the Possibilities for Renewal

Assessing the work to be accomplished—The second call for spiritual renewal is to pursue the possibilities for involvement with people all around us who have such desperate needs. Genuine service for the Lord does not mean to simply sit down in our usual services at 11:00 A.M. and leave at noon or later without any sense of commitment to serve our generation. Perhaps Vance Havner's pithy assessment is all too true in many instances: "Our services begin at 11:00 A.M. sharp and finish at 12:00 dull!"

Apathy was not Nehemiah's choice. As soon as he arrived in Jerusalem, the record indicates he "got up during the night, I and a few men with me. I hadn't told anyone what my God had put in my heart to do for Yerushalayim" (Neh. 2:12). What did he do? He rode around the city walls on his horse to assess the need. It would be no simple task to plug the breaks in the walls and rebuild some of the gates, but before he ever approached any of the city's leaders about any talk of rebuilding anything, he already had pursued the possibilities to see what needed to be done. Having this information in hand, he then presented the specific need to the elders and leaders and sought to encourage them in the task.

Quite frankly, assessing needs in order to serve our congregations and communities better is always difficult and risky. Apathetic believers more than likely will resist change in their lives and will not promote change for other people. But some must take the initiative to constantly evaluate what we do for the Lord and seek a better way to accomplish it. What is hindering the effort in the attempt to reach out in our communities? Are the services tailored to be most helpful to seekers who come within our walls? And, if unbelievers will not seek out those who have come to faith, then how does one most effectively go to them? Our efforts often are far from perfect, but the need is always to have a positive and open mind, seek better ways to relate to people's needs, and then to do so.

At exam times, I always used to tell students, "Now, you are going to share with me, and both of us will find out how much you know." But often, when correcting the papers, I found where I had failed to communicate specific points in the education process. Then came the time to make changes in order to constantly sharpen the teaching process. But any similar effort in the spiritual realm also requires examining all the possibilities in order to do the job more effectively.

Enlisting a people's involvement—Nehemiah also challenged the people of Jerusalem, but not with any dictatorial airs. He did not say, "Now I'm going to tell you what you have to do." No, he identified with the leaders in what they and the people had to do, saying, "You see what a sad state we are in, how Yerushalayim lies in ruins, with its gates burned up. Come, let's rebuild the wall of Yerushalayim, so that we won't continue in disgrace" (Neh. 2:17). He went on to describe how God already had cared for their needs; the Persian king had promised all the provisions necessary for the task. Nehemiah inspired the people to do what needed to be done.

I remember when Dr. George Sweeting assumed the presidency of the Moody Bible Institute in 1971. A new leader always finds it difficult to take a position of this nature, as he knows very well that people will compare his work to that of his predecessor. So everyone on the faculty, and the entire student body, was eager to hear what was on Dr. Sweeting's heart and mind. As he spoke, he identified with us in the sense that we all needed to work together. He described what is to be our part in world evangelization in this generation. His words became an inspiration to mesh the gifts and talents of the faculty, the student body, and the staff at the Institute to meet the challenge set before us. Coming away from that initial address, I felt I could take his challenge and fit it into the work God had led me to do as well, among Jewish people.

Recording the effort of rebuilding—Almost everyone responded and set about to rebuild Jerusalem's walls (see Neh. 3). Don't skip reading the third chapter of Nehemiah, assuming that it is just a boring long list of difficult-to-pronounce names. Particular phrases reflect the inspiration Nehemiah was able to infuse into the people of Jerusalem as they went about their task. For example:

1. "Eliashib the *cohen hagadol* [high priest] set out with his fellow *cohanim*, and they rebuilt the Sheep Gate" (vs. 1).
2. Hananyah, one of the *perfume-makers*, made repairs (see vs. 8). (One might wonder how a perfume maker could effectively be involved in heavy construction, but he did it.)
3. "Shalum the son of HaLochesh, leader of half the district of Yerushalayim, *he and his daughters made repairs*" (vs. 12).

4. "Barukh the son of Zakkai worked *diligently* making repairs on another section" (vs. 20). (We might wonder whether, in his *diligence*, he ever hit his thumb with a hammer.)
5. Even those who failed to be involved in the work also were recorded for posterity: "Their nobles [those of Tekoa] would not put their shoulders to the work" (vs. 5).

This chapter makes tremendous reading because all except for a few were working together, and this beautiful example of willing workers is an encouraging lesson for us as well. If spiritual renewal is ever to come to our congregations, we must all labor together as we relate to people's needs in our communities.

Facing up to the opposition—We can expect formidable opposition as we pursue spiritual renewal. When a person or a congregation or a number of congregations start to move for God, satanic pressure becomes all too evident. As already pointed out, Nehemiah had to endure pressures from enemies without as well as factors that almost divided his people from within. God's man met the external opposition with prayer, because he took a resolute stand for the work he had been called to do. He organized the men working on the walls into teams so that they were also prepared to rebuild, as well as for any battle that might arise (see Neh. 4:7–9).

The danger from within was even greater (see Neh. 5). Successive years of drought led to a moral breakdown. The poor had to sell their sons and daughters to rich nobles in order to have food and even grain to plant crops. Nehemiah had to deal with the possibility of a revolt against the rich by the poor. He had to take a stand for righteousness against some of the rich nobles and rulers in order to break the stranglehold they had on the poor. His tactic was to shame them:

I also said, "What you are doing is not good! You should be living in fear of our God, so that our pagan enemies won't have grounds for deriding us. Moreover, my brothers and my servants, I too have loaned them money and grain. Please, let's stop making it so burdensome to go into debt. Please! Today! Give them back their fields, vineyards, olive groves and homes; also the hundred pieces of silver and the grain, wine and olive oil you demand from them in interest.

(Neh. 5:9–11)

When he had to, Nehemiah could be a forceful leader, withstanding social abuse with a firm and resolute stand for righteousness.

As believers mature, they experience all kinds of pressures. Some have been the targets of opposition by their families. Perhaps some have not been entirely able to withstand the conflict, but the Lord is faithful. He can enable every embattled soul to overcome and be victorious. But every believer needs to remember—as he takes his stand for God—he is greater than all opposition. He will never let his witness cease; and we need not fear, we can continue undaunted, reaching out to people in their needs.

Preaching That Challenges People for Renewal

The third call for spiritual renewal involves challenging preaching. The walls and gates were completed after fifty-two days, but after that, what? Were completed walls the objective of Nehemiah's work among the people of Jerusalem? No! God had something better.

Gathering the people on an auspicious occasion—The record indicates that, "When the seventh month arrived, after the people of Isra'el had resettled in their towns, all the people gathered with one accord in the open space in front of the

Water gate and asked Ezra the *Torah*-teacher to bring the scroll of the *Torah* of Moshe, which ADONAI had commanded Isra'el" (Neh. 8:1).

The timing was significant because it was the beginning of the New Year on the civil calendar. By this point, Israel has two calendars—the religious one when the first month occurs in the spring and Passover is celebrated, and the civil one, mentioned in this chapter, which begins in the seventh month of the religious calendar, in the fall. Ten days after the beginning of the civil new year is the Day of Atonement, and from the fifteenth until the twenty-first day is the Feast of Tabernacles, which commemorated the general harvest of the land.

It was customary for people to gather for the first of the month, anticipating the celebration of the end of the harvest season (see Deut. 14:22–27). But because of the unity of the people after they completed the project of closing the gaps in the walls and rebuilding the gates, the occasion of the assembly of the people was to be an auspicious one. Little did the crowd realize what God would do in its midst, as the moment had come for a gracious outpouring of his love upon Judea.

Proclaiming the truths of the Word—The people then called for the reading of the Word, so Ezra brought out the Torah and began reading aloud. He read from daybreak until noon (see Neh. 8:2, 3). The gathering consisted of men and women and "all children old enough to understand." And "all the people listened attentively to the Book of the Law." The people recognized an authority in the Law, that is, in the Word of God, because, as they began to listen they "bowed their heads and fell prostrate before ADONAI with their faces to the ground" (Neh. 8:6). By acknowledging God's sovereignty, the people knew the importance of the Scriptures given to them by the God of all creation.

The Levites instructed the people, making the Word clear, enabling them to understand its meaning. Not only was it necessary to read the newly transliterated version of the

Scriptures, but the content must be understood, so it was provided in Aramaic. When the people took hold of the Word, they sensed a power transmitted to their hearts. But this potency of the Word is the same today, and as believers take the time to read the Word and permit the Holy Spirit to search their hearts, he can stir everyone as well.

What were the results as Ezra read the Word? The people began to weep as it penetrated the deepest recesses of their hearts, causing a division of soul and spirit (see Heb. 4:12). Conviction set in to such an extent that everyone simply broke down and cried before the Lord (see Neh. 8:9). The governor finally had to declare in the midst of the work of the Spirit, as people acknowledged their needs and wrongdoing, "Go, eat rich food, drink sweet drinks, and send portions to those who can't provide for themselves; for today is consecrated to our Lord. Don't be sad, because the joy of *ADONAI* is your strength" (Neh. 8:10). All of his prayer and fasting for four months back in Susa had come to a climax as God's Spirit began to work in hearts.

Offering the sin offering on the day of atonement—The Word was read again on the second day of the month—it seems that daily public reading, from daybreak until noon, became the practice. While the Scriptures do not mention it, the tenth day was the Day of Atonement, and we can imagine the people's keen anticipation when the high priest offered the bull of the sin offering sacrifice on behalf of himself and his family (see Lev. 16:6).

The sin offering on behalf of the people was designed to teach vividly the truth of atonement (see Lev. 16:15–22). Two goats had been made ready, one as the goat of sacrifice, and the second as the scapegoat. The first one was slain, and its blood was presented in the holy of holies, to care for the sins of the people. Then the high priest prayed over the second goat, whereby the sins of the people were laid on it. Next, this second goat was led out into the wilderness, and the symbolism became quite clear: The people's sins were taken away so that they would never have to face them again. One almost can hear the wellspring of "Hallelujahs" from the hearts of those restored in their fellowship, as well as from many unbelievers who came to faith as they saw the new work of God in the hearts of those who professed genuine faith. A great culminating event took place in front of the Water Gate, affecting a tremendous renewal of the people of Judea; but again, this response by the people all began when Nehemiah began to pray for his brethren. Little did he realize how God would answer his prayer.

Celebrating the feast of tabernacles—The people also heard from the Word concerning the Feast of Tabernacles (see Exod. 23:16; Deut. 16:13–17), when people are to take time, reflect, and rejoice because of all God's goodness (see Neh. 8:14). Everyone willingly went out to obtain branches of various trees to make booths in which to sit and take their meals and bless God for his bountiful blessings of the general harvest. No doubt, many talked of what the Lord had accomplished in their midst in the days leading to the Day of Atonement, when God's Spirit so mightily touched their hearts. Their sense of thanksgiving was deep as they observed the Feast of Tabernacles for seven days. On the twenty-second day was the Holy Convocation, the Crowning Day when the people celebrated the climax of all the feasts of the year in accordance with the Mosaic regulation (see Lev. 23:36).

Waiting upon the Lord—Even after the celebration of the holidays, the people were of no mind to leave. The Scriptures further explain, "On the twenty-fourth day of this month the people of Isra'el, wearing sackcloth and with dirt on them, assembled for a fast" (Neh. 9:1), which means the Judeans had been there already for more than three weeks. They were not ready to return to the ordinary humdrum of everyday life, but instead sought further to dedicate themselves to God, worship him with a full heart, and seek for the many ways to serve him. People rejoiced and praised the Lord as they thought of all that God had done in their hearts, and they wanted to demonstrate their love for him. Though they were under Persian domination and, therefore, not politically free, they were free in the Spirit. They confessed the evil deeds of their forefathers, which brought about the exile to Babylon, but they also rejoiced that God had preserved a remnant to glorify and praise him (see Neh. 9:5–37).

Once more, the Judeans ratified the covenant made at Mt. Sinai (see Deut. 28). They promised God they would never again be involved in idolatry nor would they intermarry with pagan peoples, they would keep the Sabbath Day, remember their tithes to the Lord's work, and not neglect the Lord's house (see Neh. 10:28–39). As already noted, this covenant was to have been ratified as follows:

1. Every seven years, as a reminder to Israel of their relationship to the Lord (see Deut. 31:10–13);
2. Every time a new king came to the throne (see 2 Kings 11:17);
3. When God's Spirit brought renewal to the nation (see 2 Chron. 34:31).

And so, even in the time of Ezra and Nehemiah, the covenant was acknowledged again by a repentant people who were touched in such a special way by the Holy Spirit.

The people also were of one mind to maintain Jerusalem's reputation as a holy city. They cast lots to decide which tenth of the people were to remain in Jerusalem while the other nine-tenths could return to their own towns and villages. The ten percent chosen to live in Jerusalem was charged with the responsibility of guarding the sacred character of the city, which was a special task indeed (see Neh. 11:1, 2).

Nehemiah's final action was a grand dedication on Jerusalem's walls (see Neh. 12:27–43). Arrangements had been made for the choirs to sing their songs of thanksgiving, glorifying God for what he had wrought for the people of Judah. With an elaborate procession of the choir, dividing into two groups and each taking their place all around the walls of the city, the entire experience was a testimony to God, as men, women, and children rejoiced. The record indicates, "the celebration in Yerushalayim could be heard far off" (vs. 43). God had given his people a victory that would long be remembered.

I pray that our congregations will, likewise, enter into such a blessed renewal, with the effect being felt far and wide in our nation, among the household of Israel, and among the national congregations of many countries and God's people everywhere.

Perfection in the Spirit

Here is the fourth call for maintaining and expanding spiritual renewal. The renewal that began during that seventh month continued on among many of the believers, but again we need to remember that these special works of God are never self-sustaining. Nehemiah returned to Persia after being governor in Judah for twelve years; but, sadly, by the time he came back to Judea, some of the spiritual renewal had begun to dissipate. Much of this deviation was due to the many in Judea who were unrepentant and who had not come to Jerusalem when the spiritual renewal was underway. In addition, a new generation was beginning to come on the scene. So some Judeans again transgressed, committing the evil of mixed marriages, and resisting the testimony of believers who had participated in the renewal (compare Ezra 10:16; Neh. 6:17–19; 13:4–9). Tragically, unbelievers can and do resist God's grace, even though they can see it before them plainly, day by day. As a result, they fall prey to ungodly influences.

So Nehemiah had to encourage God's people to sustain the renewal; he had to remind everyone that it was necessary always to seek for perfection of the Spirit, whereby the Lord's will can be honored. Nehemiah had the unpleasant task of chiding people who had not consecrated themselves, yet he did not flinch from his call to be a leader of righteousness. Once more, he emphasized the terms of the covenant: that the Sabbath was a time to worship and not to carry on with everyday business, that the people of Judah must not intermarry with pagans, and that God's Word and its directives must be supreme. Likewise, believers today need to work continually at the perfection of the Spirit in order to keep up a warm-hearted, devotional relationship with the lover of our souls.

Watchman Nee, a believer in China, spent more than twenty years in Communist prisons after the Marxists had seized complete power on Mainland China in 1949. He fought a government that was more hostile to his beliefs than anything that most of us in the West will ever have to face. One day he took a biscuit from a plate and broke it. Then he tried to put it together again and did such a good job with it that he said to a companion, "You see, it looks almost like it was before." But, he added, "You and I know that it is not."

Every believer is similar to the broken biscuit. As God begins to work in hearts and leads in life's experiences, he knows we are as frail as the biscuit Nee held in his hands. Every one of us who are of the Messiah has to learn to yield and stand in the Lord's strength. Our earthly bodies can crumble and break apart; the only genuine strength we have is when his Spirit fills our houses of clay, renews us, and helps us to reach out to others who are hungry in their souls.

CHAPTER TEN

From the End of the Period of the Tanakh and During the Intertestamental Period

"Judas [Yehudah] replied, 'Many can easily be overpowered by a few; it makes no difference to Heaven to save by many or by few. Victory does not depend on numbers; strength comes from Heaven alone. Our enemies come filled with insolence and lawlessness to plunder and to kill us and our wives and children. But we are fighting for our lives and our religion. Heaven will crush them before our eyes. You need not be afraid of them.'"

1 Maccabees 3:18–22 (NEB)

The renewal under Ezra and Nehemiah marks the end of a consideration of the spiritual renewals of the Tanakh (Old Testament), but certainly this is not the end of the way God has worked with Israel from generation to generation—from the close of Tanakh until now. God had his ways to speak to the people Israel so as to bring the nation to himself. In this chapter, a thumbnail sketch will be provided of what occurred at the end of the Old Testament period, and on through the inter-testamental period to the great *Shavu'ot*, the Day of Pentecost, and to the end of the first century C.E.

From the Biblical Period to the First Century

In the last chapter, the work of God under Ezra and Nehemiah was noted, and near the end of the book of Nehemiah, the record mentions that the governor returned a second time to Jerusalem, in about 430 B.C.E. He discovered that some of the effects of the renewal already had begun to wear off, and many unbelievers were violating God's Word by intermarrying with pagans and breaking the Sabbath day. Nehemiah had to rebuke the unbelievers severely because of their disrespect for the covenant God had with Israel.

Malachi (circa 420 B.C.E.), the last of the Old Testament prophets, had to charge that the nation was no longer in spiritual renewal, which had occurred only a generation before. Once again, God had to speak to his people as he sought to renew believers' hearts and to rebuke unbelievers in an attempt to bring them to a born-again experience. After Malachi's ministry, for almost 400 years, there was no further direct revelation from God. That curtain reopened with Israel's Messiah, Yeshua.

While God gave Israel no special Word during the 400 years, by no means were people void of the knowledge of salvation history and the nation's religious moral literature. God always was involved in outreach, although, without specific revelation from him, it is difficult to ascertain the purposes in his providential rule.

Correspondence did occur between Jewish people in Egypt and the high priest in Israel, as contained in the Elephantine Letters (420–400 B.C.E.).[50] The Egyptian Jews had a temple in which a synthesis had been created between the worship of Israel's God and some of the pagan deities. For whatever reason, Egyptian priests destroyed this Egyptian-Jewish temple, and in these Elephantine Letters, the Jewish people in Egypt asked Jerusalem for help to rebuild their temple. While this house of worship was reconstructed by 402 B.C.E., no aid came from the Jewish people in Judea. The high priest and others correctly assessed that the only temple allowable under scriptural guidance was to be in Jerusalem, indicating that, in this respect, the religious leadership of Jerusalem was faithful to God's Word.

Alexander the Great and the Egyptian Rule over Judea

Not much information is available regarding the Persian occupation of Judea. In 331 B.C.E., Alexander the Great took Judea from the Persians and, while he destroyed Tyre, he did no harm to Jerusalem. Josephus explained the encounter between Alexander and the high priest of Jerusalem: As Alexander the Great overlooked Jerusalem from the northeast, standing on "The Hill of the Scouts" (Mt. Scopus as it is known today), the high priest came out to meet the Greek conqueror. He was dressed in his full regalia, attended by other priests, and as the procession approached Alexander, the conqueror dismounted and gave his right hand to the Jewish high priest as a sign of honor, much to the dismay of Alexander's lieutenants.[51] Josephus explained this strange behavior of a mighty Greek conqueror by relating the curious story that when Alexander was a child he had a dream that, during his conquests, he would one day meet a priest dressed in such great splendor. When the dream came true, the Greek warrior acknowledged what he felt to be a revelation of the gods. If the account is true, it would be another instance of how God protected his people of Judea as they lived in accordance with his Word, and, as a result, Jerusalem was spared any destruction.

Little information is available of what occurred immediately after Alexander's death and during the time when the Egyptians (Ptolemies) controlled Judea (301–198 B.C.E.). This period was relatively quiet, yet one significant event occurred when authorities in Jerusalem gave permission for the translation of the Old Testament into Greek. The project began at about 250 B.C.E. and was not completed until about 150 years later.

Toward the end of the Egyptian rule, many in Judea, especially the younger generation, had become *Hellenized*. They embraced the Greek lifestyle with its philosophy, athletics, plays and, in general, its love for beauty, which in too many cases stood sharply opposed to the Torah's call for holiness. In particular, competition at the games by naked athletes and art that displayed the naked human body were particularly offensive to those who adhered to a Torah lifestyle. Also outrageous was the undoing of circumcision by some of the Jewish athletes so as to be accepted by adherents of this foreign culture!

The Syrian Rule over Judea

In God's providence, Judea was conquered by the Syrians (Seleucids) in 198 B.C.E. and, under Antiochus Epiphanes, went through one of its worst persecutions (175–164 B.C.E.). If Judeans wanted to taste the forbidden fruits of the seductive Hellenistic ways, God permitted his people to have a good exposure to it; while at the same time he allowed them to suffer its consequences.

After Judea came under Syrian control, the latter continued to battle with Egypt. But to sustain a war machine, Antiochus Epiphanes needed money, and the best way to obtain it was to raid the temples, where money was stored. When the Syrian king tried to confiscate monies stored in the Jerusalem Temple, many of the people of Judea resisted this invasion of their religious sanctity. The Syrians then understood correctly that they were actually fighting the Judeans' religion, so they issued edicts to eliminate it. One of Antiochus Epiphanes' worst acts was his desecration of the Jerusalem Temple by offering a pig on its altar, thereby causing all worship to cease. The entire worship area was defiled, the priesthood was rendered unclean, and the people of Judea no longer had a place where sacrifices could be offered. In addition, the Syrian king ordered Hellenistic pagan altars set up in many parts of the country and ordered the Jewish people to worship the Greek gods.

These anti-Jewish acts and others put extreme pressure on the Judean people, but we must conclude that God permitted this horror to cause his people to turn back to him in renewal. We can surmise that Judea's time of sorrow was a repetition of what took place during the period of the Judges. In the midst of this trial, godly people began then to assert themselves in prayer that their fellow countrymen should turn from the strange Hellenistic ways to the Lord's covenant with his people.

The revolt against the pagan occupiers began in a little town of Modiin in 167 B.C.E., when an elderly, godly priest, Mattathias, killed a renegade Jew who wanted to worship according to the Syrian demands. A Syrian officer also was killed and, subsequent to these acts of defiance, Mattathias and his five sons fled to the hills, calling on their fellow Judeans to revolt against Syria. What is more important, however, is that this aged man was a priest; he saw the necessity for Judea to return to the God of Israel and give honor to him. For about three and a half years, this family who came to be known as the Maccabees—and others who joined them— battled the Syrians and won one battle after another. Eventually, the people of Judea were able to negotiate with the Syrians for religious freedom, and in 164 B.C.E. the Temple was rededicated. In a sense, Mattathias acted as courageously as the Levites, Moses' brethren, who had to take up the sword against their brethren (see Exod. 32:26–29), and as Phinehas when he killed the renegade Israeli and Midianite woman (see Num. 25:6–8). In each case, the purpose of the violent action was to preserve God's righteousness. The alternative would have been for God's people to be exposed to his judgment.[52]

Under the Maccabees

But religious freedom was not enough for some in Judea. The fight for political freedom continued, and by 128 B.C.E. Judea won her freedom from the Syrians, allowing John Hyrchanus I to preside over a free nation.

Only a bare sketch will be mentioned of this complicated period of Judea's freedom.[53] The first years of freedom were good, as Judea expanded its territory by military conquest. Spiritually, however, the course was downward, because once again the renewal was not sustained, as it was when Mattathias stood firmly for the things of the Lord. In its place came dissension, greed, and intrigue among the Jewish political leaders. Many religious people broke away from the main parties and formed a number of sects, some of which felt that the nation sorely needed a spiritual revitalization. Eventually, Rome backed Herod the Great and, by 37 B.C.E., Judah became a Roman province under Herod. During the last year or so of Herod's reign, Yeshua the Messiah was born.

Judea under Rome

By the first century, Judea was a Roman province, no longer free, and burdened with taxes collected by a foreign power. People found life miserable. Into just this situation, John the Immerser appeared as the forerunner whose preaching pointed to Yeshua the Messiah. Many believers sensed an anticipation of what was about to happen, so they went down to the Jordan where he was preaching, and he immersed them for repentance, and to await the Kingdom. Then, at the onset of his proclamation of the Messianic Kingdom, as described by the prophets, Yeshua presented himself for immersion as well. Yeshua also proclaimed that through his death, the atonement for sin would be possible. He had a following in the thousands, but the climax came when the Sanhedrin could not live with his testimony that he is Messiah (a human) as well as the son of God (deity) (see Matt. 26:64–65). He was condemned and turned over to Pilate—who did not act on his own recognition that Yeshua had not committed any wrong worthy of death (see Luke 23:13–17, 20)—and then gave him over to be crucified by his own soldiers. Luke assigned guilt for his death to all mankind—Herod, ruler of Israel, Pilate, governor of Judea, and "the *Goyim* [nations] and the peoples of Isra'el" (Acts 4:27).

Even if the Sanhedrin had accepted Yeshua as Israel's rightful King/Messiah, as well as the Son of God, the Romans would have put him to death. One can easily imagine that the Romans could never live with Yeshua as the King over Israel. He still had to die as an atonement for our sins, as the Scriptures declared, and as Yeshua himself had announced (see Matt. 16:21). He would have been resurrected on the third day and then would have asserted his sovereignty over Rome and the entire Roman government; the Messianic kingdom as envisioned by the prophets then could have commenced. But, events did not turn out in this way, and God had to commence the kingdom and fulfill his promises to Israel in another way.

The First Century as a Workshop of the Holy Spirit

The Great *Shavu'ot*

The Pentecost experience, as seen in Acts 2, affords a good understanding of how God's Spirit worked in the lives of so many people. A spiritual renewal took place among believers in the period between Messiah's resurrection and *Shavu'ot* (Feast of Weeks/Pentecost). This post-resurrection ministry was necessary for the disciples to realize the truth of what Yeshua had told them over and over again; he was to be delivered into the hands of the religious leaders, he would be put to death, and he would be raised on the third day.

Remember, however, that no such concept existed in Israel of the Messiah—son of David—who, when he came, would die as the atonement for our sins, be resurrected, and still be the same son of David with authority to bring in the kingdom. Even Yeshua's disciples had great difficulty with this concept, refusing to accept it. Take Peter's reaction (see Matt. 16:22), for example, or the display of grief by the disciples at such a dismal prospect (see Matt. 17:23). And, thereafter, no response at all appears in the next round of Yeshua's statements. Even at Yeshua's last Passover, the disciples made no comment regarding his strange statements over the bread and third cup of the Seder. Not until after the resurrection, with Yeshua's appearances to his disciples, did they begin to perceive the truth of what Yeshua had declared all along.[54]

So the post-resurrection ministry was, in a sense, a new revelation to Yeshua's followers. This was the time he also prepared them for their peculiar ministry on that special *Shavu'ot*. This time of ministry was a time for spiritual renewal. The disciples were being readied for God's purposes when the Holy Spirit finally would come to inaugurate the kingdom, but under a different program than the disciples had expected before.

Israel's Response to Yeshua the Messiah

Beginning with that auspicious day of *Shavu'ot*, when the Holy Spirit came in power, the records provide information on the work of evangelism as well as the numbers of people who came to know the Lord. The first response includes some 3,000 persons (see Acts 2:41), a statistic that was not provided during other responses after the spiritual renewals seen in the Tanakh. In the following references, we find these descriptions:

1. "The Lord kept adding to them those who were being saved" (Acts 2:47).
2. Five thousand "men" believed the message and, in addition, women and young people also could have been included (see Acts 4:4).
3. "The number of disciples increased rapidly." In addition, a large number of priests also became believers. After Paul's three journeys to the major cities of the Roman empire,

some twenty-five years after the resurrection, he came back and stayed with Ya'akov (James) who then informed Paul that present in Jerusalem were "tens of thousands" of believers (see Acts 21:20).

This account of numbers gives us some idea of the evangelistic outreach after the disciples' spiritual renewal. But the account also can be a testimony of the numbers of people who came to know the Lord as a consequence of the renewals in previous times, as seen in the Tanakh.

While no figures are available afterward, we may surmise that the interest continued. When the revolt broke out against Rome, that empire's legions came, fighting their way to Jerusalem and surrounding it. The believers then remembered what Yeshua had predicted, "When you see Yerushalayim surrounded by armies, then you are to understand that she is about to be destroyed" (Luke 21:20). He further declared that they should flee to the mountains, or at least get out of the city. And so, instead of remaining to fight with the Jewish defenders, the believers fled to Pella, on the other side of the Jordan.[55] Tragically, the Temple was destroyed, exactly as Yeshua had predicted.

With the Temple gone, and with most building stones pushed off the Temple mount, Jewish people were in a quandary as to how worship should take place. Many religious leaders wept with despondency because the very center of Mosaic worship was gone. However, at the same time, a group of rabbis went into a council at a small town of Yavneh and restructured Israel's worship, taking some twenty years for the process. The result of decisions regarding the loss of the Temple was Judaism without any substitute atonement, which the sin offering, as seen in Leviticus 4 and 16, had made possible. Atonement became a matter of self-effort, of repentance, prayer, study of Torah, and living a godly lifestyle.[56]

During these thirty or so years—until the decisions of Yavneh began to take hold after 100 C.E., and while the common people were mourning for their Temple—a gracious window of opportunity opened for Jewish believers who had come back from Pella. Moving into this religious void, these believers began to reach their brethren with the message of Yeshua as the sin offering for atonement. They could have stressed that Yeshua had predicted this calamity of the Temple's destruction. They may have encouraged the people of Israel to take note and respond to Yeshua's death as the atoning sacrifice—a sacrifice that followed the Mosaic principles of atonement.

Who knows how many Jewish people became believers as a result? Some have estimated that by the end of the first century, the response was perhaps twenty percent of the nation, although no hard figures are available. And yet, if the earlier figures are any indication of a response, think of how a trauma such as the loss of the Temple could have opened many hearts to Yeshua's message. The response could have been high indeed. And these numbers of believers persisted until the 400s C.E., causing the religious leaders to adjust a number of facets of religious beliefs and practices in reaction to the Messianic Jews.

CHAPTER ELEVEN

A Brief Overview of Renewal During the Age of the Body of Messiah

"For he has set a Day when he will judge the inhabited world, and do it justly, by means of a man whom he has designated. And he has given public proof of it by resurrecting this man from the dead."

(Acts 17:31)

"The Lord is not slow in keeping his promise, as some people think of slowness; on the contrary, he is patient with you; for it is not his purpose that anyone should be destroyed, but that everyone should turn from his sins."

(2 Pet. 3:9)

What Happened to the Jewish Believers?

My intention in this chapter is to provide only a brief overview of renewal within the body of Messiah. Many other books deal with the history of the Church, in general and with renewal in particular.

If as many as twenty percent of the nation did come to the Lord by the end of the first century, what happened to the Jewish believers afterwards?

When the council of Yavneh had completed its work in 90 C.E. every effort was made to separate Messianic Jews from the main body of Israel. The edict of adding the malediction to the *sh'moneh esreh*—where the Jewish person gives thanks to God he is not a *min* (an apostate)—went a long way toward barring Messianic Jews from the synagogues.[57] In this case, being an apostate primarily meant believing that Yeshua is the Messiah.

However, the presence of Jewish believers continued well into the third and fourth centuries. Based on the existent testimonies about Yeshua to various leaders and people in the Jewish community by Messianic Jews, it seems clear that many of those believers were well-trained and knowledgeable in the Written and Oral Torah.[58] Sadly, however, the distinctive Messianic Jewish testimony slowly began to diminish.

But the more telling blow against the Messianic Jews came with the decisions by the Council of Nicea in 325 C.E. Some three hundred non-Jewish bishops[59] attended this conference, and their major concern was the question of Yeshua's deity. Many among the non-Jewish folk who attended were ready to do battle against the claim for the deity issue, but the majority finally decided for it, giving it a distinctively philosophically Greek cultural dimension. This expression of the doctrine of the tri-unity of God reflects a biblical truth, but Messianic Jews will want to express this truth in a more Old Testament setting, as did the New Testament writers.

But two other decisions by this council had an adverse bearing on Messianic Jews. The first conclusion was that Messiah's death, burial, and resurrection was to be centered on Good Friday and Easter, and, henceforth, no church ever was to observe the Passover. The second determination was that weekly worship must no longer occur on the Sabbath, but on the first day of the week. These two decisions went a long way to marginalize the Messianic Jews, marking them as heretics. To add to the developing rift, Jewish leaders in turn set themselves apart from Christendom; that is, they particularly drew a line also between themselves and Jewish believers. By the sixth century, the number of believers from Jewish stock no longer could carry on a witness as *Jewish* believers. Instead, their witness had to be from within a Greek/Roman cultural context.

And yet, Jewish believers were present in almost every generation, since the councils of the 300s and 400s. Then, in the nineteenth century, their numbers began to grow again. Across the decades until now, Jewish believers have attempted more and more to express faith from within a Jewish perspective, while keeping it biblical. Messianic Jews now number in the thousands in North America, with at least two hundred congregations. And there are at least fifty-seven congregations in the land of Israel as of this writing.

An Overview of Renewal

The major emphasis of this book is concentrated on the renewals of Israel and Judah in the days of the Hebrew Scriptures (Old Testament). But it is also good to see how these renewals impacted the body of Messiah, which meant so much for the history of Europe and North America. The same principles of renewal also have occurred in our more immediate history. And while believers were filled with the Spirit, and many unbelievers were reached with Messiah's love, the consequences took on such significance that believers, in and out of government, had their hand in changing the political, social, and economic life of their respective countries.[60] Again, our attempt is not to be exhaustive with this treatment, but to select some of the more prominent renewals that occurred from the Middle Ages to the present.

The Work of God within Roman Catholicism

Spiritual renewal touched wide areas within Roman Catholicism and Evangelical areas. Among the former were those of the Brethren of the Common Life. One member of that order, Thomas a Kempis (1380–1471), gave to the body of the Messiah the book called *The Imitation of Messiah*. Many became involved in the "strange world of the Bible"—as Sidney A. Ahlstrom referred to it in citing these examples:

1. Savonarola (1452–98) turned the city of Florence into a penitential city.
2. Cajetan (1480–1547), a forerunner of sixteenth-century Catholic Reformation, sought to call laypeople and clergy to a more earnest personal moral lifestyle and service to the poor.
3. Pietro Caraffa (1476–1559), and later as Pope Paul IV (1555–1559), throughout his ministry, tried to call for a change in the clergy, challenging them to develop a deeper spiritual level and greater concern for the parish ministry.
4. Erasmus (1543–83) provided a resurgence in the study of Greek and specialized studies in the Greek New Testament. His labor laid the groundwork for the Protestant Reformation, although he himself did not leave the Catholic Church.

Many more can be mentioned, but one must take note that a movement of God existed even within this church, sparking a number of renewals that affected thousands of people.[61]

The Impact of the Reformation

Among those who laid the foundations for the evangelical movement of the Reformation—people who had experienced God's power in their lives—were Martin Luther (1483–1546), John Calvin (1509–1564) of Geneva, and Ulrich Zwingli (1484–1531) of Zurich, each of whom in turn impacted many believers.[62] Another son of the Reformed tradition was John Knox, known for his prayer, "Give me Scotland, or I die," which expressed his deeply heartfelt and Spirit-led interests in encouraging believers and thereby reaching out to unbelievers. England of the 1600s also had its movement for God when, in particular, the Puritans in England stood for a Calvinistic reformation, which called for an emphasis on the preaching of God's Word, leading to "household prayers, sanctification, and strict morality." Although they tried to have a strong impact on English religious society during the Elizabethan period (beginning in 1558), by 1604 they had become divided. The Puritan spirit continued, however, among the non-conformists in England as well as among those who came to the New Word to establish a "purified Church of England as an example to the homeland."[63]

The work begun by Luther sagged during the Thirty-Years' War (1618–48). But God began a new thrust in the pietistic movement in Germany and Moravia as his answer to the war and to the immediate post-Reformation era of heresy hunting and creedal Protestantism, which seemed to have lost some of the original fire of renewal. Pietism became the effort to recover the Bible as spiritual food and nourishment; and at the University of Halle, Spenner (1639–1709) provided the context for Bible study, devotions, and prayer, which was to have a wide influence on the evangelicals.

Franke (1663–1727) continued the work in Halle, while Zinzendorf (1700–1760)[64] led in a similar effort from which came the Moravian brethren. In turn, they had a profound influence in Central Europe as well as in North America, where many of them migrated. As a party of Moravians were sailing to Georgia in 1735, they had a strong influence on John Wesley (1703–1791), who was also bound for the same destination to minister among the colonists and Native Americans. What was begun in Wesley's heart on the way to the new world continued when he returned to England and shortly thereafter: As Wesley was listening to a reading of Luther's preface to the book of Romans, a moving sense of joy of God's Spirit flooded his heart. The Moravians' example and Luther's words accomplished a work of renewal in John Wesley. And through his preaching, and the hymns of his brother Charles Wesley (1707–1788), revival swept England in the 1700s, turning that country away from a devastating revolution that France experienced at the end of the century.

Renewal in America

The renewal in England spilled over into the American colonies. John Wesley sent Francis Asbury (1745–1816) to labor there, while George Whitefield (1714–1770) made eleven trips to America where, in a widespread ministry, thousands hung on his words. Meanwhile, God also raised up men in America to stir the believers. The work of Jonathan Edwards (1703–1758) began with spiritual renewal when he preached a series of sermons that eventually resulted in an awakening, beginning in 1740 in New England. One of his sermons was the well-known "Sinners in the Hands of an Angry God." But many of his other messages also were empowered by God.

God also used Edwards' grandson, Timothy Dwight (1752–1817), president of Yale, in the renewal that broke out on that campus in the early 1800s. But this was only the beginning of a series of revival movements in the new country. West of the Alleghenies were the "Cane Ridge" renewals (1801) as well as the renewals of the 1830s in the eastern states and in the Appalachian country of Kentucky and Tennessee. And we must not overlook the work of Charles Finney (1792–1875) in Ohio and New York, particularly from 1832 onward. All had their effect on the young republic of the United States. After Finney, the spiritual climate began to wane, but once more a new renewal broke out in 1858, sweeping every state. J. Edwin Orr commented on this movement that at least a "million converts [came into the] church, accomplishing untold good."[65]

Revival and Social Action

Often, secular interests are prone to think that movements of spiritual renewal are only fanatical religious outbursts that make no contribution to society in general. Timothy Smith has documented the powerful influence for social uplift following the American renewal from 1800–1830s:

What happened was that the American Christians had created a new pattern of church-state relations unknown since the first century. It was called the "voluntary system," to distinguish it from the state-church tradition in Europe. Thoughtful visitors from the Old World expressed amazement at its success. Alexis de Tocqueville pointed out in 1833 that the efforts American clergymen made to avoid political strife actually increased their hold upon society. Religion, he said, regulated the community through its power over manners and morals. It was, therefore, "the foremost of the political institutions of the country." Tocqueville noted that citizens of all classes and shades of political opinion held Christianity to be indispensable to the maintenance of republican government.[66]

Smith's assessment was not limited to the nineteenth century context; renewal movements always affect social uplift.

Revival and Evangelism in Many Areas

Shortly after the American renewal in 1858 and 1859, the British Isles experienced another awakening, which swept Ulster in Northern Ireland, Scotland, Wales, and England, revitalizing believers and bringing thousands into the congregations as new believers. Orr said this movement brought "a million accessions to the evangelical churches."[67] Furthermore, as a result of this movement, believers became interested in Scripture distribution, welfare of slum children, establishing orphanages, evangelizing children, establishing the Young Men's Christian Association in the United States, the Temperance movement, and a host of other religious and social concerns.[68] In fact, the renewal in England became the answer to Marx's economic and political proposals as expounded in his *Das Kapital* in 1859. When people's hearts were changed upon becoming believers, the societal structure was turned around for the good, and there was no need in England for any social revolution as envisioned by Marx.

God's work in the United States in 1858 became the springboard for the evangelistic ministry of D.L. Moody (1837–1899) in the latter part of the 1800s.[69] He called for "the evangelization of the world in this generation." His ministry stirred up believers who in turn reached out to those who had no belief, affecting the lives of many, not only in the United States, but also in Great Britain. God worked auspiciously, providing Moody and Sankey (his musical associate) with great "victories in Edinburgh and Glasgow." When "they invaded London for a four-month period, total attendance at their meetings reached more than 2.5 million."[70]

Moody's work greatly contributed to strengthening existing evangelical societies, as well as formation of new ones. The outreach of the YMCA was revitalized and had a significant impression on students in America's colleges and universities, as many came to the Lord. Moody's ministries also touched lives in Great Britain, which in turn led some to become involved in missions. Two well-remembered leaders, Charles T. Studd and Stanley Smith, were led to go to China, along with five others, serving with the China Inland Mission. When Mr. & Mrs. Studd became ill, they returned to England; but as they recovered, Mr. Studd was invited to the United States to minister to university students who in turn answered the call to the mission field. Out of this effort came the Student Volunteer Movement.[71] When Studd returned to England, he founded the "Heart of Africa Mission," and even went to Africa to serve there. Later this mission became the Worldwide Evangelization Crusade. Spiritual renewal always will have an impact in various ways to touch the needs of men and women.

Once more, God worked in spiritual renewal, this time in Wales when, beginning in 1905, believers' hearts were warmed in their devotional singing. As a result, the Spirit began to move throughout the entire countryside as believers shared with those who did not know the Lord. Entire communities were transformed as people found the Lord. This movement went on to have a widespread effect over the next several decades in Great Britain and in North America.

Spiritual renewals did not cease as the century wore on. There was the revival in the Hebrides Islands in 1949, the mid-twentieth century renewals in the colleges and seminaries in the United States, the movement in Indonesia during the latter 1960s, and then the Asbury College renewal among the students in 1970 in Wilmore, Kentucky. And, ever since the opening of what was once the Soviet Union, great numbers of people also have come to the Lord, including many Jewish people.

But the question today on the hearts of many believers is, *Are we ready for a widespread renewal once more in North America and Europe?*

The Need Today

When does spiritual renewal come? Under what conditions does it take place? From the previous overview, it appears to occur in times of moral declension and breakdown. When crises come to plague a society in the political, social, educational, and economic spheres, many times God steps in and turns around the society. Usually, he begins to burden a few of the believers within the body of Messiah to pray for an awakening, and then it spreads to touch the hearts of other believers.

An Assessment from a Secular Source

The editors of *Time* magazine saw fit to devote an entire lengthy issue to "Special Project, American Renewal," in its February 23, 1981 issue. Henry Grunwald, Editor and Chief, in the opening statement, declared:

> The belief in an even better tomorrow, the conviction that obstacles exist to be overcome in that the U.S. has a strong and beneficial role to play in the world, these constitute the American secular religion. For sometime now,

that religion has been corroded by doubt. Intractable inflation seems to have turned a good life into a treadmill and has shaken our confidence in the future—America's last frontier. Our industry appears to have lost its productive magic, its daring, and sometimes even its competence. Our government is intrusive, inept—and expensive. Our democracy too often produces only mediocrity deadlock. (Page 34)

Grunwald further agonized in his perception over a number of other ills in America in the early 1980s, putting his finger on areas of specific importance:

We face a crisis of moral responsibility . . . Many people are either unwilling to take up their responsibility or unable to discern what they are. Our society as a whole is not only without an effective religious ethic: Its codes of secular morality are also in tatters. It is hard to imagine a plan of action, a practical program, for a moral revival. We can preach and listen to preachers, we can try to do good ourselves and organize good works; we can, and should, re-examine the philosophical source of our laxness. But in the end, we will undoubtedly find that a resurgence of values will not be brought about by moralizing vigilantes, by legislation, or constitutional amendment. A respect for authority, a sense of duty and a degree of self-restraint—these will never be restored in a society that has slipped too far. (Page 35)

Mr. Grunwald was somewhat pessimistic, although he did have hope the "great reservoirs of sound moral strength" would be restored as people make right decisions. But it is interesting that even the spokesman of a secular magazine put his finger on what was wrong in the late 1970s and early 1980s.

With the heightened presence of the evangelical, *Time* magazine's September 2, 1985 issue, in a section titled "Thunder on the Right," again addressed the issue of spiritual renewal. Richard N. Ostling, *Time*'s religion editor, wrote the article in which he offered a number of penetrating observations on "Jerry Falwell's Crusade." Here are some of those conclusions:

1. Fundamentalist preachers used to denounce evil and insisted upon strict isolation from the world, but nowadays there is a "stern call to social action."
2. "Protestant fundamentalism has become a powerful, confident, and important force. Properly associated with stern opposition to such personal 'sins' as drinking, smoking, and gambling, Fundamentalism draws on the entire heritage of American revivalism, with its code of personal piety and insistence upon conscious commitment to Yeshua the Messiah as one's 'personal Savior.'"
3. "The opinions of the religious right are shared by large numbers of people who do not belong to the fundamentalist churches. Philip Hammond, sociologist at the University of California at Santa Barbara declares that people of all stripes now agree with the emphasis by the fundamentalists that many are concerned by the more than 16 million abortions performed since 1973, a four-fold increase of children raised by unwed mothers since 1970, the rise in drug use, and the emergence of gay liberation, and the glamorization of promiscuity."

Whereas many citations by various religious leaders in the article demonstrate questionable areas of fundamentalists, one wonders concerning the future influence of born-again believers upon their society. While historian Martin Marty says that conservatives have established themselves as an interest group that is firmly "rooted in American culture," he feels that it is only one interest among many. Norman Geisler wrote, "The conservative Protestant effort has barely begun [and he] foresees growing bonds between the fundamentalists and the large evangelical movement: 'as soon as the evangelical and fundamentalists learn how the system works, and they are learning now, they will be a very, very powerful force—if they maintain their coalition.'"[72]

A Fervent Hope by Genuine Believers

In the above article, many put their fingers on the ills of society in 1985. What about now, a number of years later, when, in some ways, the needs are even greater? We can only hope that with the rise to prominence of those who are preaching God's Word, calling for renewal among believers and pointing out society's ills—as did many an Old Testament prophet—a general spiritual renewal could begin among believers. I pray this renewal will have an impact on people in desperate need, which in turn will have wide-ranging effects throughout society.

The only way America ever will have a renewal is when God's Spirit strikes at the basic bedrock of need. When a sufficient number of unbelievers come to the Lord, America can once more be responsible in its moral and spiritual leadership, and that spiritual turnaround will have an effect on its political, economic, and social foundations.

An Observation of Today's Revival Movement

Do any sincere believers not wish to see a real movement of God today among their congregations? Some revivals have come to churches, which in turn have acted as a magnet to others. Again, while our assessment is not exhaustive, the question is asked if such a revival is in the making in this situation.

> In Toronto, a congregation nestled among airport hotels becomes a jet-age version of the frontier camp

meetings, drawing its attendance not just from the next county, but from other continents. Are events like these the overture to another great awakening—or even just a small one?[73]

There is reason to believe that the beginning of the revival had a good impact on believers there, and many came to be touched by the strong presence of the Spirit at work in the congregation. But as the revival went on, some believers have been disturbed by the phenomena of uncontrolled laughter, people barking like dogs, roaring like lions, groveling on the floor, and other strange phenomena. Some have defended this human response, indicating it is a part of the work of the Spirit in the revival movement.

From a study of the revivals in the history of Israel and Judah, we see that no such phenomena ever were recorded. Jonathan Edwards believed that "injecting spurious and disfiguring elements into a revival is a main part of demonic strategy." He would certainly have agreed with J. Edwin Orr that in any awakening, "the first to wake up is the Devil."[74] This is certainly not to say that the movement in Toronto, or elsewhere today, is demonic. It is just that one needs to be careful to question certain elements that will appear in a renewal—elements that detract from the main emphasis of the Holy Spirit's work.

Lovelace cites Jonathan Edwards again on what would be part of a genuine movement for God:

> For Edwards, the primary human catalyst for revival was always dependent on prayer. . . . For Edwards, as for Calvin, conviction of sin was the usual result of an awakening encounter with God. . . . Edwards' concern would be to verify that the experience involved real illumination and transformation of the heart, with lasting fruit in Christian faith and life, and not just transient bodily effects. . . .[75]

Lovelace comments concerning the frontier revivals in the United States in the early 1800s, when "converts were seized with contagious behavior, jerking involuntarily and barking like dogs. Peter Cartwright encouraged the phenomena as an aid to humility, but others felt that the revival was being disfigured by these elements. . . ." One Baptist minister "who was preaching when one of the jerkers began his motions made a pause, and in a loud and solemn tone said, 'In the name of the Lord, I command all unclean spirits to leave this place.' The jerker immediately became still."[76] The point is that Satan would dearly love to destroy a genuine revival, making believers look "weird" and, therefore, repulsive to unbelievers. In conclusion, as Lovelace cites Edwards once more regarding genuine spiritual renewal, "His own approach to the Great Awakening was to subject it to the most rigorous critique, on the one hand, and to solicit extraordinary prayer for its advancement, on the other. These are the strategies we need to follow today."[77]

Having made all these assessments, my deep desire is that believers experience a genuine awakening that will result in an evangelistic outreach among unbelievers, so that they too can come to the Lord, and that there can be a change in the moral and social fabric of our society.

CHAPTER TWELVE

The Coming Return of Israel to the Lord God

"Afterwards, the people of Isra'el will repent and seek ADONAI their God and David their king; they will come trembling to ADONAI and his goodness in the *acharit-hayamim* [last days]."

(Hos. 3:5)

"[A]nd I will pour out on the house of David and on those living in Yerushalayim a spirit of grace and prayer; and they will look to me, whom they pierced. They will mourn for as one who mourns for an only son; they will be in bitterness on his behalf like the bitterness for a firstborn son."

(Zech. 12:10)

"Then they will know that I am ADONAI their God, since it was I who caused them to go into exile among the nations, and it was I who regathered them to their own land. I will leave none of them any more, and I will no longer hide my face from them, for I have poured out my Spirit on the house of Isra'el,' says ADONAI Elohim [the LORD God]."

(Ezek. 39:28, 29)

The subject of how God will regather his people from a worldwide exile and bring them back to the ancient homeland is fascinating, and has engaged the interest of great scholars as they endeavor to understand Messianic prophecy. Tragically, however, most within professing Christendom do not believe in the recovery of Israel. The Church is seen as the "New

Israel," with all the promises stated by the prophets concerning Israel to be experienced by the Church. And while Jewish people may be kept as a distinct body of people, the only hope open to individuals among this body is to receive Jesus as the Messiah and find their all in all in him and with God's people in the Church. No hope is seen existing for Jewish people as a body to be regathered again in the ancient homeland. These ideas have been formulated into creeds and doctrines that proclaim the beliefs of most within Christendom.

A few non-Jewish scholars, who are believers, however, seek to soften this harsh stance. These people see Israel kept as a distinct body; and in the days just prior to Messiah's return for his body, God will pour out his Spirit on Israel. As a result, more and more among the nation will come to faith, culminating—immediately before Messiah's return—in the response by the entire body of Jewish people. So stated John Murray who for years was professor of systematic theology at Westminster Theological Seminary in Philadelphia, which holds a Reform theological position. For example, Murray noted, after answering a number of objections that only a remnant of Israel will be saved:

> If we keep in mind the theme of this chapter (that is, Romans chapter 11) and the sustained emphasis on the restoration of Israel, there is no other alternative than to conclude that the proposition, "all Israel shall be saved," is to be interpreted in terms of the fullness, the receiving, the engrafting of Israel as a people, the restoration of Israel to gospel favour and blessing and the correlative turning of Israel from unbelief to faith and repentance . . . in a word, it is the salvation of the mass of Israel that the apostle affirms.[78]

At least Murray is sensitive to Paul's proclamation that "all Isra'el will be saved" when "Out of Tziyon [Zion] will come the Redeemer" (Rom. 11:26) is a literal reference to Israel as the special people whom God wants to reach corporately. Such observations are few and far between.

Most within Christendom do not regard the State of Israel as any fulfillment of prophecy. According to this thinking, the project of founding the state by a group of Jewish people in 1948 represents the culmination of an interesting notion. And few would want to see these Jewish people harmed in any way. But it has also raised many problems.

1. How can Jewish and Arab peoples live in peace in the same land?
2. What is the solution to the question of property rights of land once owned by Arab peoples and similarly for Jewish people who have been evicted from their lands in Arab countries?
3. Who has what rights to Jerusalem—a prize claimed by both peoples? (Especially important is that part of the old city containing places of worship common to the three religions of Judaism, Christianity, and Islam.)

Some Christians actually see the creation of the state of Israel as some sort of a fluke of history![79]

It is not my intention to enter into a detailed reply to those who do not see the present state of Israel as anything other than an interesting set of historical circumstances. This book is meant to look at how God has chosen to reach his people. I believe, however, that the greatest outreach will yet occur among the people of Israel in its land when Yeshua the Messiah will come to redeem them and then commence the Kingdom of peace as envisioned by the prophets. Many religious Jewish people acknowledge this truth, and many non-Jewish believers today likewise give credence to this prophetic proclamation.

Israel Dispersed

Hosea was the last prophet to the Northern Kingdom, and it was his task to announce the nation's bleak future:

> "For the people of Isra'el are going to be in seclusion for a long time without a king, prince, sacrifice, standing-stone, ritual vest or household gods."
> (Hos. 3:4)

For many days, the nation of the north would have no king to rule over it, no sacrifice permitted in its worship of the idols. Neither would it have a priest to function for it, using either the legitimate ephod garment or the clothes of a false priest offering sacrifices to false gods. Israel ceased to be a political entity in 721 B.C.E.

The same would be true for Judah in the south, although Judah continued for another 130 years. Eventually, Judah's worship ended in idolatry, its prophets and priests turned away from God, and, in 586 B.C.E., it too ceased to be an organized nation. Because of the curse on the line of Solomon, when Judah returned from the Babylonian exile it had no king to rule over it (see Jer. 22:28, 30). Judah was permitted a Second Temple with bona fide priests, but eventually, because of the tragic impasse between Yeshua and the Sanhedrin (see Matt. 26:64, 65) as well as the ill-advised revolt by the Zealots, the Second Temple was destroyed in 70 C.E. What Hosea said of the Northern Kingdom also came true for all the people of Israel. From 70 C.E. onward, no king has ruled over Israel, no altar for sacrifice exists because Israel has no Temple, and no priest of Zadok, wearing the ephod, can minister at a bona fide altar.

The dispersion from the land of Israel did not occur all at once. Some Jewish people may have left after 70 C.E., but the great majority of the people remained in the land. The second revolt in 132–135 C.E. proved to be disastrous. The Romans were so infuriated they attacked Judea again; the Jewish people who were crucified numbered in the hundreds of thousands. Emperor Hadrian ordered Jerusalem ploughed up and a Roman city built on top of the ruins, calling it Aelia Capitolina. He also renamed the land of Judea the land of Philistia, from which is derived the word Palestine. Many more Jewish people also began to disperse throughout the Roman Empire at that time.

The final blow came with the Arab invasion in the early 630s C.E., which then led to a full Arabization of the land. As a result, most Jewish people left for other countries, and the population in the land reached its lowest in history. However, a few Jewish families remained across the centuries; and at times, Jewish people moved back to the land, as in the 1200s, when a number of synagogues were built, and also in the 1400–1600s with the presence of the Messianic visionaries in Tz'fat (Safed). But, by and large, the population in the homeland was low, and in the 1880s, when the modern return to the land began, it numbered only 25,000 Jewish people.

Some Facets of Israel's Recovery[80]

The 1800s were a turning point in God's purposes for his people Israel. The difficulty in trying to see 1948 as a fulfillment to prophecy is that so few paid attention to how God was working quietly in history all across the 1800s to bring about the formation of the state in the following century.

Some important points to consider

1. The Suez Canal was opened in 1868, once more focusing Europe's attention on the Middle East.
2. The populist movements began in Europe, in which the common people wanted more say in their country's destiny. Many Jewish people in various countries were caught up with these interests, but other Jewish people began to

think among themselves that they too wanted a say in their destiny, but that it should be *in their ancient homeland.*

3. The *pogroms* (persecutions) of Jewish people in Eastern European countries forced many to move to escape their miserable lot. In particular, some two million left Russia for the United States between 1880 and 1914. However, some Jewish people said that if they had to move, then why not to the land of Israel.

4. Of the greatest interest was the appearance of essays by various Jewish writers of many backgrounds, starting in 1843 with Yehudah Alkalai and culminating in 1896 with Herzl's essay, "The Jewish State." These writers expressed their dreams of a resettlement of the land of Israel from various points of view, religious and secular, and their topics primarily focused on a call for an emigration to the homeland, citing specific reasons for doing so. One can almost say this was a movement of the Spirit, even though the writers themselves were not all religious.

The Emigration Waves

Beginning with the 1860s and 1870s, small groups of Jewish people began their return to the land, but, officially, the first emigration wave started in the 1880s. Then, Herzl's call at the yearly Zionist congress meetings, beginning 1897, was responsible for the second wave, from 1904 to 1914, and plans for the future of the movement. After World War I, three more waves took place, until 1936. Sporadic moves still came until the beginning of World War II, when emigration ceased until after the war. The death of six million Jewish people in the Holocaust also had a decisive bearing on the necessity of a homeland for the remainder of these people.

Following World War II, most of the several hundreds of thousands of Jewish people who remained in Europe wanted to go to Israel, and some managed to get there as illegal emigrants, in spite of the British resistance.[81] Finally, the United

Nations partitioned the land in November 1947, giving part of it to the Jewish people and the other part to the Arab Palestinians, to become effective on May 15, 1948. Through this partition, Jews could move back to the homeland freely. The Israeli Jews accepted the partition; the Arabs did not, and the rest is now history.

When Israel began as a state in May 1948, 600,000 Jewish people were citizens in their own country. It is not so much the date, but the question that needs to be addressed: How did these Jewish people get to Israel? One has to recognize the inescapable fact that God had worked quietly in history for almost eighty years to bring about the fulfillment of his purposes that enabled his people to return to the land.

But this was not to be the end of emigration to the land of Israel. Within three years of statehood, the 600,000 became the hosts to twice their number as more than a million Jewish people returned home from Europe, North Africa, Yemen, Iraq, Iran, and other places. Then the emigration slacked off. But the Six-Day war in 1967 prompted Russian Jews, so that between 1967–74, about 100,000 of them emigrated to the land.[82] About 50,000 North American Jews went to Israel as well. But by 1974, the movement of Russian Jews had slowed.

From 1974 on, Jewish people came mostly in trickles: A good movement of Ethiopian Jews came for a time in the 1980s, but by 1990, when the Soviet government collapsed, the emigration picked up considerably as some 500,000 Jewish people came from the former Soviet Union. The rest of the Ethiopian Jews were brought home as well. While the volume of Soviet Jews has died down, a considerable movement still arrives. As of this writing, Israel has a population of 4.8 million people; that is more than the combined Jewish population of New York and its suburbs. And, if the movement continues as it is today from Russia, Ukraine, and other republics, then within the next twenty years, Israel will have the major portion of world Jewry—more than the United States, with its 5.5 million Jewish people! And all this occurred within the space of 120 to 130 years, after the immigration started in the 1870s and 1880s, when only 25,000 Jewish people were in the land.

But this is exactly what the prophet had predicted: "Afterward the Israelites will return . . ." (Hosea 3:5a, NIV). What does "afterward" refer to if not the "many days" of vs. 4, already noted? God had something in mind when he promised, not only to this one but other prophets as well,[83] to bring his people home again. This is not a mere fluke of history; it is his careful design to recover his people from a worldwide dispersion. Not only is he moving his people into the homeland, but he also desires to enter into a new relationship with them, a topic that will be our next consideration.

Trials and Hardships

The Outreach Today

We would be wrong to assume that all the people of the modern state of Israel are believers. Israel is a democratic state, much like many countries of the west. Sixty-five percent of the Jewish people there are secular, and twenty-five percent are religious. The balance includes Christians and variety of other beliefs.

Most who believe in the prophecies about Israel's response to God and his Messiah assert that at some time in the future—some say soon—Israel will be "born again," when the Messiah returns to earth. This is a biblical truth, yet the question persists: What is God doing in the interim to reach his people? The answer provides some interesting dimensions regarding Israel.

The Tanakh in the schools—During the War of Independence, in October 1948, educators sat down to discuss the curriculum of the schools for the new state of Israel. The item considered to be of most importance was that the Bible (the Tanakh) must be a specialized study in the schools, from the first to the twelfth grades. Even though some of the these educators were secular, each one, religious and secular, recognized that in order to know the historical and cultural background of Jewish people from their beginnings, the Bible is the only and best textbook.

So, from childhood to late teens, students must study the Bible in class. In the early years, the children learn about the heroes of the Bible, in the middle school years students can roam the countryside and many times stand on the very sites they read about. (As I viewed these classes, at times I have felt that God was marching his people around the land, getting his Word down into their hearts.) Finally, in their senior years, students are exposed to the moral system of Moses and its implications as well as what the prophets have to say. This study of the Bible is the first objective to make the people of Israel biblically conscious, and even though many end up as secular people, it is easy at times when speaking with them, to stir their memories about what they once had studied.

The New Testament as a textbook—Surprising as it may seem, all or parts of the New Testament, depending on the class, also are within the curriculum of study in the universities. Many Christians have commented that if Jewish people do not accept Yeshua, then why do they read about him? But to live in Israel and ignore Yeshua is impossible. In such a small country, one cannot avoid his presence. After all, he was born in Bethlehem, a scant four miles south of Jerusalem, grew up and lived most of his life in Nazareth, the last three and half years of his life had a ministry across the country, finally dying just outside of Jerusalem.

He also was resurrected within this land and ascended from it as well. To pretend he does not exist or that he is of no consequence in the land of Israel is preposterous. Besides,

Israelis don't stick their heads in the sands like ostriches on this issue; they must reckon with him as a part of Israel.

So, many students take courses in the New Testament. Obviously, the issue of Yeshua's deity is sidestepped, or even denied, but what is most important is that these students are being exposed to what the text itself has to say concerning Yeshua. Other students take courses in art, history of the end of the Second Temple period, literature of the period, and so on, all of which requires some knowledge of the New Testament. They are encouraged to buy Hebrew New Testaments, many times by going to the Bible shops. For whatever reason, students become acquainted with what the New Testament says.

The presence of Messianic congregations—At least fifty-seven Messianic congregations exist in Israel today, comprised for the most part of Jewish believers in Yeshua. This does not take into account Jewish believers in the denominational churches, the Baptists, Anglicans, and Lutherans, as well as smaller apartment prayer groups or various cell groups. As to how many believers are present among the Israeli population is a figure hard to determine. It is possible to count all the people attending all the groups—some 3,000 to 4,000. But there may be more. In my thirty years of traveling through Israel I have met many silent believers who are not attached to any congregation. I have conducted cell Bible classes that exist off by themselves, not associated with other believers. There may be as many as 7,000 believers in Yeshua the Messiah in Israel.

The point, however, is not to debate how many believers are present, or how many congregations exist in the land. One is enough to set many people on edge. However, seekers exist among the young population, and they are attracted to and interested in the witness concerning Yeshua the Messiah.

The Presence of books and materials concerning Yeshua—Two Messianic publishing firms in Israel publish books to attract the interest of Israelis. Within the last few years, it has become possible to advertise the presence of these books in the Hebrew newspapers and, as a result, Israelis have written and asked for them. Most of the books treat human interests, yet the authors indicate that biblical principles are the answers to life's problems. The publishers have been carrying on literature evangelism and as a result, some readers become interested in the claims of Yeshua, and have come to faith because of the truth that they read. To reach people, we need literature, and it is present today as one of the factors to engage the interests of Jewish people.

So, slowly but surely, the numbers of Messianic Jewish people are growing today, exactly as the prophet had predicted: "Afterwards, the people of Isra'el will repent and seek ADONAI their God and David their king; they will come trembling to ADONAI and his goodness in the *acharit-hayamim*" (Hos. 3:5).

But we still do not see multitudes of Israelis who profess any belief in the Bible as God's Word, even though many have studied it. What will it take to move an entire nation to finally recognize the Lord God as totally sovereign and to recognize his Messiah, Yeshua?

Israel's Coming Horror

How can we Messianic Jews speak of severe hardships yet to come on the people Israel? Have we not suffered enough already? The land of Israel was occupied so many times in the past, by the Assyrians, the Babylonians, the Greeks, the Egyptians, the Syrians, the Romans, the Byzantine who controlled the land from the 300s until the Arabs came in the early 600s, the Arabs, "Christian" crusaders, the Mameluke Egyptians who threw out the Christians, the Turkish army, and the British. And, if we throw in the suffering of Jewish people in Europe under the Crusaders, and then the expulsions, the pogroms in Eastern Europe, the degrading ghetto life, culminating in the Holocaust when six million died, it all seems too much even to contemplate any future horror.

So, how in the world can one speak of a future suffering in the land, and even capture of the land by invading troops? The modern land of Israel was supposed to provide the peace and quiet that Jewish people longed for in having their own homeland. But, we must be in harmony with what God's Word declares, even though it might mean we will be out of step with the hopes and aspirations of our own people. ADONAI will prevail. It will be under the pressure of an invasion by many nations at the end of this age (Zech. 12:14) that will finally bring an entire generation of Israelis to call upon ADONAI for help. He will then send Yeshua the Messiah with the armies of heaven to annihilate the invaders and only then will an entire nation recognize that Yeshua is indeed who he claimed to be all along in the days of his flesh (Zech. 12:10). Only then, finally will Israel be able to enjoy God's Messianic kingdom.

CHAPTER THIRTEEN

Conclusion
The Encouragement to Reach Out

The body of Messiah faces four powerful enemies that are damaging to her calling.

1. *Materialism*, which denies the supernatural and concentrates its entire interest on the physical or material conditions of human life. While many believers in the West would not call themselves materialists, we love and revel in the comforts materialism affords.
2. *Criticism*, which is an attack on the basic beliefs God's people hold dear. The proponents of criticism are very clever with their analyses, as they rip biblical beliefs into shreds. In particular, the belief in the inerrancy of God's Word is held in question. When we are unsure of what is inerrant, we lose the foundation on which genuine faith can rest. If we are unclear over the authority of God's Word, what then are we going to share with a pagan world?
3. *Humanism*, in which man is his own captain and the center of the universe. No matter whether humanism is optimistic or destructive, it is hostile to any claim for the transcendent God who alone is sovereign. Man needs a power over, beyond, and above himself—a power who alone can relate to his needs. When believers are filled with the sovereign Holy Spirit, they have the power to reach out and see the change among those who respond to the gospel message.
4. *Satisfaction of the sensual*: Many seek comfort in alcohol, drugs, and immorality; but these are only substitutes for genuine satisfaction, which God alone can offer. The

pleasures of satisfying the sensual can be enjoyed, but only for the moment; in the end, a person will be left more frustrated than ever, and with an empty heart. The body of Messiah has to vigorously press its message of salvation as the only means by which men and women can find meaning to life.

To all of these opponents, there is but one reply: Genuine believers who make up the body of Messiah cannot be compressed into a system, or a form of worship. The only power God gives us is the fullness of the Holy Spirit who can work through renewed believers, regardless of the denomination or group. Believers must reach out to unbelievers in their needs. When the Holy Spirit can work freely in and through dedicated believers, he will satisfy the hunger in men's beings and enable people to be fulfilled.

We are glad for the signs we see in our generation: Jewish and non-Jewish believers are being renewed and are getting involved in outreach to unbelievers who are coming to the Lord today in great numbers. But many yet remain to be reached: alcoholics; people trapped in drugs; young people caught up in permissive sex and suffering from the resultant diseases, including AIDS; street people and the lonely and dispossessed. Broken-hearted people, and those with wrecked marriages; single parents, trying to raise their children; materialists who choke with dissatisfaction on their gadgets; and the many others desperately need an intimate relationship with Yeshua the Messiah. Believers will have to give up our satisfied pet practices that pass for belief in the Messiah. Furthermore, we must root out the smug legalism with which we close ourselves off from our neighbors' needs. When the Holy Spirit is free to act through consecrated believers, unbelievers will accept our testimony and will respond to Yeshua as the Redeemer and realize their fullness in him.

May God graciously work in each of our hearts; may he create in our hearts the desperate hunger for more of his Spirit. May he be pleased, after renewal, to urge and use us to reach others. May he renew our congregations with an outpouring of his Spirit, whereby thousands in our nation can be brought to faith.

"Won't you revive us again,
so your people can rejoice in you?"
(Ps. 85:6)

Endnotes

Chapter One

1 Moishe Rosen, "Revival is the Ronngh Word," *Jews for Jesus Newsletter*, Volume 2:5743, page 1.

2 Philip R. Newell, *Revival on God's Terms* (Chicago: Moody Press, 1959), page 4.

3 Hebrew and English Lexicon of the Old Testament, F. Brown, S.R. Driver, & C. Briggs, eds. (London: Oxford University Press, 1968), pages 996–1,000.

4 Newell, *Op. Cit.*, page 5.

5 Charles Finney, *Revival Lectures* (New York: Fleming Revell, 1868), page 23.

6 Lewis A. Drummond, *Op. Cit.*, page 118.

7 Newell, *Op. Cit.*, page 2.

8 Louis Goldberg, *Bible Study Commentary, Leviticus* (Grand Rapids: Zondervan, 1980), pages 26–33.

Chapter Two

9 Edwin Thiele, *The Mysterious Numbers of the Hebrew Kings* (Grand Rapids: Eerdmans, 1965, rev. ed., page 53, points out that the year 931 B.C.E., when Rehoboam came to Israel's throne, is a secured date. That would have been the year Solomon died. Since he reigned forty years, his reign, therefore, began in 971 B.C.E. The dating of the exodus in 1447 B.C.E. represents the early date of the Exodus; other scholars opt for a later date, see Chapter 1, footnotes 7,8, page 13.

10 Leon Wood, *A Survey of Israel's History* (Grand Rapids: Zondervan Publishing House, 1970), p. 147.

11 Edwin Thiele, *Op. Cit.*, pages 54, 55, calculated the Exodus date on the basis of Solomon's death and the rupture of the kingdom at 931 B.C.E., which is a fixed date, then going back some forty years to when he became king. With this date of 971 B.C.E., and with the commencement of the building of the Temple in 967 B.C.E. (see 1 Kings

6:1) the record sets the Exodus at 480 years prior to the commencement of building the first temple, that is, 1447 B.C.E. Moses lived to be 120 years old (see Deut. 34:7). He was forty years old when he visited his brethren while he was a part of the Egyptian royal court. At that time he also had to run into the desert in order save his life (see Acts 7:23) and he then spent forty years in the desert, at which time God called him to go and deliver Israel from Egypt (see Acts 7:30). That would mean he was eighty years old, in 1447 B.C.E., when called to the greatest task of his life—a task that took forty years to lead Israel to the east bank of the Jordan (see Deut. 1:3). If he was eighty years old in 1447 B.C.E., he was then born in 1527 B.C.E., soon after the beginning of Egypt's 18th dynasty.

12 I opt for the early date for the Exodus, following the views of conservative scholars, for example, Samuel Schultz, *The Old Testament Speaks* (San Francisco: Harper & Row, 1980), page 49. Many archeologists and more critical scholars take the view that Israel left Egypt during the 19th dynasty, about 1230 B.C.E. Some conservatives also hold to this view, for example, R.K. Harrison, *Introduction to the Old Testament* (Grand Rapids: Eerdmans, 1969), page 177.

13 Alexander Whyte, *Bible Characters: The Old Testament, Vol. 1* (Grand Rapids: Zondervan Publishing House, 1952 reprint), page 139.

Chapter Three

14 For a further study of the period of the judges, consult Abraham Malamat, "The Period of the Judges," in The World History of the Jewish People, III (New Brunswick: Rutgers University Press, 1971), pp. 129–163; John L. McKenzie, The World of the Judges (Englewood Cliffs: Prentice-Hall, 1966); Leon Morris, Judges and Ruth (Downers Grove: InterVarsity Press, 1968); Leon J.

Wood, Distressing Days of the Judges (Grand Rapids: Zondervan, 1975).

15 What is interesting is that the same word, heavenly realms, *epouraniois*, is also in Ephesians 6:12, where, as the believers reach out for these spiritual blessings, Satan's spiritual forces are also present, ready for a battle. That is why Rav Sha'ul (Paul) reminded believers to put on all of the spiritual armor to withstand these evil forces (Ephesians 6:13–18).

16 *Sukkah* 4:9 in *The Tosefta, An Introduction*, eds. Jacob Neusner, Green, James Strange, David H. Fashing, Sara Mandell (Atlanta, GA: Univ. of South Florida, 1992), pages 356, 357, which provides detailed information on obtaining the water everyday, and then the special last day, and it was poured out at the altar, along with the wine.

17 Alfred Edersheim, *The Temple: Its Ministries and Services* (Hendrickson Publishers, updated and repr. 1994), pages 220–223. On the last day, the great day of the Feast, after the water and wine were poured out, they sang the Hallel Psalms (Pss. 113–118) and when they came to Ps. 118, the words for Ps. 118:1, "Give Thanks," and Ps. 118:25, "O Lord, do save," all had reference to the salvation the Messiah can bring.

18 Goldman, Samuel, *Hebrew Text and English Translation and Commentary* (London: Soncino Press, 1951), Page 37, who suggests this act as representative of "repentant, contrition . . . or humility." While all of these facets are a part of what was taking place among the people of Israel, dedication of life as representative of pouring out one's life was also an important dimension.

19 Edersheim, *Op. Cit.*, pages 221 (footnote 4), 222, 223. One of the views of the ceremony of water pouring, especially on the last day, was its derivation from Isa. 12:3. No wonder with this emphasis and the singing of Ps. 118:25, Yeshua's cry was certainly an emphasis on salvation and he is the source of it.

20 John Rea, "Fast, Fasting," in *Wycliffe Bible Encyclopedia Vol. 1*, C.F. Pfeiffer, Howard F. Vos, & John Rea, eds. (Chicago: Moody Press, 1975), pages 593, 595.

Chapter Four

21 Leon Wood, *A Survey of Israel's History* (Grand Rapids; Zondervan Publishing House, 1970), pages 341, 342.

22 Edwin Thiele, *The Mysterious Numbers of the Hebrew Kings*, p. 55.

23 The biblical record recounts a number of military encounters between Syria and Israel where thousands of men from both sides died in the fields of battle. And, some of the animosity of Syria exists to this day for the modern state of Israel.

Chapter Five

24 This matter of naming individuals before they even appear on the historical scene is not without precedent. At about 700 B.C.E., Isaiah named the one who would deliver Israel from exile, which occurred with the conquest of Babylon by the Persian king, Cyrus (44:28; 45:1), and Judah could then return to its homeland in 538 B.C.E. Many critics will call this naming of these individuals after the historical fact; in other words, the biblical writers were only writing history. But when we believe in the omniscience of God and his ability to communicate some of what he already knows beforehand, why should this phenomena be considered impossible?

25 Alexander Whyte, *Bible Characters, The Old Testament* (Grand Rapids: Zondervan, reprint 1952), p. 363.

26 Leon Wood, *A Survey of Israel's History* (Grand Rapids: Zondervan Publishing House, 1970), page 313.

27 Ernest Gordon, *Through the Valley of the Kwai*, (New York: Harper, 1962), pp. 213, 214.

Chapter Six

28 B. Pritchard, ed., The Ancient Near East, Vol. 1 (Princeton University Press, 1958), page 191.

29 A. Helmbold, "Jonah, Book of" refers to a legend that "he was the son of the widow of Zarephath, and was the youth whom Elisha sent to anoint Jehu to be the king of Israel" but he states that this is "historically unacceptable," in *The Zondervan Pictorial Encyclopedia of the Bible Vol. 3*, Merrill C. Tenney, gen. ed. (Grand Rapids: Zondervan, 1975), page 675.

30 Upon comparing the accounts in Genesis 11:31; 12:1; and Acts 7:2–4, it would appear that the first call to Abraham occurred in Ur in Mesopotamia. But after Abraham's father, Terah, died in Haran, God spoke to Abraham again the second time to proceed on his way to Canaan. In this sense, there appears to be a partial obedience on the part of Abraham, but he finally was in God's will when he arrived in Canaan.

31 Dan Jacobson, "The Zaida and the Zulu," Emanuel Litvinoff, ed., in *Penguin Book of Jewish Short Stories* (New York: Penguin, 1979), pages 171–185.

Chapter Seven

32 Kai Kjær-Hansen, *Joseph Rabinowitz and the Messianic Movement*, David Stoner, tr. (Grand Rapids: Eerdmans, 1995), pages 18–20.

33 Leon Wood, *Op. Cit.*, page 352.

34 Whenever the temple was shut down, either by Ahaz's policies, or when a temple was destroyed, the priests had to go through the processes of ordination and installation all over again, and the entire temple and furniture had to be dedicated for God's use (see Lev. 8, 9).

35 See again, Louis Goldberg, *Bible Study Commentary: Leviticus* (Grand Rapids: Zondervan, 1980), pages 26–33

where the subject of atonement in the sacrificial system is considered with regard to the principles: substitute identification, death of the substitute and the exchange of life. Furthermore, the believer could know he had a forgiveness of sin, see Ps. 103:12; Mic. 7:19.

36 Two burnt offerings were presented every day, one after sunup and the second was, literally, "between the two evenings," (see Lev. 29:39). During the second temple period, leaders decided that this afternoon offering was to be presented ". . . at a half after the eighth hour, and offered up at a half after the ninth hour," or, at about the ninth hour. In other words, 3:00 P.M. (Pesahim 5:1 in *Mishnah*, H. Danby, ed., London: Oxford University Press, 1933), page 141. See also Acts 3:1.

37 Hezekiah had a co-regency with his father; Wood would put this co-regency with Ahaz as early as 728 B.C.E. Once more, many commentators who have made a study of this dating of Hezekiah have plausible reasons for their dating schemes, but this represents one of the most difficult of problems.

38 Sholom Aleichem, *The Old Country*, Julius & Frances Butwin, trs. (New York: Crown Publishers, 1946), pages 138–145.

Chapter Eight

39 Leon Wood, *A Survey of Israel's History* (Grand Rapids: Zondervan Publishing House, 1970), page 36.

40 See the discussion of higher criticism's formulation of the canon in E.J. Young, *Introduction to the Old Testament* (Grand Rapids: Eerdmans, 1949), pages 146–156.

41 Jeremiah, Ezekiel, and Daniel would have been added after the exile, as well as the books of Ezra, Nehemiah, and 2 Chronicles and other books of the Writings.

42 Commonwealths were marked in accordance with the existence of the temples. As long as the first temple stood, it was designated as the first commonwealth; similarly, the

second temple marked the time of the second common-wealth.

43 Careful note must be taken that Yeshua never called any-one a sinner, unless the situation became so drastic that it necessitated a proper response. Rather, Yeshua's involve-ment with people was that of the *Zaddik*, who comes from God's presence, with God's fire from his altar, and stoops down to lift people out of their sin and misery. So the Messiah sought to gently turn people from their self-serving ways to the higher level of God's servants, as in his encounter with the religious leaders and the adulter-ous woman (see John 8:1–11).

44 Francis Schaeffer, *A Christian Manifesto* (Westchester, IL: Crossway Books, 1982, rev.), pp. 64,65.

Chapter Nine

45 Consider again the ages from 2 Chronicles 36:2, 5, & 11. Jehoahaz was 23 years old in 608 B.C.E. while Eliakim (Hehoakim) was 25 on that same date. Zedekiah who was 21 years old in 597 B.C.E. but would have been only 10 years old in 608 B.C.E.

46 Nothing is known of his burial place, no one mourned for him, and his body was as the burial of a donkey (see Jer. 22:18, 19).

47 He began his prayer vigil—while carrying his normal du-ties before the king as his cupbearer—from the month of Kislev, corresponding to November-December to the month of Nisan, corresponding to March-April, which is a period of some four months.

48 Laws were still on the Persian books that forbade rebuild-ing the walls. But, because of his prayer, God worked so graciously in response to Nehemiah's request that the Persian king overrode or ignored the former laws, thereby providing for the walls to finally be completed.

49 Anna Talbott McPherson, *Spiritual Secrets of Famous Chris-tians* (Grand Rapids: Zondervan, 1964), pp. 33–35.

Chapter Ten

50 Gleason Archer, *A Survey of Old Testament Introduction* (Chicago: Moody Press, 1974 rev. ed.), page 414, footnote 12. "Letter 30 was addressed by Jedoniah, religious leader of the Elephantine Jews, to Gov. Bagdi (also vocalized as Bigvai) of Judea, complaining that Johanan the high priest at Jerusalem, had ignored the need for rebuilding the recently destroyed temple in Elephantine."

51 Flavius Josephus, *Antiquities of the Jews* (Grand Rapids: Kregel, 1960 reprint), Book 11, Chapter 8, Section 5, page 244.

52 For the thrilling story of the fight for religious freedom by the Hasmonean family (the Maccabees) see the historical record preserved in the apocryphal book 1 Maccabees, which has a fairly accurate historical account.

53 For a one-volume rapid overview of the history, see Solomon Grazel, *A History of the Jews* (New York: New American Library, Mentor, 1968 reprint).

54 This is not the place to enter into a discussion of what was official Jewish belief at the time concerning the Messiah. But already, Targum Isaiah was well known and particularly, the targum paraphrase of Isaiah 53 tells the story: 1) all the passages that describe suffering are relegated to the nation that suffers 2) the passages that picture exaltation relate to the Messiah who is personal. See S. Stenning, *Targum Isaiah* (London: Oxford, 1949). This spells out exactly what Yeshua had to contend with in the days of his flesh.

55 Into the area known in Roman Times as Perea.

56 Jacob Neusner, *First Century Judaism in Crisis, Yohanan and the Renaissance of Torah* (Nashville: Abingdon, 1975), pages 167–171, describes how ben Zakkai led the Council of Yavneh, meeting from 70–90 C.E., about how to reconcile Jewish belief and practice without the temple. According to Shimon HaSaddik in 200 B.C.E., the world rested on three prongs: "The Torah, the temple rites, and acts of pi-

ety," but after the temple was lost, . . . through hesed the Jews might make atonement, and that the sacrifices then demanded of them were mercy and love," acts of compassion he derived from Hosea 6:8.

Chapter Eleven

57 Bellarmine Bagatti, *The Church from the Circumcision, History and Archeology of Judaeo-Christians*, Engl. Tr., Fa. Eugene Hoade (Jerusalem: Franciscan Publishing House, 1971), pages 98–103, discusses this topic under the title, "The Malediction in the Liturgical Prayers."

58 Bellarmine Bagatti, *Ibid.*, pages 106–111, points that most rabbis maintained a sharp line between themselves and the *Minim*, that is, the Messianic Jews. However, a few of the rabbinic authorities had good relations with them, refused to curse them, and one, R. Shimon ben Lakish remarked, "They were full of commandments as a pomegranate is full of pips."

59 Although Bagatti, *Ibid.*, page 86, points out that some eighteen Jewish bishops were present in Israel, of whom the rest of the Church were completely unaware. Whether this is so, it is difficult to check, although another possibility is that Constantine and many of the other bishops did not want them to attend. But if they had attended, one wonders if the climate of the council regarding Jewish people would have been different.

60 The history of revival awakenings is monumental, and one feels guilty in attempting in a few lines to provide the overview of God's special works. Only a few volumes were consulted, but these provide further extensive bibliographies. They include, Sydney E. Ahlstrom, *A Religious History of the American People* (New Haven: Yale University Press, 1972); Lewis A. Drummond, *The Revival that Must Come* (Nashville: Broadman Press, 1978); J. Edwin Orr, *The Second Evangelical Awakening in Britain* (London: Marshall and

Scott, 1953 reprint); Timothy L. Smith, *Revivalism and Social Reform* (Nashville: Broadman Press, 1957).

61 Sydney E. Ahlstrom, *Op. Cit.* pages 23–32.

62 Certainly, these men can be faulted for some of their beliefs and practices: the Lutheran bodies have repudiated Luther's deplorable observations concerning Jewish people today. And many today would not accept Calvin's position that the Church has taken over all the blessings yet to be experienced by the people Israel. And yet, we cannot overlook what these men did in awakening people's interest in the Scriptures and thereby turning many back to God.

63 Norman, "Puritans; Puritanism," in J.G. Douglas, gen. ed., *The New International Dictionary of the Christian Church* (Grand Rapids: Zondervan, 1974), pages 814, 815.

64 The *hasidic* movement began within Jewry also in the early 1700s with Rabbi Israel ben Eliezer, the Ba'al Shem Tov (Master of the Good Name, also know by the acronym "Besht") (1700–1760), who also spawned a mystical element within Judaism. Was there some kind of influence upon Jewish people by the German Pietists and Moravian Brethren, or did the two movement begin simultaneously with no links? This question might provide a fruitful field for research by some scholar.

65 Edwin Orr, *The Second Evangelical Awakening* (London: Marshall, Morgan and Scott, 1953 reprint), page 5.

66 Timothy L. Smith, *Revivalism and Social Action* (Nashville: Abingdon Press, 1957), page 35.

67 Orr, *Op. Cit.*, page 5.

68 *Ibid.*, pages 208, 229.

69 Lewis A. Drummond, *The Awakening that Must Come* (Nashville: Broadman Press, 1978), page 18.

70 Bruce L. Shelley, "Moody, Dwight Lyman," in J.D. Douglas, *Op. Cit.*, page 674.

71 Norman Grubb, *C.T. Studd* (Chicago, Moody Press, 1962), pages 96–102.

72 Richard N. Ostling, "Jerry Falwell's Crusade," *Time* magazine, September 2, 1985.

73 Richard F. Lovelace, "The Surprising Works of God," *Christianity Today*, September 11, 1995, page 28.

74 Lovelace, *Op. Cit.*, page 30.

75 Lovelace, *Ibid.*, page 32.

76 Ibid.

77 Ibid.

Chapter Twelve

78 John Murray, "The Epistle to the Romans" in *The New International Commentary on the New Testament* (Grand Rapids: Eerdmans, 1968), page 98, although one must note the entire discussion on "The Fullness of the Gentiles and the Salvation of Israel" (11:25–32).

79 These assertions have been amply answered by Louis Goldberg, *Turbulence Over the Middle East* (Neptune, NJ: Loizeaux, Bros., 1982) and in a manuscript soon to be published, Louis Goldberg, *The Man Ezekiel and his Prophecies*.

80 For a concise review of the events of this facet of investigation, please note, Louis Goldberg, "Historical and Political Factors in the Twentieth Century Affecting the Identity of Israel," in *Israel: The Land and the People*, H. Wayne House, gen. ed. (Grand Rapids: Kregel Publications, 1998), pages 113–141.

81 In 1939, England declared the White Paper proclamation, which would allow 10,000 Jewish people to emigrate to Israel for five years, and as an expression of grace, stipulated that an additional 25,000 could also be permitted as well. But after the five years, all emigration was to cease, and any who entered, exceeding these figures, would be classified as illegal. With this decision in the light of what

had happened to Jewish people in Europe in the holocaust, the White Paper was intolerable for Jewish people
in Israel as well as elsewhere.

82 It was about that time when, for the price of having favor-
able trade relations with the United States, the Soviets
agreed to allow Russian Jews to emigrate to Israel. That
too was within God's providential work.

83 Note also, "They will no longer . . . bear the shame of the
Goyim," (Ezek. 34:29). And "I will make them one nation
in the land, on the mountains of Isra'el . . . one king will
be king for all of them. . . . I will save them from all the
places where they have been living and sinning; and I will
cleanse them, so that they will be my people, and I will be
their God" (Ezek. 37:22, 23).